The Great Navy Wreck Scam

Being a History of
**Double Dealing,
Double Standards,
and Unethical Actions**

by Gary Gentile

Bellerophon Bookworks

Copyright 2015 by Gary Gentile

All rights reserved. Except for the use of brief quotations embodied in critical articles and reviews, this book may not be reproduced in part or in whole, in any manner (including mechanical, electronic, photographic, and photocopy means), transmitted in any form, or system or recorded by any data storage and/or retrieval device, without express written permission from the author or his duly designated executor. Address all queries to:

Bellerophon Bookworks
3 Lehigh Gorge Drive
Jim Thorpe, PA 18229

Additional copies of this book may be purchased from the same address by sending a check or money order in the amount of $20 U.S. for each copy (plus $4 postage per order, not per book, in the U.S. Inquire for shipping cost to foreign countries). Alternatively, copies may be ordered from the author's website and paid by credit card:

http://www.ggentile.com

Picture Credits

All uncredited photographs were taken by the author. The front cover photograph shows depth charges in the rack of a sunken warship.

In the event of the author's demise, provisions in his will guarantee continued publication in perpetuity.

International Standard Book Numbers (ISBN)
1-883056-51-9
978-1-883056-51-3

First Edition

Printed in U.S.A.

Table of Contents

List of Appendices	4
Author's Foreword	5
Demolition of the YMS-14 in 2009	8
The Navel of Naval History	35
Naval Historical Center	36
USS *San Diego*	51
Ships History Branch	62
Naval Photographic Center	81
Judge Advocate General	84
Warship Case Files	
USS *Cumberland*	93
CSS *Florida*	99
CSS *Alabama*	115
Hamilton and *Scourge*	125
U-352	129
U-85	139
USS *Murphy*	141
H.L. Hunley	148
Into the Deep Blue Yonder	165
Fabricating the Future (Part 1)	181
Fabricating the Future (Part 2)	190
Fabricating the Future (Part 3)	199
Point and Counterpoint	208
The Lady or the Tiger?	225

List of Appendices

Appendices   227

Appendix 1 (1999)   228
Application Guidelines for Underwater Archeological Research Permits on Submerged Cultural Resources Under the Jurisdiction of the Department of the Navy

Appendix 2 (Undated)   241
Archaeological Research Permit Application Guidelines for Ship and Aircraft Wrecks under the Jurisdiction of the Department of the Navy

Appendix 3 (2005)   253
H.R. 4200 - Ronald W. Reagan National Defense Authorization Act for Fiscal Year 2005 (Enrolled as Agreed to or Passed by Both House and Senate)

Appendix 4 (2012)   260
Application Guidelines for Archeological Research Permits on Ship and Aircraft Wrecks under the Jurisdiction of the Department of the Navy

Appendix 5 (2014)   268
Guidelines for Permitting Archaeological Investigations and Other Activities Directed at Sunken Military Craft and Terrestrial Military Craft Under the Jurisdiction of the Department of the Navy

Index   317

Books by the Author   328

Author's Foreword

The U.S. Navy is seeking legislation that will grant it control of more than 17,000 wrecks worldwide: from the halls of Montezuma to the shores of Tripoli. If this Act is passed, divers will no longer be able to dive on these wrecks, and anglers will no longer be allowed to fish on them. And not only shipwrecks, but ditched and crashed aircraft.

Wreck-diving and wreck-fishing will then be activities of the past, when America was the land of the free and the home of the brave. The underwater America of the future will belong almost exclusively to a handful of civilian staff members who are paid for their unarmed robbery by the U.S. Navy.

The purpose of this book is to alert American citizens about this wholesale annexation of public property, whose unlawful seizure is not in their best interests. The only people who will benefit by this misappropriation will be the self-appointed controllers, and those sycophants they select to help them in their ongoing program of creeping jurisdiction.

By documenting the manner in which the Navy has mistreated wrecks and citizens in the past, the current generation will understand the kind of treatment that will be forthcoming once the Navy takes absolute control of these abandoned derelicts.

The Navy has raised the banner that it wants to preserve wrecks. Yet, it may come as a surprise to many that the Navy has destroyed or disinterred more historical wreck sites than it has ever preserved. In fact, the Navy has never done anything – *anything* – to preserve shipwrecks: not so much as a *single* shipwreck.

Wrecks exist in a corrosive environment that dissolves their hulls and internal parts the way nature ravages an abandoned building. Wood-boring mollusks and other marine organisms consume wood the way termites eat joists and wallboards in a house. Water converts steel and iron to rust, which flakes off hull plates and bulkheads to the point of collapse, and beyond, until nothing remains of the original structure.

Buildings are preserved by means of ongoing upkeep: painting surfaces, reinforcing sagging beams, replacing worn carpet and shingles, and so on. Without this constant care and maintenance, wrecks likewise cannot survive under water. Every boat owner knows this. Wood and metal hulls must be scraped and painted on an annual basis, else they rot or rust through to the interior.

Imagine how much worse the process of destruction must be for a wreck, which has lain underwater for years, or decades, or centuries. Submerged wood *can* be partially preserved by the application of anti-fouling paint on exposed surfaces. Metal corrosion *can* be arrested by means of cathodic protection: an electrochemical process that involves the installation of sacrificial anodes, the same way propeller shafts are protected on small boats and large vessels.

Despite its cry for so-called preservation, the Navy has never employed any of these time-honored preservation techniques on any wreck anywhere in the world. Instead, the Navy is trying to make the public believe that it can "preserve" wrecks by enacting legislation, as if the Navy could convince Congress to repeal the law of gravity.

The truth of the matter has little or nothing to do with physical preservation. It has all to do with *control*.

The first priority of any government entity is to justify its existence. That is the primary motivation behind the agency that has come to honor itself with the grandiose cognomen of the Naval History and Heritage Command. For decades it has been working toward the overthrow of its original mandate – to archive and share historical information. Now it has damped that public service, and instead works diligently toward expanding its authority beyond the pale, like an insane despot who

Author's Foreword

invades his neighboring countries with an eye toward world domination.

I have a special interest in the matter. For forty years I have studied, researched, and written books about naval history and wrecks. During that time I have personally witnessed the depraved metamorphosis, the heinous devolution, of the Naval Historical Center and its associated centers – from a center for archiving and distributing naval documentation to the aggrandizing threat of unfettered control over wrecks. In the following pages I will provide overwhelming evidence of this thesis.

I will commence by stating the most recent incident, involving the World War Two minesweeper *YMS-14*. Briefly the story is this: I discovered the previously unknown site in 2007. I identified the wreck by its location and its physical layout. I conducted a thorough examination of the remains, and took photographs of its most salient features.

I published the results of my survey work in 2008. When the Navy learned of my discovery, it dispatched a team of Navy divers to demolish the wreck – a job that they did with spectacular relish and efficiency. They literally blew the wreck to smithereens.

So much for historic preservation. So much for naval history and heritage.

Now the Navy wants to "preserve" (read "control") thousands of additional shipwrecks.

This book will look past the façade, the false image that the Navy has placed before the American people; will show how it has concealed and manipulated the dispersal of public information to the public; will disclose the truth about its wreck shenanigans; and will ultimately reveal the dark design that lurks inside the emperor's new clothes.

Captain James Lawrence is probably twitching in his grave at the way his dying command has been perverted. The modern Navy's slogan for conquest is, "Don't give up the wreck."

Demolition of the *YMS-14*

Historical Summary

The *YMS-14* was a U.S. minesweeper that collided with the U.S. destroyer *Herndon* in Boston Harbor on January 11, 1945. There was no loss of life. For full particulars of the collision and its aftermath, see *Shipwrecks of Massachusetts: North*.

After the collision, the Supervisor of Salvage of the Navy Salvage Service took charge of salvage operations, but "about or after 1 Apr." contracted Merritt-Chapman & Scott to do the actual work. "The wreck or such portion as may be recovered should be delivered to" Boston. On April 3, the Navy tug *Accelerate* (ARS-30) was dispatched to the scene "for the purpose of conducting a survey and making arrangements preparatory to salvage of *YMS-14*."

Merritt-Chapman & Scott never got to the job because the Supervisor of Salvage "advised there was no salvage value to the wreck and requested approval to demolish it or remove it as a menace to navigation." This advice was approved. "Explosives in the amount of 750 lbs. were placed in and around the wreck and a charge was set off at 1505Q [Queen time] 12 Apr. 45."

The U.S. Army Corps of Engineers conducted sweeping operations of the wreck site on June 13 and 14. At mean low water, the wire-drag cleared at 23 feet and hung at 33 feet. According to their report, "In view of the relative small variance in the controlling depth between the wreck area and the existent natural shoal (channel edge) located south of the south limit of the 40 ft and westerly of the demolition area, further wreck removal operations will not be required by this office."

In other words, the minesweeper drifted out of the shipping channel before she sank.

The *YMS-14* was stricken from the Navy Register on

Demolition of the YMS-14

April 28, 1945. This action constituted legal abandonment, which was intended to relieve the Navy of liability with regard to the wreck.

Discovery of the Wreck

When I commenced intensive diving surveys for the Massachusetts portion of my Popular Dive Guide Series, local lore had it that the only feature of the YMS-14 that remained extant was the deck gun. I was told that the main hull of the wreck had been wire-dragged and dredged out of existence when the shipping channel had been widened to accommodate larger, deeper-draft vessels. In the process of wire-dragging, the gun had been snagged and dragged several miles from the original location of the wreck. I had my doubts that this was the case.

Later research led me to conclude that after the war the channel had been moved – not because the wreck posed a hazard to navigation, but to straighten the channel and eliminate the dogleg that abetted the collision. Thus a new channel segment was dredged: one that put the minesweeper even farther away from the inbound and outbound shipping lanes.

I saw no sign of a hull when I dived on the gun (a 3"/50 caliber antiaircraft gun). The gun lay on its side with the breach exposed; the barrel disappeared into the sandy bottom so that the muzzle was buried. The gun was still secured to its mount: a circular platform that

YMS-14. (Courtesy of the National Archives.)

measured seven feet in diameter. This gave the site a relief of seven feet. Two beamlike supports stretched eight to ten feet away from the bottom of the mount.

These beams pointed to a small debris field that stretched ten to twenty feet from the gun mount. This debris consisted of partially buried 3-inch gun shells, occasional 50-caliber shells (for machine guns), and fat electrical cables that had the appearance of thickly insulated degaussing cables.

The maximum depth was fifty-five feet at high tide, although other areas were shallower, particularly at low tide.

A scenario in which the gun had been dragged from the wreckage by a wire-drag could not account for the accumulation of miscellaneous debris and exposed gun shells. I concluded that the wreck must lie nearby. Also, because the seabed in some places consisted of coral-encrusted rock instead of sand, I found it difficult to accept that the entire wreck had settled out of sight. I thought that there must be other sections exposed.

Together with Marcie Bilinski, owner and skipper of the *SeaDuctress*, I decided to conduct sand searches in the vicinity of the gun, by dropping anchor in nearby locations and doing bottom sweeps to the end of a line reel. She and I took turns in the water, with one of us minding the boat while the other made an exploratory dive.

In two such sweeps (each lasting an hour and a half), I found numerous rock piles, isolated bits of metal, and one debris field that measured about ten feet by twenty. In this debris field I found a dozen 20-millimeter gun shells. Marcie made similar finds.

The rocky seabed hampered bottom searches because, as one made circular sweeps at the end of the guideline, the line hung up on protruding rocks. Often, when I thought I was swimming in a large circle, I came across my own line. I then had to backtrack along the line and unhook it from the rock on which it was hung.

Although my sand searches were somewhat productive, Marcie really hit pay dirt. She found a large section

Demolition of the YMS-14

of wreckage that, in her excited words, consisted of "white round things and tall things" which she did not recognize. After her return to the boat, I followed her guideline to the spot. I immediately recognized the "white round things" as depth charges. The metal containers had long since rusted away, leaving the white explosive material exposed to the elements. The surface of this explosive material was scalloped the same way I had seen on other wrecks that were armed with depth charges at the time of their demise.

The minesweeper's exposed stern area measured about twenty feet in width and thirty feet in length. Five depth charges were exposed. The two "tall things" were bronze rudderposts. The port rudderpost stood about five feet high, the starboard one about six feet. At times, depending on the season, some of the boulders in this stern section were covered with long strands of kelp which obscured wreckage that the kelp was using as a substrate to anchor its roots.

About thirty feet forward of the rudderposts, I came across a nest of thick electrical cables that led to a large metal structure that stood four feet off the bottom and measured some five feet in width by fifteen feet in length. One side of this structure was flat and nearly vertical, with regular cutouts in the metal; it reminded me of a bedplate. At first I thought this was a degaussing generator. When I saw it again under better viewing conditions, I noticed what appeared to be a flywheel at the forward end. I then concluded that this was one of the propulsion engines, especially as, according to the layout on the deck plans, the generator room was located forward.

Continued Exploration

In order to put the exposed but disarticulated pieces into perspective, and to obtain a measurement from the deck gun to the rudderposts, I strung a guideline from bow to stern. The length of this line conformed to the length of the *YMS-14*. The presence of the deck gun, machine gun cartridges, and depth charges, left no doubt in my mind that the wooden hull was intact and contiguous, although it was mostly buried under a thick veneer of sand and loose rocks that had been carried over the site by the tides during the intervening years.

On subsequent surveys, I secured my guideline to the bow-stern line, which I used as a starting point from which to explore to port and starboard. A guideline was necessary because visibility was often five feet or less. In order to explore the debris fields on both sides of the wreck, I placed the snap hook of my guideline somewhere along the length of the bow-stern line, then proceeded into the distance perpendicular to the wreck's centerline. I then returned to the survey line and proceeded on the other side. Finally, I returned once again to the survey line, slid the snap hook to a new position, and repeated the process. In this manner I was able to explore a broad area on both sides of the centerline.

The *YMS-14* was a fabulous find: a rare remnant of emergency naval construction from yesteryear, when steel was at a premium and the hulls of certain warships were knocked together from wood.

Marcie and I kept returning to the wreck in order to document it in full. My final underwater photo shoot of the season took place on December 2, 2007. We had tried to reach the minesweeper a few days earlier, but a storm had prevented us from reaching the site. We left our gear on board for the next opportunity. In the meantime, a cold front moved into the area, and the temperature dropped to below freezing.

Harry Dutton joined us on December 2. The air temperature was 28°. The dive gear on the boat was bitterly cold. My drysuit and regulators were coated with ice particles. My neoprene hood and gloves were frozen solid. Marcie and Harry decided not to dive. When we arrived at the first dive site (the *City of Rockland*, which I needed to survey and photograph for the book), I struggled into my ice-cold drysuit.

When I dived with Marcie during the warm summer and autumn months, I often joked, "Just remember. You're having fun. I'm working." This time I wasn't jok-

Demolition of the YMS-14

ing when I remarked dryly, "This is why I get the big bucks." I definitely was not having fun.

It was so cold on the after deck that my fingers went numb as I donned my tanks and strapped on my accessories. My frozen hood was as flat as a pancake. I had to knead it open in order to tug it over my head. When I sat fully dressed except for my gloves, I held out my hands so that Harry could help me with my gloves. But *his* hands got so cold in the open air that he had to shove them into his pockets to get them warm. After he was able to flex his fingers, he picked up a glove and spread the opening over my left hand – which had been left out in the cold while he warmed his hands. After a decidedly painful experience, he managed to get both frozen gloves onto my frozen hands.

I was happy to get into the water because it was warmer than the air: 40° as opposed to 28°. Gradually I thawed out, conducted my survey, and took a bunch photographs.

Next stop was the *YMS-14*. I spent the travel time between wreck sites in the heated cabin. Marcie had a brilliant idea: she de-iced my hood and gloves in the microwave oven. This made it easier and less painful to don them.

My goal on this dive was to photograph the depth charges. I had taken pictures of them before, but always when the wreck was plagued with poor visibility. The resultant images were marred by backscatter: the reflection of the strobe's flash off particulate matter in the water. We had timed this dive for the end of the incoming tide, when clean (or clean*er*) ocean water flowed into Boston Harbor. After the incoming slack, sewage and detritus from Boston and the inner harbor reduced visibility significantly, sometimes to zero (which was called a Braille dive).

This time I was fortunate to have 10 feet of visibility. This enabled me to obtain publishable quality photographs.

As noted in the Author's Foreword, in 2008 I published the results of our findings in *Shipwrecks of Mas-*

sachusetts: North. Marcie and I continued to make occasional forays to the minesweeper throughout that summer and the next.

The Demolition Derby

Then came bad news from Vic Mastone. He was the Director and Chief Archaeologist of the Massachusetts Board of Underwater Archaeological Resources. He had been extremely helpful in my research by allowing me to access and photocopy the historical files and shipwreck holdings in his department. In return I surveyed several wrecks for him, on my own time and at my own expense, and turned in reports and drawings of the sites.

Now he informed me that he had heard through the grapevine, through a long circuitous route, that the Navy had demolished the wreck of the *YMS-14* with explosives.

I was appalled. I could hardly believe it. I didn't *want* to believe it. The destruction of a sunken Navy vessel went against everything that the Naval History and Heritage Command claimed to stand for.

Vic couldn't be sure if the rumor were true or not. He was just reporting what he had heard: not second hand, but so many hands down the line that he had no way to trace the origin of the rumor or to verify its truth.

It is important for the reader to understand that the disturbance of any historical or archaeological site in Massachusetts required a permit from the MBUAR, of which Vic was in charge. Therefore, before any demolition could legally be conducted in Massachusetts waters, the Navy should have gone to him for permission – permission, I should add, that he had the authority to deny.

If the story were true, then the Navy had ignored Vic and the MBUAR entirely, and took it upon itself to tear up the seabed and destroy State property. To use a popular slang phrase, they just snuck out and did it.

Because rumors so often proved to be false or exaggerated, I took my time about spreading the word until

Demolition of the YMS-14

I could confirm it for myself. Marcie and I returned to the wreck in the summer of 2010. Sadly, we found that the rumor was true. Worse yet, the rumormonger had not understated the severity of the crime.

That December, I alerted thousands of interested people about the dire situation by publishing an account in my free online newsletter:

Another Boston Tea Party

My New England readers, and others who have cosmopolitan interests, might have read what I wrote about the destruction of a minesweeper in Boston Harbor. To recapitulate, the *YMS-14* was sunk by collision with another warship during World War Two. The wreck lay unmolested until I featured it in *Shipwrecks of Massachusetts: North.*

Marcie Bilinski and I discovered the site where the remains of five depth charges lay exposed among rocks and kelp. I photographed the depth charges, and used one of the photos to illustrate the back cover of the book.

I joked about how official heads would turn when they discovered that inert explosive charges lay only one hundred yards from the main shipping channel, which was plied on a regular basis by supertankers that transported liquid natural gas. In a knee-jerk reaction, those official heads turned way too far: more like a victim of possession and exorcism than a cool-headed administrative figure.

The U.S. Navy took it upon itself to demolish the wreck – without authorization from the Massachusetts Board of Underwater Archaeological Resources.

The largely eroded depth-charge remnants could not have exploded on their own. Nor could they have been of any use to terrorists. Explosive material deteriorates over time, the same way in which food rots and medicine goes bad – by means of chemical breakdown.

Marcie and I conducted extensive surveys of the wreck during the summer of 2010. If I claimed that the Navy blew the wreck to smithereens, I would be understating the case. Hardly any smithereens remain to mark the site.

Fortunately, Marcie had accurate GPS coordinates, else we might have thought that the wreck had been blasted to oblivion and hauled away to the scrap yard. Only by searching for hours at the end of a line reel were we able to locate what used to be the site of an historic landmark that now hardly exists.

Navy divers detonated so many pounds of explosives around the depth charges that the wreck now looks like a moonscape. The seabed was unearthed by the blast, large boulders were shattered and the pieces were tossed great distances, and marine life was obliterated.

One bronze rudder post is completely missing. The other one was laid down horizontally by the explosion, and a deep pit was gouged out of the rocky substrate beneath it. The bottom contours are so altered that the broad patch of sand that extended outward from the depth-charge area is gone; the seabed is now a debris field littered with shattered rocks.

If there is any saving grace to this travesty, it is that some of the timbers of the wooden hull have been exposed by the removal of overburden. That is small recompense for the destruction of a fascinating shipwreck.

You can thank the Navy for demolishing an important piece of America's past.

There is irony to this situation. Had the witch-hunters at the Naval Historical Center caught an American citizen removing as small an item as an iron bolt from the blasted wreck, they would have sicced the Naval Criminal Investigation Service on him – as they have done in the

Demolition of the YMS-14

past – for stealing what they perceived to be government property. Go figure.

Navy Ground Rules

Let me quote a few items from the Navy's 1999 "Proposed Rules" about "Application Guidelines for Underwater Archeological Research Permits on Submerged Cultural Resources Under the Jurisdiction of the Department of the Navy" (see Appendix 1 for the full text):

"The diving public is encouraged to report the location of underwater ship and aircraft wrecksites to the NHC. Documentation of these wreck locations allows the Navy to evaluate and preserve important sites for the future." And:

"Federal property law dictates that no portion of a government wreck may be disturbed or removed. The Navy strongly encourages cooperation with other agencies and individuals interested in preserving our maritime and aviation heritage." And:

"Submerged Navy cultural resources will be left in place unless artifact removal or site disturbance is justified and necessary to *protect* Navy cultural resources, to conduct research, or provide public education and information that is otherwise inaccessible." Emphasis added.

There is no need for me to gild the lily. The intelligent reader can easily comprehend the inferences from these quotations without my having to elaborate on them.

After confirming that the *YMS-14* had in fact been totally destroyed, I tried to ascertain how the Navy had allowed such a travesty to occur. The first place to seek this information was obviously the Naval Historical Center. But there I was stymied: first by excuses and then by outright prohibition against access. In the former instance, the NHC claimed to have no information in this regard. When I tried to press my case from a different angle, I was denied entry to the facility. (See the following chapter for more information in this regard.)

Letter of Opposition

I persisted in my research in a roundabout fashion, finally achieving some results: first by accident and then by intent. It was not until late in 2014 that I obtained an expurgated version of the story. The first version was in response to my July 9 letter to Senator Pat Toomey with regard to the Navy's latest territorial demand. Now is as good a time as any to introduce this letter into evidence for the public:

> Re: Guidelines for Permitting Archaeological Investigations and Other Activities Directed at Sunken Military Craft and Terrestrial Military Craft Under the Jurisdiction of the Department of the Navy
>
> I strongly oppose the proposed Guidelines for a number of reasons. For one, the U.S. Navy has proven itself unworthy of protecting sunken naval craft. Consider the case of the *YMS-14*. The location of this World War Two minesweeper was unknown until I discovered it in Boston Harbor in 2007. The following year, I published a history of the wreck and the circumstances of its loss in *Shipwrecks of Massachusetts: North*. After reading my chapter about the wreck – whose location I published in the book – the Navy deployed an underwater demolition team to the wreck site and demolished it with explosives. The wreck was so torn up after the Navy blasted it apart that it was no longer recognizable as a ship. The entire seabed was overturned. Remains of the hull lay scattered across the bottom in disarticulated pieces that resembled a junk pile.
>
> This is the way the Navy treated its WW2 naval history. This is the kind of respect, or lack thereof, that the Navy has exhibited for its naval history. This is how the Navy cheated the American people of their past.
>
> The manner in which the Navy treated the

Demolition of the YMS-14

YMS-14 has demonstrated its disdain for the preservation of history. The Navy has demonstrated its irresponsibility with regard to historic sites. The Navy is the *last* organization that should have jurisdiction of any kind relating to sunken craft, lest it deploy its vast resources around the world to destroy other shipwrecks.

Another reason for my opposition is the manner in which the Naval Historical Center – which is staffed and operated by the same people who now wish to control shipwreck access – has repeatedly withheld historical and archaeological information from me, on numerous occasions when I visited the facility in the Washington Navy Yard. The NHC is supposed to hold historical naval documents in trust for U.S. citizens, and to share those documents with the public. Instead, it decides who shall and who shall not have access to the records in its holdings.

This situation was brought to my attention during one of my visits to the NHC, when I requested to see half-century-old documents from WW2, and a senior staff member instructed an intern to withhold the documents that I had requested. The intern did not agree with this philosophy of not sharing information with the public, so he informed me about the instructions that he had received. The senior staff member kept watch over him to ensure that he did not let me see those documents.

This made me wonder how many times in the past – during more than 30 years of conducting historical research at the NHC – other documents had been maliciously withheld from me.

In another case, a senior staff member informed me that the documents that I requested were not in their holdings. I had to return to Washington at a later date and prove that those documents were in their holdings, by showing her pages that I had photocopied from the file years before. She then begrudgingly "found" the file and let me view them again.

Furthermore, the "Sunken Military Craft Act of 2004" was passed by unethical means. Neither the American people nor their elected representatives knew of the existence of the Act until after its passage. At the last minute, before Congress was aware of its inclusion, the Navy inserted the Act as a rider to the military appropriations bill. Thus the Act was not brought before Congress for discussion, and the American people had no voice in its ultimate passage. This unscrupulous means averted the opposition that the proposed bill had received in previous years.

The Navy has since used this Act as a means to extend its control over the underwater world, and to persecute people who possess a long history and vested interest in shipwrecks.

Aside from the Navy's dishonorable intentions with regard to shipwrecks, aircraft, and naval history, the newly proposed Act would impose an incredible hardship on people the world over. The Act seeks to control access to tens of thousands of wrecks by granting access authority to a handful of civil servants who are employed by the Navy. How are these few naval employees supposed to handle the issuance of permits to thousands of historians, archaeologists, anglers, and scuba divers from all over the planet – people who study, fish on, visit and photograph wrecks? On what basis will permits be issued? How long will it take to obtain a permit should these civil servants deem to grant one?

The Navy has a disreputable history with regard to wrecks and naval history. To better serve the American public, and people across the globe where wrecks reside, the proposed Act should be vetoed. The Sunken Military Craft Act of 2004 should be repealed. The historical records in the NHC should be turned over to the National

Demolition of the YMS-14

Archives, where they can be viewed freely by the public without arbitrary and capricious restrictions.

The U.S. Navy should utilize its resources for its mandated directive: national defense.

Accidental Admission

The last line of my letter was the direct result of thirty-year-old correspondence. On April 17, 1984, I wrote to the Navy Department to request historical information about Navy vessels *Tarpon*, *Wilkes-Barre*, and *S-16*. To explain the nonexistence of the data that I requested, T.T. Marchitelli (Director, Congressional and Public Affairs Office) wrote (in part): "The mission of the Naval Sea Systems Command is to build and maintain the ships and weapons systems of the U.S. Navy."

What Marchitelli affirmed in no uncertain terms was that abandoned naval shipwrecks were largely irrelevant to Navy concerns when compared to defense of the homeland and national interests. It made perfect sense to me. The Naval Historical Center, which was run by a handful of hired civilians, was little more than a burden that the real Navy suffered to exist.

My letter to Pat Toomey had unexpected results. I wrote to inform him why I opposed the Navy's gross expansion of authority, and its perverse acquisition of military craft that had long since been abandoned by being stricken from the Navy Register. I wanted to make him aware of the Navy's irresponsibility in those regards so that he would vote in my behalf against the proposed legislation.

Toomey must have been intrigued by my charges against the Navy, for he forwarded my letter to the Department and demanded a timely response. In due course (September 29) he received a rhetorical attempt to explain away the Navy's unlawful actions and impulsive or whimsical behavior. He sent the Navy's justifications to me.

The three-page September 24 letter was signed by J.K. Kuhn, Director, Naval History and Heritage Command, Acting. The letter was quite an act. It read (in part):

> "In the specific case of the YMS-14, referenced by Mr. Gentile, the ship sunk in January of 1945 in approximately 48 ft of water in the North Channel of Boston Harbor with no loss of life. However, it was laden with up to eight 300-lb depth charges.
>
> "In the spring of 1945, the Navy Supervisor of Salvage detonated 750 lbs of explosives on the site to neutralize the ordnance hazard and the Navy considered the matter closed. However, in 2009, Navy became re-acquainted with the site and discovered five unexploded depth charges intact and present on the seabed.
>
> "Due to the age and instability of the ordnance, which was located adjacent to an active ship channel whose traffic includes liquefied natural gas tankers, Explosive Ordnance Disposal Mobile Unit 12 (EODMR-12) undertook a controlled detonation of the depth charges to ensure public safety and eliminate the hazard to navigation.
>
> "Navy took this step aware of the historical significance of the wreck, but mindful of the potential threat posed to the harbor. In this case, the decision was made to conduct a controlled detonation of the explosive to mitigate the risk to people, shipping, and the environment."

Before I parse the above paragraphs, I want to assure my readers that I will deal with Kuhn's other whining rationalizations in subsequent chapters. The ways in which I was mistreated by staff members at the Naval Historical Center will be examined in full in the following chapter section entitled "Naval Historical Center." A full discussion of the unethical passage of the Sunken Military Craft rider of 2004, as well as the 2014 proposal for autonomous Navy control, will be found in the three

Demolition of the YMS-14

chapters that are entitled "Fabricating the Future" (all three parts) and "Point and Counterpoint."

The Cop-out

Kuhn's historical information about the *YMS-14* was taken straight out of my book, yet he or she neglected to cite me as the source. This lack of citation made it seem as if he/she (and by extension, the Navy in general) was aware of these facts all along, and had them on the tips of his/her (and the Navy's) fingers. On the contrary, this information is not to be found in the Navy's primary historical reference, *The Dictionary of American Naval Fighting Ships*. (More in this regard will be found in the next chapter's section entitled ("Ships History Branch.") It is obtainable only by intensive research into primary sources.

To compound Kuhn's lack of citation, he/she then stated that the "Navy became re-acquainted with the site and discovered five unexploded depth charges intact and present on the seabed."

This so-called "re-acquaintance" was not a miraculous event. It was the purchase of my book. Furthermore, not only did the Navy did not "discover" the depth charges (Marcie Bilinski discovered them, and I identified them for what they were), but the depth charges were not "intact;" they were only "present," as the Navy learned from reading my book and became "re-acquainted" with the site.

Making the fictitious claim that the depth charges were "intact" gave the false impression to the senator that they could self-detonate at any moment. This was far from the truth. The metal canisters had largely rusted away, else the explosive material would not have been exposed, partially dissolved, and decomposed the way Marcie and I found them: a water- and mineral-impregnated material whose remaining outer surface was scalloped, as if someone had gouged the explosive chemical with an ice cream scoop. Every depth charge that I have seen on other wrecks possessed the identical appearance, and were likewise inert.

Demolition of the YMS-14

Right: The HMCS *Sackville* in Halifax, Nova Scotia. The cylindrical "ashcan" is a depth charge that the Canadian Navy calls "intact."

Below: One of the depth charges on the *YMS-14*. This is what the U.S. Navy calls "intact."

Demolition of the YMS-14

The standard World War Two depth charge consisted of a cylindrical metal canister that was filled with an explosive chemical that could be detonated only – and I stress the word *only* – by a fuze or exploder. The blast could not be initiated by purely mechanical means, such as beating the explosive material with a hammer.

As for instability, there are *no* reports on record of any submerged World War Two depth charges detonating spontaneously – or in any other fashion for that matter. Divers swim around depth charges all the time, the same as they would walk past rifle cartridges in a gun store. A cartridge is not in danger of exploding unless the primer is punched, or if the cartridge is dropped into a fire. Underwater fires are rare events (I am being facetious).

No shipwreck depth charge that I have ever seen had the fuze in place, and for a very good reason.

On February 28, 1942, the U.S. destroyer *Jacob Jones* was on anti-submarine patrol when she was torpedoed by a German U-boat. The ship broke in two and the forward section sank immediately with loss of life. The survivors remained on the still-floating after section for several hours, until it too began to sink, at which time the survivors were forced into the water.

The onboard depth charges had been armed for rapid deployment. They exploded when the stern reached the pre-set depth on the fuzes. The concussion killed every sailor who was floating in the water at the time of detonation. The only men to survive were those who were in life rafts: eleven of a complement of one hundred forty-five.

The Navy protocol was changed after this avoidable catastrophe. From that time onward, depth charges were never armed until an attack became imminent. The fuzes were not inserted into the depth charges until the skipper gave the order to do so. Fuzes were stowed elsewhere on the vessel in order to prevent accidental or premature insertion.

I repeat: of the dozens of depth charges that I have seen underwater, none was armed, and that includes the depth charges on the *YMS-14*.

Kuhn implied that 64-year-old depth charges were a hazard because of the proximity of a shipping channel that was habitually used by liquefied natural gas tankers, and that such a tanker could detonate a depth charge by striking it. This concoction appears to result from either faulty reasoning or an attempt to hoodwink a senator who lacked particular knowledge about depth charges and supertankers.

The reason that LNG tankers stay in the shipping channel is because of their draft, which is so great that they would run aground long before they reached the vicinity of the *YMS-14*.

Kuhn further stated that the depth charges were "detonated," as if they were "live" or "active" depth charges. I beg to differ. The Navy protocol for ordnance disposal is not to self-detonate the ordnance. Old inert ordnance won't detonate on its own. So the EOD packs live and active explosives around the ordnance to be disposed, so as to disintegrate the inert ordnance by means of an exterior explosion. The resulting explosion originates from the recently packed live explosive material, not necessarily from the long-dead ordnance.

The falsification of this and the other two issues in Kuhn's letter seems like an attempt to snowball the senator into believing factoids that the Navy created as mechanisms to disguise the truth. The Navy's false image with regard to shipwreck preservation could not stand up to scrutiny. Hopefully the senator was smart enough to read between the lines and know when he was being buffaloed. After all, he was a politician.

If the Navy truly cared about the "historical significance of the wreck," it would have moved the explosive material off-site before it destroyed the depth-charge remnants. This is what the Navy did on the *U-352* (which see in a later chapter).

Instead, the Navy reacted with evident disdain for historic preservation, resulting in the loss of what the Navy claimed it wanted to preserve, thus exposing its true attitude toward cultural resources. This bolsters my

Demolition of the YMS-14

contention that the Navy's true goal is not to preserve shipwrecks, but to justify its ambition to control them.

Last Chance Saloon

After I gave up trying to ascertain the truth about the demolition of the *YMS-14* through the usual Navy historical channels that were (or used to be) open to the public, I resorted to the Freedom of Information Act. FOIA is the Court of Last Resort that is employed to obtain information that government agencies refuse to release voluntarily.

In other words, a FOIA request is an expedient to use when all else fails. The response to a request is as onerous as the agency wishes to make it. Much depends on the honesty of the agency and its FOIA officers, and on how much information the agency wants to conceal from the public.

I submitted my FOIA request to the Navy's Office of Judge Advocate General (JAG) on July 19, 2014 – five days after I submitted my letter of opposition to Senator Pat Toomey.

What followed was a long-time (and so far unended) ordeal through disorganized Navy Department bureaucracy. I wrote my request succinctly:

> Pursuant to the Freedom of Information Act, 5 U.S.C. Sec. 522 et seq., I hereby request copies of all reports, correspondence, emails, notes, telephone transcripts, inter-office memos, photographs, and any other form of documentation, relating to the demolition of *YMS-14*.
>
> Digitized documentation is acceptable and may be sent to me as email attachments or on compact disks.
>
> As information, in 2008 or later (likely 2009, possibly 2010), the U.S. Navy demolished the shipwreck *YMS-14* by means of explosives. *YMS-14* was a minesweeper that sank in Boston Harbor after collision with USS *Herndon*, on January 15, 1945. There was no loss of life.

FOIA requests should not be complicated or overly verbose. The request should be stated simply and explicitly, and should provide any information that may help the FOIA officer to locate documents that are responsive to the request (to use agency FOIA lingo). The reason for submitting the FOIA request is irrelevant.

On the other hand, a FOIA request must be inclusive. For example, were I to leave out "emails" or "interoffice memos," a FOIA officer would decide that those forms of documentation were not responsive to my request, and would exclude them because I did not specify them. This is a common game that agencies play as a way to circumvent the law.

To give the Navy credit where it is due, I must admit that at first it appeared to me that the Department was willing to cooperate in handling my request. The initial problem, as you will soon learn, was that the Navy mechanism for filing and retrieving information was badly fractionated.

The first stumbling block that I had to overcome was this initial response to my FOIA request: "Please advise if you are willing to pay fees and if so the amount you are willing to pay."

This is a gambit that is now employed by agencies that do not want the public to have access to public information. But in this case the request was somewhat perfunctory. A flurry of emails transpired:

Me: "I am willing to pay a reasonable fee."

Navy FOIA paralegal: "How much is reasonable to you? Typically requesters list a dollar figure and we will not process over that dollar figure without notifying you first."

Me: "Fair enough. What is the most common dollar figure?"

Navy FOIA paralegal: "Most people start at $25.00."

Me: "I will start at $50."

On August 11, 2014, I received the following letter from the Navy (in part): "Our search for records determined that our office does not possess documents that are responsive to your request. Naval Sea Systems Com-

Demolition of the YMS-14

mand may have documents responsive to your request. A copy of your request has been forwarded to that office for direct response to you. If you consider my response to be a denial of your request, you are entitled to appeal this determination in writing to the Secretary of the Navy. . . . "

I did not appeal but waited for developments.

On August 25, I received the following letter from the Naval Sea Systems Command (in part): "Although the FOIA stipulates a response to you in 20 days, in 'unusual circumstances' an agency can extend the twenty-day time for processing a FOIA request if it informs the requester of why it needs the extension and of when it will make a determination on the request. The FOIA defines unusual circumstances as (1) the need to search for and collect records from separate offices; (2) the need to examine a voluminous amount of records required by the request: (3) the need to consult with another agency or agency component and rely upon them to locate and review these records. In this case, there is a need to consult with other agency components to conduct a review of these records. We will provide a final response to your request in the most prompt manner possible.

"Meanwhile, you have the right to file an appeal to our delay in issuing a substantive response. . . . "

I did not file an appeal. I let the Navy take whatever amount of time it needed.

August 29: "This is our final response to your Freedom of Information Act (FOIA) request dated July 19, 2014, for about [sic] the demolition of the YMS-14. We conducted a thorough search of this Headquarters files, specifically those located in the Program Executive Office Ships, Inactive Ships Office (SEA 21), and the Ocean Engineering, Supervisor of Salvage and Diving (SEA 00C) and were unable to locate any records responsive to your request. However, personnel with those offices suggested you check with the Naval History and Heritage Center and the Navy Expeditionary Combat Command. To save time, we have taken the liberty of forwarding your request to those activities for action and direct response to you."

I never heard from the Naval History and Heritage Command except indirectly through the letter to Senator Pat Toomey, which I quoted above. But that response did not include any documentation, only a summation that was lifted from my book, and parenthetical information about which unit was responsible for demolishing the wreck.

On October 3, I received a response from the Navy Expeditionary Combat Command. In part: "Your request was forwarded to our command by Commander, Naval Sea Systems Command. We received your request on September 22, 2014 and it was assigned FOIA case file number DON-NAVY-2014-008834. In an effort to assist you, Naval Sea Systems Command personnel suggested that the Navy Expeditionary Combat Command (NECC) may have records responsive to your request. However, NECC does not maintain documentation regarding Minesweeper warships. Therefore, we do not have any documents pertaining to the USS TMS (YMS-14) or its demolition.

"If you have a specific file or event related information that leads you to believe we would have such records, or if you can identify a particular office that you believe would hold the documents, please resubmit your request, including as much detail as possible."

Luck was on my side. Only one day before I received the above letter, I received the letter that Senator Pat Toomey forwarded to me from the Naval History and Heritage Command, in which the unit that demolished the wreck was given.

As the Naval History and Heritage Command possessed the information that I was seeking, and as my original FOIA request had been forwarded to that command, it should have responded directly to me and furnished responsive documentation. But it was playing hardball.

It seemed to me that there were two major problems with obtaining information from the Navy. First, the command structure within the Department was so mud-

Demolition of the YMS-14

dled and disarranged that one command did not have access to another command's files, despite the fact that data storage and retrieval were computerized; or to coin a cliché, the left hand didn't know what the right hand was doing. It was left to me and John Q. Public to know beforehand which command within the complex Navy hierarchy held the documents I wanted, and to submit my FOIA request to that particular command. This is plain stupid. How is an uninformed outsider supposed to know what the Navy itself doesn't know?

This observation is no indictment on the individuals who tried to fulfill my request. They gave the appearance of having been defeated by the system. But it *is* a reflection on the overall conduct of Naval Intelligence.

Second, the command that *did* possess the information – the Naval History and Heritage Command – refused to provide it to me. And this is the command that is primarily responsible for Navy history, and that now wants to take possession of tens of thousands of shipwrecks worldwide. This is definitely a reflection on the individuals within that command.

As the Naval History and Heritage Command was either dragging its feet or ignoring me intentionally, I appealed to the Navy Expeditionary Combat Command, and furnished the information that Kuhn had given to the senator.

On November 12, I received an email acknowledging that my appeal had been received. When December arrived with no response to my FOIA request despite my appeal, I decided to write directly to the Naval History and Heritage Command – to which the Navy Expeditionary Combat Command had forwarded my FOIA request two months earlier:

> J.K. Kuhn, Director   December 4, 2014
> Naval History and Heritage Command
> 805 Kidder Breese Street SE
> Washington Navy Yard, DC 20374-5060
>
> Some three months ago, on August 29, 2014,

the Naval Sea Systems Command responded to my July 19, 2014 FOIA request (see enclosure) for information regarding the demolition of the *YMS-14* in Boston Harbor. (See enclosure.) That letter informed me that my request was being forwarded to your command for "action and direct response." The Naval Sea System Command is located only a few blocks from your office.

Although you responded to Senator Pat Toomey in regard to my letter in opposition to your proposed legislation (see enclosure), and although you referred to me and acknowledged your familiarity with the demolition of the *YMS-14*, I have not received a direct response from you in regard to my FOIA request. Your familiarity with the demolition of the *YMS-14* indicates that you possess the information that I requested, that you know where the information is located, and that you have access to all the information that is responsive to my request.

In either case, if you have already sent this information to me, please be advised that I did not receive it. Please send it again. Digitized documents may be sent either as email attachments or on compact disks, whichever is easier. Printouts are also acceptable.

I hoped that one of these two Navy Commands would finally deliver the documentation that I had requested four months earlier.

The Navy "Lost in Limbo" Dance

On January 6, 2015, I sent a reminder to the Navy Expeditionary Combat Command, to which I had submitted Kuhn's first-hand knowledge three months earlier.

Coincidentally, the very next day I received a response from the Naval History and Heritage Command in reference to my month-old reminder: "Your request is being worked on. We are currently working on a 400+

Demolition of the YMS-14

case FOIA backlog with requests dating back several years, with older cases receiving priority. Therefore, it may be 60-90 days or more before your request is completed."

This was a dreadfully telling statement. As you will read in the following chapter, in 2013 the Command stopped providing all historical services to civilians. Both the Naval Historical Center and the Naval Photographic Center were closed to the public. In all the decades in which I conducted research in those facilities, I never saw any Navy personnel doing research or requesting historical documentation.

The active Navy – that is, the part of the Navy whose occupation and concerns involved homeland defense and the protection of American lives and interests around the world – had no need of historical reference materials. The active Navy was engaged with the present, not with the past.

In other words, the primary purpose of those Centers was to provide historical research services to the non-Navy public: to civilian historians and academics. This begs the question: What were all those employees doing now that they were no longer complying with their Congressional mandate?

According to the statement that is quoted above, one thing that the Naval History and Heritage Command was not doing was responding to FOIA requests within the 20-day timeframe that the Naval Sea Systems Command informed me was stipulated. (For that matter, neither was the Naval Sea Systems Command adhering to its own acknowledgment of that stipulation.)

So if the Naval History and Heritage Command was not providing research services to the public, and was not fulfilling FOIA requests, just what the hell was it was doing? I could go farther and ask: What purpose was it serving? Or: Why did it even exist?

In my opinion, the Naval History and Heritage Command served no public purpose and had no justifiable reason to exist. As for what it was doing: it was writing rules and legislation that would benefit no one but its

Demolition of the YMS-14

staff members, by maintaining their jobs and by giving them control over vast resources such as abandoned and deteriorating shipwrecks and aircraft, none of which they were doing anything to protect or preserve from the harsh environment that they inhabited.

The Naval History and Heritage Command was a self-serving entity, and nothing else.

I had no doubt that no matter how much the Command caught up with its backlogged FOIA requests, my low-priority request would be given a permanent place at the bottom of the heap.

As this book goes to press, my seven-month-old FOIA request is still in limbo.

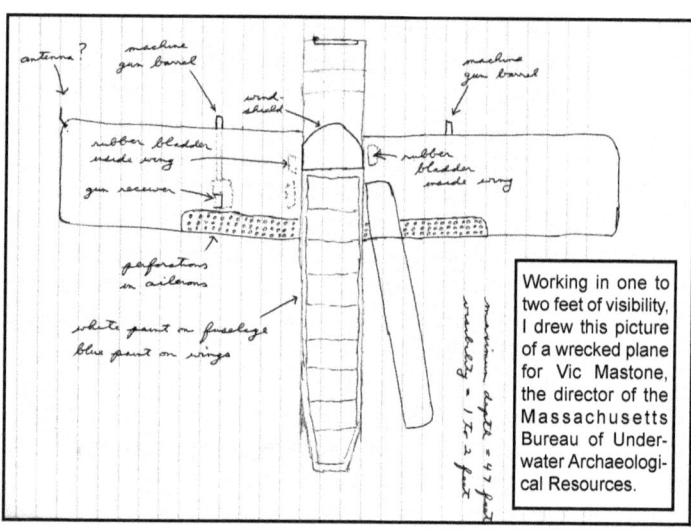

Working in one to two feet of visibility, I drew this picture of a wrecked plane for Vic Mastone, the director of the Massachusetts Bureau of Underwater Archaeological Resources.

The Navel of Naval History

The Washington Navy Yard is the main repository for U.S. Navy archival records. The Yard is an active Navy base that is located on the shore of the Anacostia River, a few miles upstream from the confluence with the Potomac River.

I have been doing research there since the 1970's. The research assistants from those days have all retired or died. That is too bad for modern civilian researchers because those folks were honest and sincere about their duties as public servants. I have lived and conducted research long enough to witness the gradual degeneration of the attitudes of the new staff, and the increasing restriction of access to public records by the public. Today the doors to Naval history are nearly all closed to the public.

Touching All Bases

There are four facilities in the Yard in which to conduct research. All four of them used to be housed under the same roof – although, technically speaking, they were located in three different buildings.

The Ships History Branch and the Operational Archives were located in Building 57: Ships History Branch on the first floor (to the left of the lobby), and Operational Archives on the third floor (with offices on the second floor). Both of these facilities were known collectively as the Naval History Center.

If you walked straight ahead from the lobby of Building 57, and proceeded down a flight of steps, you would pass through what appeared to be a short hallway but which was actually a roofed-over connecting corridor that led to Building 44, which housed the research room of the Navy Department Library. You could then reach the Naval Photographic Center by climbing up a flight of steps from the Library, and proceeding along a narrow covered passageway to Building 108, whose floor was the ceiling of the open shelves where the Library's books were stored (separate from the research room). If you were to visit all four facilities in a row, you would never know that you moved from one building to another.

Nowadays the Ships History Branch is located in a different building.

Operational Archives of the Naval History Center

In the 1970's and 1980's, when Bernard Cavalcante and Mike Walker ran the show, the Operational Archives was a virtuous and valuable institution that was devoted to the dissemination of historical information to researchers of all denominations. From there I gathered a massive amount of material not only on Navy vessels and operations, but on merchant vessel losses during both world wars.

Cavalcante handled most of the mail order queries, while Walker took charge of identifying and pulling records for visiting researchers. I explained to Walker what I was looking for, then he located the file boxes and brought them to the Research Room. If he was uncertain about which records to pull, he either asked me for clarification or he pulled all file boxes that might contain information on the topic that I was researching.

On occasion, Cavalcante and Walker took me into the stacks where the records were stored, so I could read the descriptive labels on various file boxes in order to determine which ones I could discard outright or suggest others nearby to pull. Both of them went out of their way to help researchers find the information they sought. Sometimes Walker brought file cards or carts full of file boxes on the off chance that they might be of some help.

Those were the good old days.

There was a copy machine in the room, but researchers were not allowed to operate it. I had to tab documents for Walker to copy. If he spent too much time on pulling records for researchers, and did not have enough time to make photocopies before closing time, I totaled my tabs, paid ten cents a copy in advance, and he mailed the copies to me within a few days.

I needed plenty of copies because I was conducting bulk research on vessels that were sunk all along the eastern seaboard, not just on one or two isolated shipwrecks. Toward the end of the 1980's, I stepped up the quantity of my research because I signed a contract with Avon Books to write *Track of the Gray Wolf*, which focused on World War Two U-boat depredations from Maine to Florida.

Around this time, the administrators of the Operational Archives (not Cavalcante or Walker) started tightening the reins on the productivity of researchers by allowing them to order only fifty photocopies *per year*. They kept count. The working staff was hampered by regulations that were made higher up.

Gina Akers, new kid on the block, was assigned to work with me on my book project (although Cavalcante and Walker were there to lend their able assistance and long-time expertise). She had to obtain special dispensation to enable me to make more than my allowable quota, and to her I owe a great debt of gratitude.

In retrospect, it eventually came to light that another newby, Kathy Lloyd, had a hand in my research. But more on that later.

The *Gentian* Report – Turnabout is Fair Play

One of the most heartwarming aspects of shipwreck research is meeting kindly people in the pursuit of historical research. One such person was Denny Breese. In 1990, when I was researching *Shipwrecks of North Carolina*, someone in Wilmington gave me his phone number and suggested that I contact him. I called him, told him who I was, and what I was doing. Breese was a treasure salvor who was living on a salvage vessel that was moored off Wilmington.

He invited me to visit for a chat. One of his employees picked me up at the dock in a motorboat, and drove me to the site that Breese was working. He and I hit it off well. Obviously we shared an interest in submerged maritime history, but it was more than that. Because we both knew so much about the subject, we were able to converse intelligibly in a way that neither of us had much opportunity to do with other people. There aren't many shipwreck scholars in the world. We had so much to talk about that I ended up staying overnight.

Breese had information on a number of local wrecks that he was happy to share with me. He didn't have a photocopy machine onboard, so he gave me his original files and told me to mail them back to him after I made copies ashore. This was extremely gracious and trusting of him; he didn't know me from Adam. The only other person to ever trust me with original documents was Clive Cussler – on more than one occasion.

Anyway, in addition to documents about specific local shipwrecks, Breese loaned me a large report about the *Gentian* survey of 1944. The *Gentian* was a Coast Guard cutter that served as a platform for a group of scientists from the Lamont-Doherty Geological Observatory. These scientists were testing their state-of-the-art underwater camera and flash system on shipwrecks off the coast of North Carolina. The *Gentian* located many of the tankers and freighters that were torpedoed by German U-boats in the first half of 1942: the so-called Operation Drumbeat. The scientists took photographs of wreckage with a drop camera in a waterproof housing.

The report was more than one hundred pages in length. It was replete with information about wrecks that I was covering in my various books. The report referenced a report about an earlier cruise aboard the *Gentian*: one that occurred in 1943. On my next visit to the Naval Historical Center, I asked Mike Walker for the 1943 report. Throughout the day, he kept telling me that he was still looking for it. Finally, late in the afternoon, he admitted that he was unable to locate it. Bernard Cavalcante joined in the search, but to no avail. In ex-

The Navel of Naval History

asperation, Walker asked me where I found the citation for the report.

Fortunately, I had brought with me the photocopy that I had made from Breese's copy. (By then I had mailed all of Breese's documents back to him.) I took the report from my briefcase in the outer office, showed it to Walker, and indicated where it referred to the earlier report. Armed with the citation information that was given in the 1944 report, both he and Cavalcante delved deep into the stacks. Just before closing time, Walker returned to the Research Room with two three-by-five file cards that referenced the *Gentian* reports. According to the notations, both reports had "disappeared" about ten years earlier.

Cavalcante joined us. He asked to see my copy of the 1944 report. I showed it to him and explained how I had obtained it. As an historian, he was obviously excited about the reappearance of a report that had been lost for so long. He asked me if I would let him make a copy for their files.

Now here was a decided turn of events: I was there to obtain documents, not to furnish them to an agency that was supposed to possess them already. I couldn't help but mention the irony of the situation. They both snickered.

I said, "Of course you can copy it." Then I added casually, "But you're only allowed fifty photocopies per year."

They were nonplussed for a moment, until my grin told them that I was only joking.

They wasted no time in copying the report in its entirety. The 1943 *Gentian* report is still missing.

The moral of this story is one of trust. I trusted the staff to find documents that pertained to the subjects that I was researching. The staff trusted that I and other researchers would make use of the documents that the staff willingly provided. We were all historians: some on the archiving and disseminating end, others on the receiving and distributing end.

The purpose of the Naval Historical Center was – and

I stress the word *was* – not only to stockpile documents that related to Navy history, but to share the information on those documents with anyone and everyone who could make use of it. In this manner Navy history was spread throughout the world for the enrichment and benefit of all.

The End of the Good Old Days

Long gone are those halcyon days when the staff at the Naval Historical Center was dedicated to providing historical records to researchers – going out of their way, even, to track down documents that were difficult to locate. The new guard is just that: a guard or defender against unwanted intrusion into what they consider to be their private domain.

The attitude of sharing information has given way to an oppositional attitude of concealing it from the public. Chief offensive fullback was civilian Bill Dudley, newly ordained head of the restrictive regime, with Kathy Lloyd acting as his sergeant-at-arms. She was a research "assistant" who on good days was merely abrasive; on bad days she was openly hostile toward researchers – and not just to me, but to every researcher I ever met who had to deal with her. Together they conspired to prevent researchers from having access to documents that were held by the Navy in the public trust.

The depravity of this self-serving direction was brought to my attention in October 2000. For reasons that will soon become apparent, I did not act upon the situation until six years later. What follows is a verbatim transcript of a letter that I sent to Admiral Paul Tobin, then Director of the Naval Historical Center, on January 1, 2007:

> I am presently writing a book about U-boat warfare off the American eastern seaboard during World War One.
>
> On December 19, 2006, I visited the Washington Navy Yard for the express purpose of accessing a manuscript entitled "U-boat

Operations in the Western Atlantic During World War I," written by Richard A. von Doenhoff and Harry E. Rilley. I have accessed this manuscript often over the past twenty years, as my research dictated, for other book projects. Originally I asked to have the manuscript photocopied for future reference, but my request was denied because – as I was told – there was a limitation on photocopies of 50 pages per calendar year. The ongoing nature of my research demanded that I "save" my meager photocopy privileges for different relevant work.

I have always relied on reference assistants to locate the manuscript in the stacks, and to pull it from the stacks for viewing. On this occasion, no one was able to locate the manuscript – or even to confirm its existence. The "best guess" was that the manuscript (which, to the best of my recollection, was stored in two or three blue cardboard file boxes) had been transferred to the library downstairs.

The librarians were unable to locate the boxes that contained the manuscript. Nor were they able to find a transfer order. They called upstairs to obtain the number of the transfer order from Kathy Lloyd. She was unable to provide such a number, but stated that she had personally transferred the manuscript to the library. The reference assistants then stopped searching for the manuscript in the Operational Archives.

The matter ended in limbo. My trip from Philadelphia was wasted.

This brings to mind another and more serious matter that occurred in October 2000. On that occasion I visited the Operational Archives in order to obtain additional information for a revised edition of *Track of the Gray Wolf*, a book about U-boat warfare off the American eastern seaboard during World War Two. I researched and wrote *Track of the Gray Wolf* in the 1980's. I conducted much of my research at the Naval Historical Center. The book was published in 1989.

Kathy Lloyd assigned a recently hired research assistant to help me. After hearing the nature of my research, this assistant went into the stacks to obtain documents that were relevant to my research. Upon his return, he asked me to accompany him to his office so that we could talk in private. Behind closed doors, he told me that Kathy Lloyd had given him specific instructions to withhold certain documents from me. These documents were not classified; nor was there any valid reason why they should have been withheld.

He explained that he did not think that it was right for public documents to be withheld from a member of the public; that these documents were being held in trust for the American people; that he disagreed strongly with Lloyd's instructions; but that he could not bring out the documents that I asked for because he could lose his job if she caught him disobeying her specific instructions. He also asked me to protect his anonymity should I choose to lodge a complaint with her superiors.

At that time, I felt that any complaint that I lodged must implicate him directly and jeopardize his job. Now, after the passage of six years, and after not seeing him in the Operational Archives during my recent visit, the time is ripe to bring this matter to the attention of people in authority – to people who may not be aware of Lloyd's dictatorial policy regarding the release of documents to researchers; or, perhaps, to people who are part of the conspiracy to withhold public documents from the public.

The documents that were withheld from me six years ago were also withheld from me twenty years ago, when I was researching and writing

Track of the Gray Wolf. This information should have been disseminated to the public through the publication of my book. Instead, the public was cheated out of some of its heritage.

This situation constitutes a serious breach of ethics. By withholding public documents, Lloyd abused the authority that is vested in her. This is not merely a matter of inefficiency, or lack of dedication in the performance of her duties, but a conscious decision on her part to dictate who should have access to public documents, and who should not have access.

This is not her decision to make. Nor is it the Navy's decision to make. These documents are merely held in trust by the Navy for the public. This is a Congressional decision to make. Congress has long since deemed it proper that researchers, historians, and the public at large have access to public documents.

Furthermore, mine are not isolated incidents. On more than one occasion, when I telephoned Lloyd months after submitting a written request for information, she told me that there was no record of receipt; my mailed requests were mysteriously "lost." I have heard complaints from others who have had difficulties in dealing with the Operational Archives in general and with Lloyd in particular: difficulties that have now reached epidemic proportions.

Fortunately for my continued research, many of the World War Two documents which the Naval Historical Center controlled when I wrote *Track of the Gray Wolf* were transferred to the National Archives in 1996. These documents are more accessible to the public at their new premises, not only due to the policies of the National Archives and to the able help provided by research assistants who are honest and sincere in their endeavors to aid researchers, but because there is no limitation on the number of photocopies that a researcher may make. The new custodians of these documents are simply that: custodians, not self-appointed despots.

I want these matters investigated at once. I want to be kept apprised of any action – or inaction – that is taken to rectify the extremely important matter of willfully withholding public documents from the public. Of secondary importance, I also want to be notified of the "discovery" of the location of the von Doenhoff and Rilley manuscript.

Perhaps the Naval Historical Center is not a suitable agency for archiving national historical documents that pertain to the American heritage.

So that co-conspirators at the Naval Historical Center do not sweep this complaint under the rug, I am sending copies to my representatives.

Copied to: Captain Peter Wheeler, Deputy
Director, Naval Historical Center
Representative Mark Cohen
Representative Allyson Schwartz
Senator Arlen Specter
Senator Robert Casey

Lame Excuse

As you can see, I didn't pull any punches. I call 'em as I see 'em.

One purpose of my letter was to determine how far the conspiracy went in the hierarchy of the Naval Historical Center. Here is Tobin's reply:

We apologize for our inability to provide you with access to the Richard A. von Doenhoff and Harry E. Rilley manuscript, "U-boat Operations in the Western Atlantic During World War I," which as you correctly indicated has been in the custody of the Operational Archives for many years. The five boxes of material have not been moved from their location in the archives but we did fail to list the title in our TRIM database that is the primary reference tool of our archivists. That oversight has been corrected.

With regard to your visit to the Operational Archives in October 2000, we regret that your experience was not a positive one and that you were unable to gain access to materials related to your research on U-boats in World War II. Please be assured that our policy is to withhold no unclassified archival documents from the public. Mrs. Lloyd, Head of the Operational Archives, is a dedicated and professional civil servant who would only withhold documents bearing a security classification or covered under Privacy Act restrictions. If you can identify those documents you require for your research, we will do all we can to locate them and once assured they are releasable to the public offer them to you. Moreover, we no longer have a policy of limiting 50 photocopied pages per researcher in a given year.

We regret your unfortunate experience in the Operational Archives and welcome your future research visits to the Naval Historical Center.

Conspirators Unite

In my opinion, Tobin was either totally ignorant of how Lloyd operated under his command, or he was part of the conspiracy. It will soon become apparent why I suspect the latter.

Tobin was being either facetious or absurd when he suggested that I "identify those documents you require for your research." This is a classic catch-22. A researcher cannot know when documents are being withheld from him if he has no knowledge of their existence, and if the research assistant goes out of her way to hide that knowledge from him.

As for the records that had been maliciously withheld from me on two occasions – first in the late 1980's after Lloyd started exerting her authority, and second in 2000 at her direct intervention – I no longer needed them. A few weeks after my October 2000 visit, I received a one-inch-thick packet of photocopied documents in the mail. The package was sent by the research assistant whose anonymity I promised to protect: a retired ex-Navy officer whose principles contradicted those of the watchdogs who kept a lid on information from me and my readers.

That day in his office, my anonymous benefactor said that Lloyd told him not to give me anything with wreck locations. She kept a close watch on the records that he pulled for me, and examined them before she let him show them to me. In *Track of the Gray Wolf*, I appended a chronological list of every U-boat attack in the Eastern Sea Frontier, along with attack positions in latitude and longitude. The packet that I received contained hundreds of attack locations that I could have used in compiling my appendix. None of these documents was classified.

The Ministry of Love

At this remove, fifteen years after the incident, I don't think that the career of the research assistant can be adversely affected if I reveal his name: Kenneth Johnson. In any case, the Navy must have employment records for the time period in question. It would easy for Navy revengers to ascertain his name and have their thought police launch a vendetta against him for his honesty, and as a way to prevent him from confirming the truth of the incident.

As a precautionary measure, to forestall the witch-hunters from harassing him, here is his cover letter (dated October 21, 2000):

Dear Gary,

I have enclosed the geographic coordinates for the World War II ship sinkings from 20° N through 49° N latitude. This information was coped from 3 x 5" index cards that we hold in

The Navel of Naval History

our finding aid card file. Technically, these cards are a cross-reference to an alphabetical file (on 5 x 7" cards); the geographic locations are, of course, approximate. You and I know they should be made available to researchers as they are in the public domain. Cal Cavalcante agrees but he is no longer the branch head. Kathy Lloyd has assumed the position and it was fortunate that she was on leave the last two weeks, otherwise I would have been unable to copy the cards.

Please keep this information on close hold with your colleagues. The last thing I need is a FOIA from one of them intimating that you received preferential treatment. If you need any further information my address, home telephone and e-mail are listed above. I would give you my e-mail at work but that is on a network and subject to monitoring by our Information Management Branch. Also, due to an office shuffle, I'm ensconced at one of the two front desks in the entrance foyer and therefore my telephone conversations are no longer private. I am currently job hunting and probably will not be at the Naval Historical Center after the beginning of the year. You can read between the lines and understand why. If you need any additional information, please let me know soonest.

Warm regards,
Ken

Further affiant sayeth naught.

The Missing MS

I had to make a special trip to the Washington Navy Yard to see the von Doenhoff and Rilley manuscript. It was still located in the Operational Archives under Lloyd's control. Had it been transferred to the library downstairs in the 1980's, I could have copied it in its entirety, because the library never had a limitation on the number of photocopies that a researcher could make.

The library had three self-operated photocopy machines that researchers were allowed to use. I used to make as many photocopies as I wanted, count the number of pages, and pay the librarian. The librarian did not count the photocopies, but trusted me to be honest and pay the correct amount.

As long as I am on the subject of the "lost" or "misplaced" manuscript, I will take this opportunity to relate the saga of its research, writing, and eventual shelving, because it relates directly to Navy censorship and suppression of information.

First, some background information to set the stage.

In 1920, the Government Printing Office published a book entitled *German Submarine Activities on the Atlantic Coast of the United States and Canada*. It was called Publication No. 1. This was the official version of the U-boat war, complete with photographs, statistics, and foldout charts. The book was not without errors. Later editions added four pages of errata totaling more than seventy mistakes (although most of the mistakes were misspellings or typographical errors). Also, some of the information regarding U-boat movements was speculative.

For many years in the late 1970's and early 1980's, von Doenhoff assisted me after he transferred to the National Archives to work as a research assistant in the Navy Records Branch. Because we talked a great deal about our shared historical interests, he told me how the manuscript came into being.

The project that was known as "U-boat Operations in the Western Atlantic During World War I" was initiated by Vice Admiral Edwin Hooper, then Director of Naval History. At the time of its inception, in 1973, von Doenhoff and Rilley were civilian historians who were employed at the Naval Historical Center. Admiral Hooper charged them with producing the above-named book.

The manuscript was pieced together with snippets that were photocopied from Publication No. 1, along with the addition of official statements from survivors and U-boat deck logs, to which von Doenhoff and Rilley added

The Navel of Naval History

connecting narrative.

U-boat deck logs were not available to Navy historians in 1920, when Publication No. 1 was published. After the Allies invaded Berlin and ended World War Two, the British dispatched a staff of technicians to microfilm German military records, in order to compile a two-sided history of the war. As part of this process the Brits microfilmed all the U-boat deck logs that they found in German archives – and not just deck logs from Hitler's Third Reich, but also deck logs from the Kaiser's previous bid for world domination.

The British provided the American government with copies of the microfilms. These copies are now stored in the Microfilm Research Room of the National Archives at College Park, Maryland, and are freely available to the public.

The addition of U-boat deck logs to the von Doenhoff and Rilley manuscript added a new and correlative perspective to the history of the U-boat war in American waters. Now this aspect of the war could be seen from both sides, with deck log entries often correcting the misinterpretation of events that were seen by Allied observers and intelligence agencies.

No problems arose until the manuscript reached the paste-up stage. Admiral Hooper wanted the completed book to show how U.S. citizens had been traumatized by U-boat activity so close to American shores. However, the facts belied the admiral's pet theme. Even a casual perusal of contemporary newspaper accounts demonstrated the contrary. If anything, the people were galvanized to action against the arrogant invading Huns.

Neither von Doenhoff nor Rilley backed down from their position. Frustrated by his misconceptions, the admiral refused to permit the publication of the manuscript. And so the only copy has languished on a shelf ever since, practically forgotten.

For me the manuscript was an invaluable resource – not for the snippets from Publication No. 1 (of which I owned a copy), nor for the official statements of survivors (of which I had copies of the full and unedited versions courtesy of the National Archives), but for the U-boat deck logs. The microfilmed originals were written in German. Von Doenhoff and Rilley had them translated into English.

Despite Lloyd's interference, I was eventually able to incorporate the U-boat deck log translations into *The Kaiser's U-boats in American Waters* (2010).

Never let it be said that research is easy. It is made more difficult, sometimes impossible, by selfish and self-appointed guardians who place obstacles in the way of honest researchers who seek only truth – and often encounter intentional obstructionism.

"I'll Save You, Nell"

The morning of November 31, 1995 found me doing microfilm research on the 4th Floor of the National Archives in DC. Because of the self-retrieval process, I squirreled my microfilm research into odd moments when I was waiting for the delivery of records to the Central Research Room. I studied the finding aids, then went into the stack area to locate the aisle, cabinet, and drawer in which the reel that I wanted was stored.

Just as I wrapped my fingers around the drawer handle, another hand grabbed the other end of the same handle. We looked up at each other in surprise. What are the chances that two researchers wanted reels out of the same drawer at the same time, when there are thousands of drawers? But that was only the beginning of the coincidence.

No, we did not both want the same reel. But we were working in the same microfilm group: T-925 – U.S. Coast Guard Casualty and Wreck Reports, 1913-1939.

In accented English, he introduced himself as Patrick Lize, a freelance researcher from Paris, France, who had been hired by a French treasure salvage outfit to conduct research in American archives.

When I told him my name, he looked stunned for a moment. Then he told me that he had just seen my name on the cover of a book in the Central Research Room. Since he too was doing shipwreck research, he

The Navel of Naval History 51

spent some time talking with the gal who was using my *San Diego* book as a reference guide. The *San Diego* was an armored cruiser that had struck a mine laid by a German U-boat in World War One, off the coast of Long Island, New York. She told him that she was a private researcher from California, and that the Navy had hired her to confirm the facts in my 1989 publication.

This was a bizarre twist of events. Lize and I chatted for a while about our research projects, exchanged contact information, then proceeded with our separate research.

A postcard picture of the *San Diego*.

Reverse Research

Later that morning, in the Central Research Room, I surreptitiously sauntered past the workstations until I saw my book on the desktop in front of a woman who had a cart full of file boxes that related to Naval activities during World War One. She was going through the book, and checking my facts with archival documents. She was doing "reverse research." This is much like "reverse engineering" that is conducted by a company that purchases a product from a competing company with the idea of duplicating the product. She was locating the originating sources of the facts that were in my book.

The way she did this was to show my facts to a research assistant, and ask to see the records where I found those facts.

I knew what she was looking for, and I could have

told her precisely where to find it. The Navy could have saved the taxpayers a great deal of money by hiring *me* to provide the documentation whose existence she was trying to confirm.

I had done extensive research on the *San Diego* prior to writing the book on the warship's history, and I had photocopied every relevant document that I had found. I knew from current Navy scuttlebutt which individual document she was hoping *not* to find; or, if she found it, was hoping that I had misread, misinterpreted, or intentionally misconstrued the information that the document contained.

For years, minions at the Naval Historical Center had been trying to make all sunken Navy vessels off-limits to divers – not to protect or to preserve the collapsing hulks, for mankind is powerless against the inevitable forces of nature and the corrosive undersea environment – but to exercise their control: for no better reason than, like little Hitlers, they wanted to dominate the underwater world.

Control Freaks

The commonly accepted belief is that the "Navy" wants to prevent divers from seeing that part of their cultural history that exists in the form of sunken Navy vessels. This is not exactly the truth.

Remember this from the previous chapter: when I wrote to the Navy Department in an attempt to obtain historical information that I was unable to obtain from the Naval Historical Center, the person who replied was blunt when he wrote that the purpose of the Navy is national defense, not the preservation of history. He was right.

The "Navy" has little or no interest in its submerged fleet of yesteryear. The faction that is hell-bent on the shipwreck power play is a handful of *civilians* who work in the Operational Archives. This handful – literally five people at the time – continually abuse the authority of their association by utilizing Navy funding and resources to promote their collective personal agenda.

These people do not represent the Navy, nor do they represent the *wishes* of the Navy. They are employees of the Navy who have taken it upon themselves to control abandoned vessels for which the Navy has no further need.

As noted above, the leader and chief conniver of this group was Bill Dudley, then Director of the Naval Historical Center. Dudley is now retired, but his legacy of underwater territorial demand lives on in the minds of indoctrinated underlings who carry the torch to burn present and future generations of divers. This civilian but uncivilized cancer within the Navy is solely responsible for the ongoing efforts to oppress freedom under the guise of historic preservation.

The disreputable part that the real Navy plays is one in which it unwittingly supports the renamed Naval History and Heritage Command by financing its fanatical ownership demands, and by providing unlimited legal services which the Command exploits in order to achieve its nefarious goal of aggrandizement, and which it manipulates to act as a cat's-paw in order to threaten and browbeat all those who oppose its self-appointed directive toward absolute control of submerged wrecks.

The Witch-Hunters

It seemed to me that Dudley worked hard to brainwash his compatriots about the harm that recreational scuba divers were doing to Navy wrecks. In effect, he created a witch-hunting fleet whose sole aim was to maintain control over all wrecks of Naval origin. Ostensibly, the individuals in this radical fleet were equivalent to privateers who signed letters of marque that legitimatized their confiscation of enemy vessels. In actuality, they acted more like pirates.

The witch-hunters delighted in threatening or prosecuting salvors for alleged illegal underwater activities. They were extending their authority far beyond the pale of ethics.

The prime target on their hit list of shipwrecks was the *San Diego*: perhaps the most often dived U.S. Navy shipwreck in the world. It irked the witch-hunters to no end that divers visited this wreck nearly every weekend and often during the week.

Unfortunately for Dudley and his malicious cronies, the Navy had sold the *San Diego* to Maxter Metals for its scrap value. The purchase price was $1,221.00. The sale was consummated on October 27, 1957. I noted these facts in my book (*U.S.S. San Diego: the Last Armored Cruiser*). If the wreck had been sold to a private salvage outfit, then the Navy – and by extension, the Dudley group – could not claim dominion over it.

For Dudley and his group to have exclusive control over the *San Diego*, they had to disprove my claim that Maxter Metals bought the wreck legally. Unfortunately for the powermongers, I did not invent or imagine the Maxter Metals ownership. In my files I had a copy of the Navy document that qualified as a bill of sale.

Idly, I wondered if the hired hand from California would try to steal or destroy the historic sheet of paper, so as to enable the Navy's legal team to contradict my statement of ownership in a court of law. If that happened, I opined, I could produce my copy to bolster the truth of the situation. I knew that if she looked as hard as I did, she would find the incriminating evidence.

The Naval Hysterical Center

Back to the Archives on November 31, 1995. After seeing the gal with my *San Diego* book, I checked out of the room temporarily so I could read the names on the sign-in sheet. You can't do this today with the card swipe system, but in those days everyone had to print and sign his or her name upon entry to the Central Research Room.

Several women were in the room that day, so I didn't know which one was the gal in question. The next day I went to the Naval Historical Center. I got there only minutes after it opened, but already there was one name on the sign-in sheet, and it was one of the names that had been printed on the Archives sign-in sheet the day before. The woman was doing research at the Operational

The Navel of Naval History

Archives, but I never saw her because she had special dispensation to do her research in private. Her connection with the Navy explained how she managed to carry my book into the Central Research Room.

Kathy Lloyd was on duty that day. She was in her typical abusive mood. Nonetheless, I managed to obtain some materials for my ongoing research for my Popular Dive Guide Series. Word quickly circulated that I was in the building. I had barely started looking through documents when an individual entered the Research Room and said that he had heard that I was there, and that he wanted to meet me. He introduced himself as Otto Orzech.

Orzech was ex-Navy. He now did consulting work for the Navy. He told me that he was the leader of a team of researchers from California, all of whom the Navy had hired to conduct archival research on the *San Diego*. He knew of me through my book on the subject. The woman I saw in the National Archives was one of his associates. He cheerfully tuned me in to the big picture.

The Naval Historical Center had hired him and several others to work on the *San Diego* project. Because Orzech was ex-Navy, and a diver, he was also in charge of the Navy divers who were examining the wreck and the munitions that it contained, endeavoring to ascertain if the munitions were dangerous, so as to use that as an excuse to prohibit divers from visiting the site. He and his associates had been working on the project since July. I shook my head at the monumental waste

Separate ammunition canisters deep inside the *San Diego* where few divers could reach.

of taxpayers' dollars that were being spent to gratify the whims of a few sanctimonious civil servants who were serving themselves instead of their country.

Orzech had no axe to grind. He did not know that the witch-hunters held me in contempt. It was through this forthright conversation that I learned so much about the *San Diego* project.

The Lion's Den

Orzech returned at noon with an invitation for lunch from Bill Dudley. I could have declined, of course. As usual, I had brought my own lunch with me. I was not naïve enough to believe that Dudley was offering me an olive branch. He and I were implacable enemies, and would remain so until the end of time. He wanted control; I believed in freedom. There was no middle ground between us, any more than there was between Nazi Germany and Poland.

Dudley was the ring leader of the Naval Historical Center. Did he want me to share his lunch, or did he want to *have* me for lunch: to chew me up and spit me out in little pieces? All these thoughts raced through my mind in the seconds before I hesitantly uttered, "Okay." I knew what I was getting myself into.

I had never eaten in the cafeteria because it was operated only for Yard personnel. Orzech led the way. He introduced me to Dudley and three of his henchmen who would be sharing the table with us; one of them was his number one protégé, Bob Neyland. Then we went through the self-service line and chose our food. Dudley's invitation did not include paying for my lunch. I had to purchase my own meal.

Dudley and his minions fired questions about my many explorations into the hull of the *San Diego*. I was cautious with my replies, looking for innuendoes and implications that were not implicit in the wording or phrasing of the questions. Yet I have to admit that, although they were not overly friendly, they were neither aggressive nor accusatory. I expected to be crucified, but they were never less than civil. That didn't mean that

The Navel of Naval History

their attitude toward me (or recreational divers in general) had moderated, only that they had more oligarchic ways of achieving their goals. Or perhaps they thought that they could kill more bees with a honey trap.

I explained how my primary purpose in diving on the *San Diego* was to document it photographically. I took pictures of its artifacts, and I published many of them in *U.S.S. San Diego: the Last Armored Cruiser*. This was how the Navy – to use its own terminology of sixteen years later – became "re-acquainted" with the shipwreck. Even back then, they read my books in order to learn about shipwrecks that the Navy had forgotten, and to stay informed about new discoveries and recreational diving activities.

As no Navy personnel had ever dived on the *San Diego*, everything they knew about the wreck they learned by reading my book.

Mission Impossible

Ultimately, Navy lawyers must have advised the witch-hunters that their case would never stand in court. The Navy had indeed sold the *San Diego* to Maxter Metals. The Navy could not reclaim it legally.

One of the many shell rooms deep inside the *San Diego*.

Orzech's diving team spent *months* in removing munitions from the *San Diego*: munitions whose pictures they had seen in my book. The excuse the Navy gave for this costly salvage operation was that the projectiles (with warheads) and separate ammunition containers (which held the powder charge) presented a hazard to recreational scuba divers who habitually visited the site.

All along the Navy contended that the *San Diego* was an important archaeological site: a non-renewable cultural resource that needed "protection." Yet there was no accredited archaeologist on the salvage team to oversee operations. The Naval Historical Center conducted no archaeology on the wreck. The Naval salvors did not follow standard archaeological procedures – or *any* kind of archaeological procedure.

The monumental task was strictly a snatch-and-grab military mission that was conducted with no thought given to historic preservation.

The Navy could have hired me as a consultant for a fraction of the money that it cost to employ a group of researchers from California: paying not only their salaries but their travel and temporary living expenses; hotels in the District of Columbia are not cheap.

The archival documents that the Navy's paid researchers took months to unearth from moldy record groups, I could have produced in a day. And I wouldn't have limited the Navy to photocopying privileges of only fifty pages per year!

Because I had explored every inch of the *San Diego*, inside and out, and knew precisely where the munitions were stowed and how much armament the wreck contained, I could have told the salvage team everything they needed to know in order to conduct a safe and thorough salvage operation. Instead, they had to learn everything from scratch.

For that matter, I could have overseen the entire undertaking. After all, I was the expert who wrote the book on the wreck. Instead of paying me pennies, the Navy spent hundreds of thousands or millions of dollars on a senseless task that ultimately failed to achieve anything

The Navel of Naval History

of consequence.

There were *tons* and *tons* of munitions onboard the wreck. After all, the only ammunition that the *San Diego* ever fired in anger were the few shots that gunners managed to fire in the twenty minutes that passed between the explosion of the mine and the capsizing of the vessel.

After wasting the entire summer, the Navy divers abandoned the idea of recovering all the munitions. They hardly made a dent in the most accessible magazines, and never even reached some of the shell rooms and powder rooms that lay farther inside the hull. Nor did they touch the fixed ammunition for the saluting guns.

As soon as the Navy salvage team packed up and left in humiliation at their defeat, recreational scuba divers returned to the wreck for the sheer love of exploring it. No one has ever been harmed by alleged unstable and dangerous ammunition.

Poor Losers

Instead of letting the matter drop, however, the witch-hunters spearheaded efforts to take the wreck away from recreational scuba divers by claiming that the inverted hull was an important marine habitat, and by having the wreck designated as an underwater preserve. That stopgap status did not prevent divers from diving on the wreck, but it did make it illegal to take souvenirs of their dive, for example, by spearing fish, catching lobsters, and collecting scallops and knick-knacks.

With all these secret machinations going on behind the backs of American citizens, you can understand why the Naval Historical Center was not a healthy climate for researchers who were known to the witch-hunters as scuba divers. The witch-hunters now spend prodigious amounts of time in surfing the Internet and reading newspapers from around the country, in order to find potentially incriminating evidence that could be used to harass scuba divers and bona fide commercial salvors.

All too often, they achieved their nefarious aims by

making threats of prosecution, despite the lack of merit in a case. They know that most people are easily intimidated, and will fold a winning hand because of the cost of litigation. Time and again, using the unending cornucopia of taxpayers' money, these witch-hunters have tracked down recreational divers who have made claims on the Internet – either in forums, in discussion groups, or on personal websites – that they possess items that the witch-hunters try to construe might possibly have been recovered from so-called Navy wrecks.

The witch-hunters have gone as far as to dispatch Navy investigators and agents of the Federal Bureau of Investigation – who have better things to do in the fight against *real* crime – to people's private residences or places of business, in order to confiscate alleged Navy property, or to make arrests and haul people to prison in handcuffs. It *has* been done, and the process is ongoing and getting worse.

Afterward, the accused individuals must prove their innocence beyond a shadow of a doubt, and at their own expense. Constitutional rights notwithstanding, in these cases a person is guilty until he establishes his innocence beyond unreasonable doubt. I will cover some of these cases later in the book.

These aggrandizing political maneuvers have nothing to do with the preservation of historical documentation, and the dissemination of information to the public: a fact which the Naval Historical Center has apparently chosen to ignore was its sole rationale for existence.

The Emperor's New Clothes
According to the spurious Vision Statement of the Naval Historical Center, "We envision the Naval Historical Center as the indispensable resource for the U.S. naval history and heritage. We shall maintain the highest standards of our professions and shall be known for our knowledgeable and responsive staff."

What this Vision Statement neglected to mention was that the Center held its resources for only selected individuals, not for the public at large. Civilian re-

The Navel of Naval History

searchers were definitely not among the chosen.

Once, in the 1990's, when I needed some trifling item of information, and thought that it would be more efficient to write for it instead of making an all-day trip to the Washington Navy Yard to obtain it in person, I sent a request to the Operational Archives – the way a researcher from the other side of the country would have to do it, especially if he or she had a job that prevented him or her from taking off sufficient time to conduct the necessary research in person. That was when I learned how fortunate I was to live only three hours away from the facility, and could schedule recurring research trips. I learned how the rest of the public was treated.

The letter I received stated, in part: "Replies are taking between three and four months to process." Before the predicted time, I had already visited the Operational Archives and obtained the information in person.

The handful of people who dictated Navy archival policy have underhandedly reserved for themselves the right to decide which historic documents they shall dispense, when, and to whom. The significance of these double-dealings to civilian researchers is obvious. And the situation of dealing with this incestuous Navy fiefdom has gotten worse with the name change to the pretentious sounding Naval History and Heritage Command.

Consider the most recent response to the list of complaints that I sent to Senator Pat Toomey in 2014.

Kuhn: "Mr. Gentile's concerns with respect to the historical and archeological records held by NHHC are more difficult to address, since the time period of his engagement with our command spans nearly 30 years. However, we do want to assure him that our intent is to ensure access to the records maintained in our physical custody, within the constraints established by Freedom of Information Act (FOIA) and given the need for protection of classified materials.

"If in our interactions with Mr. Gentile, we gave the impression that access to records is based on personal philosophy or individual preference, that is categorically incorrect. Our permanent professional staff is knowledgeable of the law, regulation, and policy governing documentary access, and their determinations are based on the application of the mandates of the FOIA program and on the requirements for handling classified or otherwise restricted data which may be contained in the documents being requested."

In short, Kuhn pretended to a congressional representative that everything in the Naval History and Heritage Command was hunky-dory. As in the 2007 apologia, he chose to deny the actions of subordinates instead of correcting the situation, perhaps so as not to cast aspersions on the (subversive) policies of the Command. Based on my actual experiences, I found it difficult to accept that the Director(s) was not an active participant in the conspiracy to maintain preferential mistreatment against civilian researchers and historians.

As the old saying goes, the proof of the pudding is in the eating. Access to Naval records has gotten more restrictive in recent years. The first step in this direction was the implementation of stricter office hours: the Operational Archives was closed to civilian researchers on Wednesdays.

Then, civilian researchers could no longer visit the Operational Archives unannounced. Civilian researchers were required to make an appointment far in advance. The last time I made a research trip to DC, in 2013, I called for an appointment and was told that I could not come in for a week or two. This was not because of who I was because I did not give my name.

When I tried to make another appointment a couple of months later, I was told that the Operational Archives was closed to civilians.

Ships History Branch

If a researcher asked about a particular Navy vessel in the Operational Archives, he was immediately directed downstairs to the Ships History Branch.

Harry Rilley was in charge of the Ships History

The Navel of Naval History

Branch when I started my lifelong research into shipwrecks. He was a gruff individual who did not like to be disturbed from whatever he was doing behind the desk in his office. He never smiled, so perhaps he was unhappy with his lot in life, instead of being gruff.

When I first met him in the 1970's, he tore himself away from his paperwork, took me into the stacks where the ships' history folders were stored, showed me how the system was organized, and never bothered me again – for the next couple of decades. The Ships History Branch was completely self-service. The less interference Rilley had, the happier he was (if he was ever truly happy).

From that point onward, whenever I wanted a vessel's history folder, I paused at his office doorway to make him aware of my presence, he acknowledged my "Hello" with a nod, and I pulled whatever folders I wanted on that particular visit. I also replaced the folders when I was finished with them. The only time we spoke was on those rare occasions when I needed to ask a question – which I dreaded.

I had free use of the photocopier that was tucked into a corner of the stacks, next to a desk and chair that I could use as I perused the files.

The stacks were dark and dank. Often I had to switch on the lights in order to read the name tags on the file drawers.

Sometimes Rilley wasn't in his office when I arrived. I went about my business unattended. Sometimes I finished my research, refiled the folders, and departed without ever having seen another person in the room. I felt like a ghost researcher.

Rilley is now gone. Sometime around the turn of the century, the Ships History Branch was plucked from the tree and re-rooted a couple of blocks away, in the basement of Building 200. Security has been tightened considerably, but the new atmosphere is lighter and brighter.

Researchers can enter the vestibule but the inner door is locked. They have to press a buzzer for assistance. A staff member will unlock the door, instruct visitors to leave their outerwear and personal belongings in a locker in the vestibule, and escort them to the specialty of their choice: ships or aviation. Researchers can bring notepapers with them. Gone are the days when I kept my briefcase by my side. Researchers now have to sign the sign-in book.

Staff members at the Ships History Branch are friendly and accommodating. Researchers no longer have access to the stacks, but the staff members are so fast and efficient that they can retrieve requested folders in a matter of minutes. They even let me use the photocopier without charge.

The Ships History Branch supposedly keeps a folder on almost every major Navy vessel that was ever commissioned. Folders on eighteenth-century and early nineteenth-century vessels may be slim. Folders on small auxiliary craft may be non-existent. This latter category includes unarmed tugs, oilers, and yard craft, plus small warships such as patrol boats, minesweepers, and sub chasers.

Unfortunately, the Ships History Branch was closed to civilians in 2013, when the Operational Archives closed its doors to the public.

DANF

Entries in the *Dictionary of American Naval Fighting Ships* were written from records in the Ships History Branch and the Operational Archives (two floors upstairs). However, more detailed information will sometimes be found in the file folders than what was published in DANF.

Initially I thought that DANF was gospel. But I soon came to learn that the 5,270 pages in eight large-size printed volumes were rife with errors, omissions, and blatant inaccuracies that a thorough researcher could not have made accidentally. Some minor errors might have resulted from sloppy research, but the omissions were intentional, and many inaccuracies showed a lack of dedication in tracking down or copying information.

The Navel of Naval History   65

All too often, facts that I obtained from alternative primary sources disclosed a different picture of events the way they were portrayed in DANF. Sometimes I discovered facts that contradicted DANF. And sometimes I unearthed facts that were totally missing from DANF. Here are a few of the most egregious examples:

Errata Maxima

DANF has only four lines of text in its entry for the *YMS-14*: one for the builder, one for dates of construction, one for disposition, and one for the date when it was officially abandoned and stricken from the Navy Register. For disposition: "Sunk in collision Boston Harbor 1/11/45." The website of the Naval History and Heritage Command omits the *YMS-14* altogether.

The chapter on the *Herndon* in DANF omits all mention of the collision and sinking of the *YMS-14*. This is akin to a biography that fails to mention that the subject accidentally killed someone: a major event in a person's life.

Furthermore, both the 1978 reprint edition and the current online version of DANF state that after the war, the *Herndon* "arrived Charleston 28 January 1946 and decommissioned there 8 May and entered the Atlantic Reserve Fleet. She was moved to Philadelphia January 1947 and at present is berthed at Orange, Tex."

In fact, the *Herndon* was stricken from the Navy Register in 1971, and was scuttled off the coast of Florida in 1973. This historical reference is more than forty years out of date. This oversight doesn't speak well for the "historians" (or political advocates) in the revamped Naval History and Heritage Command.

Take the Navy tugboat *Nina* as another example. According to DANF (both printed and current online versions): "At 0630, 6 February 1910, *Nina* departed Norfolk for Boston and was last sighted off the Capes of the Chesapeake in the midst of a gale. She was never heard from again. The warship was declared lost and struck from the Navy List 15 March 1910, the 30 crewmen and one officer on board being listed as having died on that day. Her loss is one of the continuing mysteries of the sea."

The *Nina* is no mystery to recreational scuba divers. The wreck was discovered off the coast of Delaware in 1977, and has been a popular dive site ever since. I published a full account in *Shipwrecks of Delaware and Maryland*.

On September 6, 1918, the USS *Hisko* rammed and sank the passenger-freighter *Almirante*. Two hundred forty-five passengers and crew members survived the sinking; five crew members perished.

In the resulting lawsuit, the *Hisko* was found responsible for the collision because she was running without showing navigation lights, while the *Almirante* was showing side lights that were dimmed in accordance with wartime restrictions. The U.S. government appealed the decision, and lost the appeal. Not to give up easily, the government then found fault with the methods that were used to determine the value of the *Almirante* at the time of the collision. Appeal followed appeal. The United Fruit Company was finally reimbursed for the full value of the vessel – $1,750,000 – but the case was not settled until 1931: thirteen years after the event!

What does the *Hisko* entry remark about this catastrophe and incredibly lengthy court case? Absolutely nothing. The *Almirante* isn't even mentioned, as if the collision and resulting lawsuit never occurred. For details, see *Shipwrecks of New Jersey: South*.

The submarine *S-5* sank accidentally on her sea trials in 1920. The entire crew was saved after a remarkable and dramatic rescue operation: the men escaped by cutting a hole in the portion of the hull that bobbed above the waves, then crawling through the opening one by one. According to DANF (both printed and current online versions): "Later, the battleship *Ohio* (BB-12) secured a towline to the stern of the *S-5* and proceeded to tow her to more shallow water. The towline, however, parted and the loosed sub bobbed, then plunged to the bottom. No attempts were made to salvage *S-5*, and she was struck from the Navy list in 1921."

The Navel of Naval History

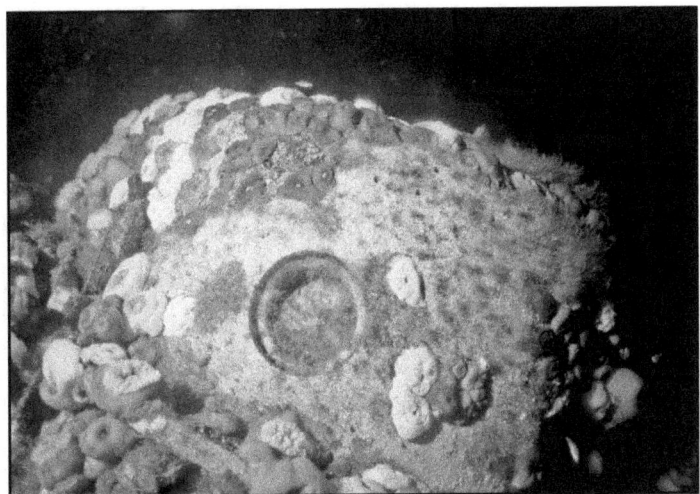

Note the porthole above the breakwater in this picture of the leading edge of the *S-5's* conning tower. Navy salvors blanked the portholes in an attempt to make the conning tower watertight. See the next page for a picture of the cutout in the Navy museum.

In fact, the Navy made two attempts to salvage the submarine. In 1920, divers from the minesweeper *Mallard* spent a month moored over the wreck, while divers tried to make the submarine's hull airtight. In 1921, the salvage vessel *Falcon* spent *four* months moored over the wreck, to no avail. In all, Navy divers made four hundred seventy-seven dives on the *S-5*.

The steel cutout – which was drilled and chiseled by hand from the hull, thus enabling the sailors to escape – is on display in the museum at the Washington Navy Yard, only a few blocks from the headquarters of the Naval History and Heritage Command. Navy historians displayed conspicuous ineptitude in overlooking these well-documented salvage operations. I pointed out these and other salient facts in *Shipwrecks of Delaware and Maryland.*

According to DANF, the submarine *Dragonet* was "decommissioned and placed in reserve at Mare Island 16 April 1946." In actuality, she was scuttled in the Chesapeake Bay on September 17, 1961. For full particulars, see *Shipwrecks of the Chesapeake Bay in Maryland Waters.*

The Navel of Naval History

The cutout from the *S-5* is on display in the museum in the Washington Navy Yard.

DANF proposes, "*S-49* was sold to the Boston Iron and Metal Co., Baltimore, Md., on 25 May 1931. Reduced to a hulk by that company in 1936, but not scrapped, the hulk was apparently reacquired seven years later, 'as equipment,' for use in experimental work

The *S-49* was a tremendous tourist attraction at the Chicago World's Fair.
(Courtesy of the Steamship Historical Society of America.)

The Navel of Naval History

at the Naval Mine Warfare Proving Ground, Solomons, Md." Note use of the word "apparently."

Navy historians appear to have no idea that the Boston Iron & Metals Company did not scrap the *S-49*, but sold her to Francis Chrestensen. He registered the ex-Navy submarine as a yacht named *C*, which spent the next five years roaming the Great Lakes as a tourist attraction. She was a major exhibit at the Chicago World's Fair, from 1933 to 1934. Tens of thousands of eager attendees walked through the fair's number one attraction. I told the full story in *Shipwrecks of the Chesapeake Bay in Maryland Waters*.

DANF claims that the armored ram *Katahdin* "was struck from the Navy List 9 July 1909; and designated 'Ballistic Experimental Target 'A''. *Katahdin* was sunk by gunfire at Rappahannock Spit, Va., in September." Not even close. In *Shipwrecks of the Chesapeake Bay in Virginia Waters*, I wrote four pages about the *Katahdin's* history subsequent to the date on which the Navy claims she was scuttled. She was sunk and raised a number of times over the next seven years, until she was finally left to rust on the bottom in 1916.

Katahdin: This unique Navy ram lies lost and forgotten in the Chesapeake Bay. (From the author's collection.)

DANF stated that the battleship *Texas* was "sunk as a target in Tangier Sound in Chesapeake Bay" without providing the date. DANF neglected to mention that the abandoned hulk was responsible for sinking three vessels and damaging two others. Proof that being struck from the Naval Register constituted legal abandonment came in the form of five lawsuits for which the Coast Guard was held responsible (for not adequately marking the obstruction) instead of the Navy (which now claims ownership, but which hid from ownership at the time the lawsuits were filed). The Navy can't have it both ways, by abandoning its legal obligations but later claiming ownership. Details may be found in *Shipwrecks of the Chesapeake Bay in Virginia Waters.*

On November 25, 1924, the battleship *Washington* (BB-47) was scuttled off the Virginia Capes. The printed edition of DANF mentions her in passing, but while the online version lists eight other vessels that carried the same name, it neglects to even note the existence BB-47. I discovered the wreck in 1989. An all-inclusive career account can be found in *Shipwrecks of Virginia.*

The battleship *Washington* under construction. (Courtesy of the National Archives.)

The *YP-389* isn't mentioned at all, yet its running gun battle with the *U-701* was one of the most heroic and tragic events of the entire U-boat war, resulting in the loss of the patrol boat as well as six members of her crew. The Navy sent the gunboat into harm's way without an operable deck gun, then court-martialed the skipper for failing to sink the attacking U-boat.

Certainly this was an incident that the Navy would like to forget, but the purpose of the Naval History and

The Navel of Naval History

Heritage Command is to tell the *whole* truth, not only those truths that promote an image of glory for the Navy. For the true story, see *Shipwrecks of North Carolina: from the Diamond Shoals North.*

According to the Naval History and Heritage Command, the iron-hulled Confederate steamer *Curlew* "participated in the battle of Roanoke Island on 7 February 1862. She was sunk in shoal water by the Confederates the following day to prevent capture by United States forces." The first sentence is true but the second one contradicts the facts.

The *Curlew* was not scuttled by the Confederates on February 8. She was sunk on February 7 *during* the Battle of Roanoke Island, when two Union shells struck the vessel: one exploded on deck and the other below deck, the latter one rupturing the hull. Because the *Curlew* was rapidly taking on water, her skipper proceeded toward shore, but ran aground on a shoal, where she stuck high and dry.

During the night, other Confederate gunboats rescued the stranded *Curlew's* crew, then offloaded her cannons, powder, shot, and shells. Confederate land forces torched the *Curlew* the following afternoon (February 8). These actions are well documented in *Official Records of the Union and Confederate Navies in the War of the Rebellion*, published by the Government Printing Office.

Destruction of the *Curlew*. (From *Frank Leslie's Illustrated Newspaper*.)

DANF would have its readers believe that the submarine *Tarpon* was "struck from the Navy list on 5 September 1956. She was later sunk in deep water, probably as a target, southeast of Cape Hatteras, N.C., on 26 August 1957." Note the word "probably." In actuality, the Navy sold the *Tarpon* for scrap to the Boston Iron & Metals Company. She sank under tow to the scrap yard, in 140 feet of water. I discovered the wreck in 1983, and it has since become a popular dive site. For further details, see *Shipwrecks of North Carolina: from Hatteras Inlet South.*

The *Granite State* (ex-*New Hampshire*) had a history that spanned more than a hundred years. According to the Naval History and Heritage Command, "Her hull was sold for salvage 19 August 1921 to the Mulholland Machinery Corp. Refloated in July 1922, she and was taken in tow to the Bay of Fundy. The towline parted during a storm, she again caught fire and sank off Half Way Rock in Massachusetts Bay.

Close but no cigar. She was on her way to Eastport, Maine, not the Bay of Fundy in New Brunswick, Canada. There was no storm and the towline did not part. The tug *Perth Amboy* cast the *Granite State* adrift after the vessel caught fire, in order to rescue the three men on board. For particulars, see *Shipwrecks of Massachusetts: North.*

The *YF-415* sank as a result of a munitions explosion in World War Two. Seventeen sailors died, but the casualty isn't even mentioned in DANF or on the Naval History and Heritage Command website.

Consider this entry for the *Triana*: "The tug remained in service at Newport until she was struck from the Navy list on 13 April 1891. *Triana* was sold on 2 May 1891." The real story is one of the most dramatic rescue efforts in the history of the Life-Saving Service. After the tug ran aground, it took all night for the life-savers to rescue the officers and crew. I related the events of this incredible story in *Shipwrecks of Massachusetts: South.*

The *YSD-56* didn't get short shrift in DANF; it got no shrift. After foundering in a storm, three Navy salvage

The Navel of Naval History

tugs spent nearly two weeks in a failed attempt to raise the wreck from 30 feet of water. The Navy did not include this incident in its published historical papers. For details, see *Shipwrecks of Massachusetts: South*.

The truth that contradicts the lying words of the Naval History and Heritage Command was published in DANF with regard to the loss of the submarine *G-1*: "Several attempts to raise her failed and the wreck was officially abandoned. *G-1* was struck from the Navy List on 29 August 1921." Note that the meaning of "struck from the Navy List" was given as "officially abandoned," a clear definition that the Command now repudiates even though it published the meaning on its own website.

Salvage of the *G-1*.
(From the collection of Billy Campbell.)

The newly christened Naval History and Heritage Command now wants to "reinterpret" the fighting Navy's explicit definition of "struck from the Navy List."

Nor did the Navy interfere when a commercial salvage outfit recovered large sections of the hull, including the forward compartment complete with torpedo tubes. For that story, see *Shipwrecks of Rhode Island and Connecticut*.

In the same book I told about the commercial salvage of the submarine *G-2*. According to DANF, "Too deep and too old to salvage, the submarine was struck from the Navy List on 11 September 1919." Salvors did not think that 80 feet was too deep, so they commenced recovery operations without Navy interference.

The Navel of Naval History

According to DANF, the submarine *L-8* "decommissioned there [Hampton Roads, Virginia] 15 November 1922 and was sold 21 December 1925 and scrapped." Nothing could be further from the truth.

My research uncovered a totally different account of the submarine's demise. The *L-8* was held in reserve until 1926, at which time she was scuttled as a test target for torpedoes that were equipped with newly designed magnetic exploders. The proof of this version of events lay less than *one hundred feet* from the Ships History Branch and the Operational Archives, in the Navy Photographic Center, where I found aerial photo-

The photo above shows a near miss: the torpedo passed under the hull of the *L-8* without triggering the magnetic exploder. The photo below shows a successful detonation. I found both photos in the Naval Photographic Center: half a minute's walk from the Operational Archives and the Ships History Branch. If Navy historians were not so busy writing legislation to give them absolute control over abandoned wrecks, and spent their time and energy on historical research, they would have found these pictures and learned the truth about the loss of the submarine.

graphs of the *L-8* being torpedoed. Pardon my crudity, but this gross difference between reality and the tall tale that Navy historians invented, shows piss-poor research on the part of Navy historians. Read the full story in *Shipwrecks of Rhode Island and Connecticut*.

Here is another instance in which the turpitude of Navy historians took precedence over historical research. As with the L-8 photos, I found this aerial photo of the destruction of the Bass in the Naval Photographic Center, a mere one hundred feet from the Ships History Branch and the Operational Archives. If Navy historians had been doing the job for which they had been hired, they would have found this picture and would have been able to inform the public of the truth about the submarine's loss. If only they cared.

TOP SECRET
SINKING USS BASS
DATE 18 MARCH 1945
SQUADRON PBY 29
PILOT COMDR FISS
PHOTOG CLINE ROLL

DANF fudged the last gasp of another submarine: "*Bass* was decommissioned at the Submarine Base, New London, 3 March 1945 and 'destroyed' 12 March 1945." In actuality, the *Bass* was used as a target for aerial mines that were designated Mark 24, which were dropped from PBY's "from an altitude of 200 feet at a ground speed of 115 knots." Again, the Naval Photographic Center has photographs of the destruction, which occurred on March 18, not March 12.

The hulk of the *Bass* was sold at auction in 1962. Nicholas Zinkowski made the highest bid – $1,278 – and became the new owner. I related all the above circumstances in *Shipwrecks of Rhode Island and Connecticut*.

In the same book, it took me four pages to describe the exciting events that surrounded the scuttling of the submarine *Spikefish*. DANF sloughed it off in a single sentence of seven words: "She was subsequently sunk as a target."

DANF would have its readers believe that the submarine chaser *SC-209* was simply "Sunk by gunfire 8/27/18." That is such a gross understatement and misconstruction of events that Navy historians ought to be ashamed of themselves for not telling the full story the way I did in *Shipwrecks of New York*. In the carnage of friendly fire from the SS *Felix Taussig*, both officers and sixteen enlisted men were shredded by shrapnel when a 4-inch gun shell made a direct hit on the submarine chaser and set the wooden hull ablaze. Navy historians totally ignored this accidental loss of life.

"Lost in collision 10/1/18" is the only explanation of the loss of sub chaser *SC-60* in DANF. Not a word about the two sailors who died as a result of the collision. For details, see *Shipwrecks of New Jersey: North*.

The tragic loss of the *YP-387* and six of her crew was completely ignored by both DANF and the Naval History and Heritage Command website. Read about the collision in *Shipwrecks of New Jersey: South*. One would think that the wartime loss of American sailors in the service of their country would at least deserve a mention.

DANF described the end of the *Eagle 56* thus: "Exploded and sank off Portland, Maine on 4/23/45." Such brevity is a slap in the face to the forty-nine sailors who died in the frigid waters after being torpedoed by a German U-boat. My file on this Eagle boat is more than two inches thick, yet Navy historians distilled such incredibly rich details down to a single sentence.

In *Track of the Gray Wolf* (1989), I correctly ascribed the explosion to a German torpedo. I repeated the ascription in *The Fuhrer's U-boats in American Waters* (2006). Not until then – some twenty years after my first ascription – did the Naval History and Heritage Command begrudgingly revise its website entry to read: "Tor-

The Navel of Naval History

pedoed and sunk by German submarine *U-853* off Portland, Maine, 4/23/45." At last the Command got the facts correct, although it could have paid better tribute to the sailors who perished.

The *U-2513* was Type XXI experimental Nazi supersub whose distinctive hull form was designed to move under water at more than twice the speed of conventional U-boats. It was completed too late to participate in the war. The U.S. Navy took it over after the cessation of hostilities, conducted numerous tests of its capabilities, then, according to DANF, "On 2 September 1951, the Chief of Naval Operations ordered that *U-2513* be sunk by gunfire. Presumably, that decision was carried out soon thereafter – though the exact date of the action is not recorded." Note use of the word "presumably."

In fact, the *U-2513* was scuttled on October 7, 1951, at 13:18 – not by gunfire, but by 6 rounds of 12.75' rockets that were fired by U.S. destroyer *Robert A. Owens*. Furthermore, between September 15 and 21, 1952, the USS *Petrel* conducted depth-charge and diving operations on the *U-2513*.

On the discovery dive, I spotted unexploded rockets on the seabed around the hull.

The writers of DANF believed that the *U-111*'s "battered hulk went to the bottom of the ocean sometime in July 1921." On the contrary, the *U-111* was scuttled on August 31, 1922 by the USS *Falcon*. Two scuttling charges – one in the forward battery room and one in the aft torpedo compartment – sent the U-boat to be bottom in 266 fathoms. For details, see *The Kaiser's U-boats in American Waters*.

The Great Navy Humiliation

The Navy in general and DANF in particular go to great lengths to avoid mentioning the name of Billy Mitchell, the U.S. Army general who proved in a series of aerial bombing tests that Naval vessels were vulnerable to attack from the air – twenty-one years before his demonstrations were validated in battle . . . by the Japanese attack on Pearl Harbor.

To set the stage in brief, after World War One, the U.S. Navy acquired eleven German warships and brought them to the United States. These were the battleship *Ostfriesland*; the cruiser *Frankfurt*; the destroyers *G-102*, *S-132*, and *V-43*; and six U-boats: *U-111*, *U-117*, *U-140*, *UB-88*, *UB-148*, and *UC-97*.

Interestingly, despite its voluminous in-house resources, the Navy has no idea how the *U-140* made the transatlantic crossing. According to DANF: "Accounts vary as to how *U-140* actually made the voyage to the United States. One source indicates that she made the voyage under her own power with *Bushnell* (Submarine Tender No. 2) and four of the other five U-boats of the Ex-German Submarine Expeditionary Force. On the other hand, in his account, Vice Admiral Charles A. Lockwood, Jr.—who served in and later commanded *UC-97*—stated that *U-140* preceded *Bushnell* and the four U-boats which sailed with her by several days. He also maintained that she was towed to New York by a collier, but he failed to identify the ship. Be that as it may, *U-140* arrived in New York sometime during May 1919."

I solved this long-standing Naval mystery, and wrote several pages about it in *The Kaiser's U-boats in American Waters*. The Navy tug *Sonoma* towed the U-boat to the Azores, thence across the ocean to the Portsmouth Navy Yard, arriving on July 4, 1919.

Ostfriesland sank in 380 feet of water. (Courtesy of the National Archives.)

The Navel of Naval History

General Billy Mitchell in full regalia.
(Courtesy of the National Archives.)

Billy Mitchell's tests took place in 1921, off the coast of Virginia. Over the course of eight days, three U-boats, three destroyers, cruiser *Frankfurt*, and battleship *Ostfriesland* were destroyed.

The highlight of the exercise was the bombing of the *Ostfriesland*. In attendance to observe the aerial bombardment were no less than two dozen Navy vessels, eight Senators, twelve Congressmen, three Cabinet members (the Secretaries of War, Navy, and Agriculture), and foreign observers from England, France, Spain, Portugal, Brazil, and the Honorable G. Katsuda of Japan. This was the biggest exercise in U.S. Naval history.

How does DANF treat this incredible display of explosive power? Like this: "*Ostfriesland,* with several other ex-German warships, became targets for a demonstration of air power. Bombed by Army planes from Langley Field in Va., she was sunk 21 July 1921 about 60 miles off the Virginia Capes."

The other vessels received less notice. For example, the *Frankfurt* was "sunk as a target 18 July 1921." And: "On 22 June 1921, *U-117* was sunk by bombing off the coast of Virginia, near Cape Charles."

As noted above, the website of the Naval History and Heritage Command claims that the *U-111* was scuttled "sometime in July 1921. Actually, it sank accidentally

The Navel of Naval History

Frankfurt sank in 420 feet of water. (Courtesy of the National Archives.)

in the Chesapeake Bay on June 18, 1921, then lay on the bottom for more than a year, until it was raised and towed to sea by the *Falcon* for ultimate disposition. Vacuous Navy historians are not aware of these facts.

In the early 1990's, I discovered and dived on the *Ostfriesland, Frankfurt*, one destroyer (not positively identified as to which one), and three U-boats. I articulated the historical narrative in *Shipwrecks of Virginia*, and wrote about some of my dives. Later, in *The Lusitania Controversies*, I described in great depth my historic first dives and the way they were planned and executed.

Closed for the Season – All Four of Them

I could go on and on about the deficiencies of the Ships History Branch of the Naval History and Heritage Branch, but the evidence that I have given above is so overwhelming in describing its overt mistakes, missing entries, and obvious oversights that it would be pointless to do so. Hundreds of other slipups and oversights I didn't bother to annotate.

Yet the banner of the Naval History and Heritage Command proclaims that anyone seeking "knowledge through the artifacts, documents, images and artwork available at the NHHC, you will find that this is where the history, legacy and traditions of the United States Navy come alive."

The Navel of Naval History

I beg to differ. The accounts that the Naval History and Heritage Command presents are not just superficial; they are partly fictional.

I don't understand how Navy historians could possibly have misconstrued so many documented facts unless they were lazy, careless, or creative: making up yarns in order to introduce glossy or sanitized versions of events – versions (or perversions) that glorified Navy successes and excluded its failures, faux pas, and darker moments.

The result is not history but historical fiction: a fabricated façade or false image that does not stand up to scrutiny. Uncomfortable issues should be confronted, not avoided, else the result leads people to believe in and perpetuate mythical constructs. This is how urban legends are created. Or is that the real purpose behind the reconstruction of Navy history?

This is the true legacy of the Naval History and Heritage Command. Instead of presenting history – whose definition stems from "his" or "mankind's" "story" – they formulated and fostered "theirstory:" a foundation of facts to which was blended a mixture of partial truths, erroneous scuttlebutt, vapid supposition, and a smattering of misconstrued evidence: all of which was then baked and glazed for public consumption.

If this summation sounds like an indictment of dishonest reporting, so be it.

As of 2013, the Ships History Branch was closed to the public.

Naval Photographic Center

I have many fond memories of doing research at the Naval Photographic Center.

In the old days, Chuck Haberlein and Ed Finney bent over backwards to help find photographs that I wanted. Haberlein was a fixture at the Center for as long as I can remember. He was incredibly knowledgeable about all facets of Naval history: and not just about Naval photographic history, but about all Naval history.

He showed me how to operate the mechanized card

file system: a monstrous rotating machine that rolled vertically at the touch of a switch, and that placed three-by-five card file drawers at my fingertips. Glued to each card was a small black-and-white print, accompanied by a negative number. He also showed me where to look in nearby filing cabinets for large-size prints.

Often we chatted about our favorite shared Naval subjects. I learned a lot from him. Occasionally he learned something from me, but those occasions were few and far between, and concerned mostly my recreational scuba diving experiences. We worked together for more than thirty years. Once, when I stayed until closing time, he even drove me to the train station.

Finney worked there for fifteen to twenty years. He was a bundle of energy who could find any picture in the collection, and could suggest alternative ways of looking for pictures that I couldn't locate on my own.

For more than three decades I did all my own browsing.

At first, when I found images that I wanted, I jotted down the negative numbers in my research notebook; then, after I returned home, I submitted an order and a check in payment to the on-site Navy photo lab. The lab could furnish 70 millimeter and/or 4x5-inch inter-negatives; matte and/or glossy black-and-white and/or color prints in sizes 8x10-inches, 11x14-inches, 16x20-inches, and/or 20x24-inches; 35 millimeter slides; and 4x5-inch and/or 8x10-inch transparencies. Copies were inexpensive, quick, and convenient – especially for remote researchers who requested pictures by mail or phone. This service was discontinued in the 1990's. Reproductions were then outsourced to commercial photographers at many times the price that the Navy charged.

Subsequently, I brought in my own four-bulb copy stand, which I had modified so that the socket arms would fold to a vertical position, which enabled the unit to fit through doorways without having to be disassembled.

Then I wrote the negative numbers on a sheet of

The Navel of Naval History

scrap paper so that Haberlein or Finney could pull the original glossy prints from the filing cabinets in the back-room stacks. If they were busy, they let me pull them myself – although they always refiled the pictures.

Somewhere along the line the Center acquired an antique two-socket copy stand which was placed in a nearby room along the hallway. It was equipped with ordinary household 100-watt incandescent bulbs that were barely adequate (or inadequate) for the job.

Toting a copy stand from the parking lot to the Center was inconvenient. So then, whenever I planned a photo shoot with the Center's copy stand, I brought my own photo flood lamps: 250 watts, 3,200 degrees Kelvin.

Things went downhill after Haberlein and Finney retired, and the Naval History and Heritage Command started exercising its newfound authority. The new guard (and I mean "guard" in the sense of "watch keeper" or "watchdog") immediately cut back on services – all of them.

At first I was no longer allowed to walk into the Center anytime I happened to be on base to conduct other research. I had to call and make an appointment.

When I called the next time I was in DC, the research assistant told me that another researcher had already made an appointment for that day, and although he had not yet arrived, the assistant could not handle more than person one at a time. I explained that I could do my own browsing, and that . . . I was cut off in midsentence. Under no circumstances would the assistant allow two researchers in the Center at the same time. He told me to make an appointment for another day, maybe in a couple of weeks, because he expected to be busy doing other, unspecified things.

The next time I called, in 2013, the Naval Photographic Center was closed to the public.

Throughout the years, I have continually found photographs of vessels that I had not found on previous searches. The reason for this is that retired sailors or their descendants donated isolated prints and entire photo albums to the Center, so that they could be archived for future generations. The closing of the Center has deprived the public of these one-of-a-kind images: a photographic legacy that is now lost due to work-ethic indifference and bureaucratic territoriality.

Judge Advocate General

Although the Navy Department's JAG retains Naval proceedings, those records are not shared with the Naval History and Heritage Command. JAG headquarters is located in Alexandria, Virginia: immediately outside of DC proper, across the Potomac River.

Among other records, JAG archives courts-martial and courts of inquiry. A court-martial is a military trial against an individual for offenses that fall under military law and jurisdiction. A court of inquiry is a formal, fact-finding investigation concerning any matter of grave military importance.

The kind of court proceeding that is helpful to shipwreck researchers is one that investigates the loss of a Navy vessel, or one that investigates an incident in which a Navy vessel was involved (such as collision with a merchant vessel). Unlike a civil trial – in which lawyers create mayhem by raising objections and by trying to obfuscate the truth – a Navy tribunal generally made an honest attempt to ascertain the facts to the fullest extent possible.

In its purest form, a court of inquiry was conducted like a scientific research project: one that was not biased or prejudiced by preconceived notions. Witnesses were permitted not only to answer questions freely and without qualification, but they were encouraged to offer additional information that they believed might be pertinent to the case. After court appointed legal counsel and investigating officers asked their questions, the judges might either ask for clarification, or put questions of their own to the witnesses. It is this forthright testimony that is so valuable to shipwreck researchers.

I used to visit the JAG offices regularly in the 1980's. In those days, the courts-martial and courts of inquiry were indexed on a card file system. The three-by-five

The Navel of Naval History

cards were stored in full-width drawers in a metal cabinet that measured three feet square and that stood four feet high. Thousands of cards were arranged alphabetically by name of vessel or individual.

In those days JAG research was simple and straightforward, and oftentimes rewarding. After checking into the JAG office without making an appointment, an officer or secretary would escort me to the basement of the multistory building, point to the cabinet, and leave me on my own. I found the cards of the vessels that I wanted to research, read the typed summary of the file, and jotted down the locator information on a sheet of paper. I then returned to the office upstairs, filled out forms that were equivalent to National Archives call slips, and handed them to the officer in charge.

The actual courts of inquiry were not kept in the JAG building. They were archived at the Washington National Records Center in Suitland, Maryland: about twelve miles away. It took two to three days for the paperwork to be filed and for the records to be pulled. I planned my JAG visits for the beginning of the week, so I could access the records by the end of the week.

In the beginning, the requested records were shipped to the JAG building in Alexandria. I called to make sure that they had been delivered, then showed up to review them. There was no official research room. After I checked in and announced my purpose, an officer handed the original files to me, then offered me a seat at an unoccupied desk where I could peruse them.

I had free use of the photocopy machine. Most investigative reports were a hundred pages or so in length, sometimes several hundred pages. The longest report that I ever found was on the loss of the destroyer *Murphy* (which see): it contained more than a *thousand* pages of testimony, plus photographs, charts, and diagrams.

I never copied an entire report. I copied only discrete portions in which witnesses described an actual event: collision, sinking, rescue operations, and so on. Sometimes I copied only half a dozen pages of a hundred page report.

The system was convenient for me because I made week-long research trips to DC. It would not be convenient for a distant researcher who could stay in the area for only a day or so.

After a few years the protocol changed. I still had to go to the JAG building in order to thumb through the card file index, and submit my requests to an officer upstairs, but after filing the paperwork JAG took itself out of the loop. I still had to wait a few days for the paperwork to be processed, but instead of returning to the JAG building, I had to go to the Washington National Records Center to review the original files.

Washington National Records Center

This one-floor archival facility is spread out like a mammoth multifamily ranch house. It is difficult to reach by public transportation because it lies so far away from the last Metro station. Nor is there any shuttle service. Prince George County operates a bus that connects the last station on the Green line with the Suitland Federal Complex, but because it is a different system, patrons have to pay an additional fare. It is easier to drive. There is ample parking because the number of researchers is generally so few.

I would always call the JAG office first to confirm that the records had been pulled and put on hold for me. The sign-in procedure was simple: I entered my name and the date in a book. I did not need to show identification. I did not need a research card, nor did I need to wear a badge. There were no armed guards. I simply entered the Research Room and provided my name to an aide. Within minutes an aide brought the file boxes to me.

One time I was fortunate enough to be taken into the stacks in order to help search for a file box whose locator information had been transcribed incorrectly. The mammoth warehouse consisted of aisles, rows, shelves, and tiers. The aisles were incredibly long: closing in perspective in the distance, and seeming to come together like a pair of train tracks. Each aisle was lined with inter-

The Navel of Naval History

locking shelving units that extended from floor to ceiling. Each vertical row was numbered, and each shelf on the row was numbered. The boxes that were stored on the shelves were stacked three boxes deep.

Let's say that the locator information placed a file box on Aisle 24, Row 12, Shelf 4, Tier 3. You would walk along Aisle 24 to Row 12 (which was a vertical stack). The file box in question would be found on the fourth shelf behind two other file boxes: the third one back. Inside that box there would be several folders, one of which was the one that I wanted. The other folders in the box had nothing to do with the vessel I was researching, nor were they arranged in any manner whatsoever. There was no continuity of name or subject matter. Folders were filed haphazardly until no more folders fit in the box.

Under this system, several folders could have the same locator information. The key to finding a particular folder was in knowing in which box on which shelf in which row in which aisle the folder was filed. Pay attention, because this information will soon assume considerable importance.

Standard research rules applied for reading documents. Only one file box was permitted on the table; only one folder at a time could be removed from the box.

Self-service coin-operated photocopiers were available in the room. Documents did not need to be examined prior to copying. For ten cents per page, I could make as many photocopies as I wanted.

In each case, a tribunal or panel of judges summarized their findings and made recommendations, but the foremost value of a court of inquiry to me was in its eyewitness accounts of a maritime disaster. There is nothing more primary than the actual words of the survivors, faithfully transcribed by a court reporter – instead of being misquoted, paraphrased, or hyperbolized by sensationalistic correspondents whose cardinal goal was to sell newspapers.

Accuracy was so paramount in a court of inquiry that, after a witness's testimony was transcribed, the witness was asked to review the written record and to make corrections or additions. This *never* happens in a civil court case, in which the primary goal is to obscure the truth, not to reveal or elucidate it.

The JAGuar

In the 1990's, JAG tightened its control over courts-martial and courts of inquiry. No longer was I allowed to see the original records at the Washington National Records Center. Instead, JAG had the file folders pulled and shipped to the headquarters building in Alexandria. The entire file was photocopied. A JAG officer then redacted the photocopies before permitting me to see them.

Redacting means editing text and deleting information. A JAG officer, or redactor, did this by applying indelible ink onto passages that JAG no longer wanted the public to see. The procedure is somewhat capricious and arbitrary, and is a time consuming process to implement. In essence, the redactor has to read the entire transcript word for word, and redact every passage that JAG, in its wisdom, has decided to hide from prying civilian eyes.

In some places, isolated words, partial sentences, or disunited lines were redacted. In other places, complete paragraphs or half a page of text were redacted.

As originally, I had to make two trips to JAG: one to submit my requests, and another to review the heavily redacted documents. When I arrived at the JAG office on the second occasion, an officer gave me the redacted version for which JAG had no further use: it had been photocopied and redacted specifically for me. Even if I found only a few pages relevant to my research, I was given the photocopy of the entire transcript.

The JAGged Edge of Stupidity

Later in the 1990's, JAG computerized its index card filing system. The text and locator information that were typed on each index card were input into a database for quick and easy retrieval. Unfortunately, it appears that the data input personnel who were employed by JAG to do the job were either careless or incompetent.

Since then, of the courts of inquiry that I have requested, JAG has been able to retrieve only one out of two. The other half cannot be found. The enormity of this loss to present and future generations is incalculable. Imagine: fifty percent of the transcripts of all the courts of inquiry that were ever convened, are no longer available – and likely to remain so forever.

All too often, when the boxes were pulled from the Washington National Records Center, the file folder that was the object of the search was *not* found in the box. One might presume that the folder was misfiled – perhaps the last time that it was pulled. But that was not the case. Or, if it was the case, it was only in a few rare instances. The reality of the matter was far more insidious.

I asked a JAG officer, who was one of those in charge of these materials, how such a dire situation could occur. They concluded that the most likely explanation was that a typographical error was made during the transfer of data from the file cards to the database. If only a single digit was mistyped, the box could not be located.

Referring to the hypothetical locator information given above – Aisle 24, Row 12, Shelf 4, Tier 3 – any mistake or reversal would designate the wrong aisle, row, shelf, or tier. The typist could have typed Aisle 23 instead of Aisle 24; or Row 13 instead of Row 12; or Shelf 5 instead of Shelf 4; or Tier 2 instead of Tier 3. A dyslexic typist might have reversed the numbers, and typed Aisle 42 instead of Aisle 24; or Row 21 instead of Row 12. Perhaps an entry contained more than one mismatch. There was no way of knowing. And trying all the possible permutations would be an exercise in futility.

After hearing this, I asked the officer why, when a transcript wasn't found where its locator information stated that it belonged, they didn't just go down to the basement and refer to the original file cards. Not only could they then obtain the correct locator information, but they could revise and correct the database.

Any rational human being is going to find his answer difficult to accept. After adopting the database system, the Navy – and this time I mean Naval officers and not a group of misguided civilian dictators – discarded the file card cabinet along with all its index cards.

What monumental stupidity!

In a multistory building that occupies nearly one square block, the amount of space taken by one small cabinet in an out-of-the-way basement storage room was inconsequential. Yet they threw away the cabinet and file cards instead of keeping them as a backup in case of an unforeseeable computer malfunction, or a glitch in the retrieval program, or a viral attack. Such lack of forethought was inexcusable, and inexplicable in this age of computer savvy Naval officers.

The Modern Capitalistic JAG

Once again, the good old days of independent and uncomplicated research are gone. Researchers are no longer allowed in JAG headquarters. All requests are handled by snail mail or e-mail. You can't send a simple request for the transcript of a court of inquiry; you must now submit a formal application pursuant to the Freedom of Information Act.

Upon receipt of a FOIA request, JAG will approximate the cost of conducting a "search" and "review" of the requested materials, and the "direct cost" of photocopying the documents and redacting its contents. A first-time requester must pay in advance; requesters with a good payment history will be billed at a later date, but payment is due within thirty days. A number of charges are involved, and they are cumulative.

"Search" means a computer search for the records in question, then the time that is spent on pulling them. This search may include a page-by-page or line-by-line identification of materials to determine if they are responsive to the request. The requester is charged at an hourly rate that exceeds $50 per hour (the charge keeps escalating).

"Direct cost" is the actual cost of making photocopies. This is not a standard charge per page, but an hourly rate that is charged for the amount of time that it takes someone to make the copies, plus the cost of operating the duplicating machinery. Again, the charge may be more than $50 per hour.

"Review" means redacting the text. The requester may have to pay more than $50 per hour for someone to read the entire transcript, and redact the very information that is relevant to his research.

A transcript that is several hundred pages in length may easily cost a requester hundreds of dollars. If JAG predetermines that the cost is likely to exceed $250, the requester is notified to pay in advance.

Researchers have to pay a search fee even if JAG cannot locate the requested file folder, of which, as noted above, at least half are no longer findable.

Summary Judgment

The once friendly and serviceable Naval Historical Center and its adjuncts have morphed into a despotic conglomerate that now calls itself the Naval History and Heritage Command. The preceding litany of the Command's miserable failure to provide accurate Navy history contradicts the purpose of its origination, and belies its mission statement.

Instead of foisting unwanted legislation upon an unsuspecting public – to confiscate deteriorating wrecks under the misnomer of "historic preservation," – the Command should clean up its act by correcting the misinformation with which it has been deceiving the public for decades.

The Command should also allow free access to the records and documents that it is holding in trust for the American people. To *not* do these things is an unwarranted disservice to citizens who deserve better treatment.

The Command's new direction was poles apart from mine. We both wanted to change the world. The difference was that I wanted to change the world for the better, while the Command wanted to change it for the worse. Or to put it another way, I wanted the make the world better for future generations, while the Command wanted to make the world better for itself at the expense of future generations.

Above: A shell magazine inside the *San Diego*. Below: The CSS *Virginia* ramming the USS *Cumberland* immediately after firing a broadside at the USS *Congress* at the start of the Battle of Hampton Roads. (From *Frank Leslie's Illustrated Newspaper*.)

Shipwreck Case File
USS *Cumberland*

Wood versus Iron

The *Cumberland* was a wooden-hulled warship that was built in 1842. She was armed with ten 8-inch guns and forty-two 32-pounders. She was rammed and shelled by the CSS *Virginia* (ex-USS *Merrimack*) on March 8, 1862, on the first day of the famous two-day Battle of Hampton Roads. For the full story of her background and sinking, see *Ironclad Legacy: Battles of the USS Monitor*.

The historic fight of the *Cumberland* against overwhelming odds has never been forgotten, yet her battered remains are almost never remembered today. For years after her loss, her gravesite was clearly marked not by a marble headstone but by her still standing wooden masts. This made the wreck an easy target for salvors.

Sold to the Highest Bidder

According to an 1875 newspaper account, "On the 9th of March 1862 the sloop-of-war *Cumberland* was run into by the prow of the iron-clad *Virginia*, and sunk in thirteen fathoms of water. Her destruction was so speedy that nothing could be saved from her and a number of her crew were drowned by the sinking of the ship. It was reported at the time that there was a large amount of specie in her chest, and this stimulated a number of parties to attempt its recovery. During the war a company was formed for that purpose, but after sinking several thousand dollars the attempt was abandoned. The wreck was allowed to rest for a few years, when a company composed of Governor Gilbert C. Walker, John A. Hebrew and Mr. P. C. Asserton, undertook the job. They recovered a number of the guns, and other articles of value, and used torpedoes freely, but the wished-for chest was still invisible. Mr. West, the diver, next undertook the enterprise, and worked at it with varying fortunes for about a year and a half, also using torpedoes. In the meantime other parties, employing some of the best divers in the country, had made efforts in the same direction, but without success.

"Some months ago several gentlemen in Detroit, Michigan, stimulated by the reports of divers who had visited the ship, formed a company for the purpose of recovering the safe. They purchased the right to search from the Government for $5,000, and having six or eight divers employed, worked for about two months without success. While at work they used the wrecking schooner *J. C.*, belonging to Messrs. O. E. Maltby & Co., of this city [Norfolk], and when they abandoned the work they left the job in his hands, to be prosecuted at his leisure, with the proviso that the profits were to be divided.

"Since they left, Captain Clements Brown, a celebrated diver, who is one of the firm of O. E. Maltby & Co., has been otherwise engaged, and did not visit the wreck until Wednesday last [June 9], when he made an exploration. The swiftness of the tide at that point only allows diving operations for about two hours during the change of the tide. Captain Brown had made careful inquiry as to the exact location of the chest, and on Thursday, when he went down for the second time, he found the mizzenmast; and laying his course from it almost instantly put his hand on the chest; one corner only of which was exposed, the remainder being covered with mud. A few minutes' work exposed one of the handles, to which a line was made fast, and after one or two efforts the safe was safely landed upon deck. The safe, when found, was upon a deck below where it originally stood, and its removal was probably due to the torpedoes. When the safe reached the deck from a fracture near the bottom (supposed to have been caused by torpedoes) a number of gold and silver coins, to the amount of $25 or $30, rolled out, which are now exhibited as a

Shipwreck Case File - USS *Cumberland*

proof that there is 'money in the thing.'

"As to the amount it contains, there is no means of forming even a conjecture, and the safe will not be opened until the company in Detroit is heard from. The mere fact of finding the safe, after so many vain efforts have been made, is [two words illegible] for Captain Brown who [remainder of sentence missing]. The safe was enveloped in canvas and lowered into the hold of the J.C., when she sailed for this city. It will, we learn, be taken out to-day and placed in one of the stores under the Atlantic Hotel for exhibition.

"Captain Brown also informs us that in immediate proximity to the safe he found the petrified body of a man, supposed to be, from the situation, an officer, still wearing clothing, although covered with mud. This he was compelled to leave for a future visit. This would be a great curiosity, and, if exhibited, would realize a fortune to an enterprising exhibitor. The work of wrecking the *Cumberland* and searching for another safe supposed to be in her, will be prosecuted with vigor, as soon as all arrangements are made."

There the article ends and, in typical newspaper fashion, no follow-up articles were forthcoming, leaving contemporary readers as well as today's to wonder what else the safe contained and what further salvage operations unearthed from the wreck. I must also comment that the date of the *Cumberland's* destruction was given incorrectly as March 9, instead of March 8.

After this, because the masts had been blasted apart by "torpedoes" (not self-propelled warheads but underwater bombs) and fell by the wayside, the wreck's location was all but lost.

Next mention of the wreck occurred in 1909, when the British freighter *Queen Wilhelmina* snagged her anchor in Hampton Roads. When the anchor was finally pulled free, it brought up from the bottom a thousand feet of iron anchor chain. Later it was determined that this chain came from the sunken wreck of the *Cumberland*.

Shipwreck Case File - USS *Cumberland*

NUMA Diary

In 1980, noted author, historian, and veteran wreck finder Clive Cussler decided to fund a search for the *Cumberland* and the *Florida* (which see) through his solely owned nonprofit organization called the National Underwater and Marine Agency. The two wrecks lay less than a quarter mile apart. After conducting considerable archival research, Cussler and his experienced team narrowed down the *Cumberland's* search quadrant to an area the size of a football field.

Normally, shipwrecks are discovered by electronic means: side-scan sonar, magnetometer, sub-bottom profiler, metal detector, and so on. In this case, Cussler found a local clammer who had dredged up Civil War artifacts when he was gathering clams with tongs. Wilbur Riley led Cussler to the site off Pier C, "approximately 1.4 miles northwest of Newport News Point.

According to Cussler, "Divers went down and discovered heavy concentrations of scattered wreckage of a large wooden ship, whose huge hull timbers rose out of the muck like ghosts frozen in the past. Almost immediately they observed the shaft of a large anchor, decking planks, and ordnance accessories used by the men who manned the cannon. Over a period of several days, a number of interesting artifacts were recovered from the ship that tenaciously fought a battle she could not win. One was an irregular frame that a sailor had fashioned around the broken edges of a mirror. Perhaps the most dramatic find was the *Cumberland's* large bronze bell, standing 6 inches high and 19 inches wide. When you stare at it, you can imagine it rung by an unseen hand, sending her crew to their guns at the approach of the *Virginia*. [Note: the given height of the bell must have been a typographical error. The bell actually measures 18 inches in height.]

"The one object any maritime museum would give its curator's left leg to put on display is the ram of the *Merrimack/Virginia* which still lies buried inside the hull of *Cumberland*. This is the most prized artifact of all, but its recovery calls for a very expensive and extensive proj-

Shipwreck Case File - USS *Cumberland* 97

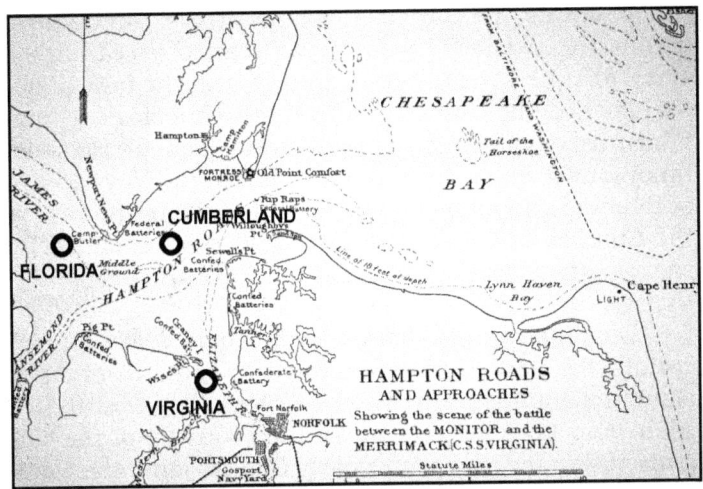

On this old map in the author's collection I have placed black circles around the sites of the USS *Cumberland*, CSS *Florida*, and CSS *Virginia*. Note that most of the hulk of the *Virginia* was raised and scrapped in 1876. In the twentieth century, when the U.S. Navy wanted the channel to the Norfolk Navy Yard widened and deepened, it contracted with the U.S. Army Corps of Engineers to dredge the rest of the *Virginia* out of existence.

ect far beyond NUMA's means."

Left unsaid was the fact that the Navy professed no interest in recovering the ram, or in conducting an archaeological survey of the site.

Cussler provided the funding for the entire operation except for the final phase: the College of William and Mary in Williamsburg, Virginia, paid most of the money to have the artifacts conserved and chemically treated before they were put on public display at The Mariners Museum in Newport News.

Cussler also located the nearby *Florida*. His divers recovered artifacts from that wreck as well, as noted in the following chapter.

Cussler: "John Sands, the curator of the museum, built a magnificent exhibit around the *Cumberland* and *Florida* artifacts. They were on display for nearly six months, when some Navy admiral and the curator of the Norfolk Naval Museum walked in, asked to see Sands, and contemptuously demanded he turn over, as they charitably put it, 'our artifacts.'

98 Shipwreck Case File - USS *Cumberland*

"It seems the Judge Advocate of the Navy had a dream. He envisioned that my two years of research, the small fortune I spent on the project, and the indefatigable efforts of the UAJV [Underwater Archaeological Joint Ventures] guys were for the navy's sole benefit. He sanctimoniously claimed the Department of the Navy owned both ships and all bits and pieces thereof. In the case of the *Cumberland*, he maintained that whoever sold it for salvage after the Civil War did not have the proper authority. . . .

"Demonstrating a definite lack of style and sophistication, the navy threatened to go to court in order to claim the antiquities, to whose recovery they contributed zilch. And because they stoke the economy of the Virginia tidewater area with nearly 30,000 jobs, the Commonwealth of Virginia rolled over and threw in the towel. John Sands's exhibit was dismantled and the artifacts trucked to the Norfolk Naval Museum, where they are now on display.

"I could have called their bluff, fought, and easily won in Admiralty Court. The navy did not have a pegleg to stand on. I have copies of correspondence from the original *Cumberland* salvors, who were sold the rights by Gideon Welles, Secretary of the U.S. Navy. If Welles didn't have the right to sell the wreck for salvage, who did?"

Cussler conceded. "So long as the artifacts went on display to the public at the navy's Norfolk museum, I decided not to create a fuss."

The morals in this story are twofold. First, the Navy showed no interest in the *Cumberland* until someone else found it and conducted a survey of its battered remains. Second, the Navy was willing to lie about the *Cumberland*'s ownership so it could have an excuse to confiscate artifacts that had been recovered legally.

To hide these facts from the public, the Naval History and Heritage Commend declined to mention Cussler's contributions in its "historical" entry on the *Cumberland*.

Shipwreck Case File
CSS *Florida*

International Incident

A somewhat detailed description of the *Florida's* complex background is crucial to understanding her present legal status, especially with respect to the Navy's machinations, which have been ongoing for more than a century and a half. A far more comprehensive account is included in *Shipwrecks of the Chesapeake Bay in Virginia Waters*.

During the Civil War, the Confederacy had commerce raiders constructed in England. One that was built under the temporary name *Oreto* was renamed *Florida* once the vessel escaped the Union blockade. After an incredible amount of teething troubles, the *Florida* commenced raiding operations.

Skip two years and more than sixty captures. On October 4, 1864, the *Florida* steamed into the port of Bahia (known today as Salvador), Brazil. Already in port was the Union sloop-of-war *Wachusett*. The *Wachusett* had spent months searching fruitlessly for the *Florida* and *Alabama* (which see). The skipper was ecstatic when he learned that the *Florida* was anchored within striking distance of his guns. Only one thing prevented him from attacking the *Florida* right away – international neutrality laws.

Brazil was a neutral nation, and Bahia was a neutral port. There were strict laws regarding the conduct of foreign vessels in neutral territory. One of the foremost laws was that, in order to protect the lives of citizens of a neutral nation, belligerents were not permitted to fight in neutral territory. The Brazilian government wanted assurances that its neutrality would be honored. U.S. consul Thomas Wilson promised that the *Wachusett*

The caption on this contemporary print in the author's collection reads: "Cutting out of the *Florida* from Bahia, Brazil, by the U.S.S. *Wachusset* [sic]."

would respect Brazilian neutrality, as did the skippers of the *Wachusett* and the *Florida*. To back his statement, and to distance himself from the *Wachusett*, the skipper of the *Florida* moved his vessel to a location in the harbor that was within easy view of moored Brazilian warships.

Nonetheless, under the cover of darkness, the *Wachusett* got up to ramming speed and crashed into the *Florida* with the intention of sinking her; then, because the *Florida* remained afloat, the *Wachusett* backed away and fired two broadsides into the *Florida's* hull. Still the staunchly built Confederate raider refused to sink, so a Union boarding party forced the *Florida's* watch crew (half her complement was ashore) to surrender. The *Wachusett* then tied a hawser to the *Florida* and towed her to sea, thence to Hampton Roads, Virginia.

This illegal capture created a diplomatic calamity. Brazil demanded that the Union return the *Florida* to Brazil. Secretary of the Navy Gideon Welles issued specific orders to ignore Brazil's entreaties and to retain the *Florida* in U.S. jurisdiction. The Union Navy stripped the *Florida* of "all of the thermometers, barometers, chronometers, spyglasses, etc., which can be of use to the North Atlantic Squadron." In addition, $20,000 in cash, which was aboard at the *Florida* at the time of her capture, simply vanished.

Three guns – the pivot, the howitzer, and one broadside – were taken to Washington, DC. The *Wachusett* transported the captured officers and crew to Fort Warren, a prison camp in Boston, Massachusetts.

Subsequently, the Union Navy either scuttled the *Florida* or allowed her to sink at her mooring, perhaps with some clandestine assistance.

The Navy's Myth of Ownership

Nor was that the end of the Navy's manipulations of events. When we jump ahead more than a century we encounter two more instances of Navy chicanery. The first one I related in the previous chapter. It concerns the endeavors of Clive Cussler in 1980 and 1981, when he funded expeditions to search for the *Florida* and the *Cumberland*, and discovered the locations of both wreck sites.

Lest my readers forget, Cussler recovered a number of artifacts to establish each wreck's identity. He donated these artifacts to The Mariners Museum in Newport News. The Navy then claimed ownership of both shipwrecks and their artifacts, and confiscated the artifacts so they could display them in a Navy museum – this despite the fact that Cussler was able to prove that the Navy did *not* own either shipwreck. In the 1870's, the Navy sold the *Cumberland* to a salvage outfit; end of story.

With respect to the *Florida*, the U.S. Navy did not own the vessel in the first place; she was never commissioned into the U.S. Navy. She was owned by the Confederate States of America, she was captured illegally, and by rights of international neutrality laws she should have been returned to Brazil, which then would have returned her to the Confederacy – except that she sank before the case could be prosecuted in court, so she was left in legal limbo under water.

As I noted above, Cussler had documented proof that the Navy no longer owned the *Cumberland* because it sold the wreck for salvage. Cussler noted, "The Navy's claim on the *Florida* was equally ludicrous. They had the wrong ship. The vessel they referred to was not the famous Sea Devil raider, captained by the redoubtable John Maffit, but a garden-variety commercial blockade runner that was captured and appropriated into the navy as a warship they named *Florida*."

It is difficult to believe that the Navy could be so stupid about its own history, but there you have it. Or was the Navy being sly instead of stupid? The Navy's eight-volume *Dictionary of American Naval Fighting Ships* lists every vessel that was ever commissioned into the U.S. Navy; five vessels named *Florida* are listed, but not the Confederate *Florida*. Perhaps the Navy was trying to muddy the waters so the courts could not see the truth.

The Navy has long tried to convince the world that after the country was reunited, the Union government assumed ownership of the vessels in the Confederate navy. This is true as far as it goes, but it does not go in fact the way the Navy would like ownership to be perceived by the courts, and by a public that is unacquainted with the law. There is a rather large gap between the Navy's portrayal of the law and the way the law is actually written. As I will clearly show, the Navy ignored the law in order to presume title to shipwrecks that it doesn't own and never did.

First, sunken Confederate vessels were abandoned by the Confederate navy at the time of their loss. This means that they were no longer part of the Confederate navy that the United States government appropriated at the end of the war. Thus the federal government did not own sunken Confederate vessels any more than it owned any other sunken or buried Confederate war materiel. Every Civil War relic hunter knows this. The fact that relics are found on or near sunken vessels instead of in widely scattered debris fields, or in fallow corn fields, does not alter the law of finds.

Nonetheless, the Navy has gone to great extremes to create the myth that it – the modern U.S. Navy – possesses title to every sunken Confederate vessel anywhere in the world. And it has done this without ever providing proof in the form of documentation. The Navy just says it is so, and intimidates courts into accepting its word.

Second, while it is true that floating Confederate vessels were appropriated by the federal (Union) government, title was not granted to the U.S. Navy, but to the General Services Administration. Therefore, and to press my point, even if the federal government *had* assumed ownership of sunken Confederate vessels, title would have been transferred to the General Services Administration, not to the U.S. Navy.

Despite these legal verities, the Navy has consistently and deliberately ignored long standing law in matters of asserting ownership of shipwrecks, and – against all reason and rationality – has managed to convince the courts to overlook it, too; or perhaps, by disobeying the law of full disclosure, the Navy has intentionally concealed these established laws, in order to assume ownership of abandoned Confederate shipwrecks. In this case, I mean "assume" in the sense of "to feign; affect" or "to take for granted."

In other words, the Navy has achieved it nefarious goals by means of fabricating evidence or intentional obfuscation. As my readers will see, this insidious Navy canard has been used in a number of shipwreck cases, with devastating ramifications for individual targets.

I should be saving this divulgence for the final chapter, but if I don't introduce it now, some of the following cases would have to be taken on faith until the ultimate revelation.

Clamor at Hampton Roads

Notwithstanding the above digression, on March 16, 1989, agents of the Federal Bureau of Investigation obtained a search warrant that empowered them to enter the premises of the Cold Harbor Civil War Museum, in Lightfoot, Virginia (outside Williamsburg), and to confiscate artifacts that allegedly had been recovered from the *Cumberland* and *Florida*. On the same day they entered the home of Larry Stevens and confiscated similar artifacts from his personal collection. It all came about like this.

Eugene Christman and Joseph Hastings were clammers. They used clam tongs to snatch shellfish from the bottom of the bay. If you have never done this kind of work, then take my word that it is one of the most physically demanding occupations in the world. Clam tongs operate like scissors or hinged salad spoons, except that the handles measure a couple of stories in length. Because the tong handles are constructed of thick treated wood, and the basket and prongs are made of strong metal, they are heavy in their own right. Add a bushel and a peck of clams to the mix, and you can easily estimate how difficult it must be to lift such a contrivance.

Clam tongs are lowered and raised by hand from the side of a boat. The clammer lets the tong into the water with the basket end down, lowers the contraption by running his hands up the two handles, spreads the handles when the basket touches the bottom by spreading wide his arms, pulls his arms together to close the opposing sides of the basket, then pulls up the tongs by means of the muscles in his arms. He does this all day, every day; in good weather and bad.

The bottom is not carpeted with clams. Most of the bottom consists of mud or shell hash. Clams tend to live together in beds. Clam beds are isolated from each other, so that finding them is a hit or miss process. Clammers move around a lot in the hope of stumbling onto a bed that has not been overworked or previously located.

Neither Christman nor Hastings were unduly surprised when they raised their tongs and found the basket filled not with clams but with Civil War objects. This was not the first time they recovered such items, nor was it the last. Hampton Roads was littered with trash and debris from the Civil War: everything from musket balls to brass spikes to timbers to keys to glass bottles to door knobs to cannon balls to pieces of wood to . . . well, you get the point.

Shipwreck Case File - CSS Florida 105

Hastings worked from his 32-foot fishing vessel *Karen Lynn*. He said, "I've been clamming for 10 years and I've found artifacts for 10 years."

Christman, who worked from his 35-foot fishing vessel *Lady Jennifer*, shared Hastings' sentiment.

All clammers knew that when you tonged for clams anywhere in the Chesapeake Bay or its tributaries, you were likely to pick up relics from every bygone age including pre-Columbian, with remnants of the Civil War predominating. You were just as likely to unearth vestiges of the Civil War by excavating a basement for new home construction. It goes with the territory and is part and parcel of the job.

Christman and Hastings accepted this situation laconically. Instead of cursing the recovery of yesteryear's discards in place of sellable shellfish, they put the manmade curiosities aside for later disposal. They could have chucked the stuff overboard, but why litter a bay that was already choked with rubbish? They kept tonging. They both had boat mortgages to pay and families to feed.

Eventually they made contact with Gary Williams and Larry Stevens. Williams owned the Cold Harbor Civil War Museum. It was filled with all sorts of memorabilia from the War Between the States: muskets, uniforms, paper money, hand grenades (with the gunpowder removed), buttons, bottles, flags, medallions, and everything else you can think of. Stevens was a private collector whose assortment was not as large but just as eclectic. Nearly all these items were hand-me-downs, family heirlooms, or trades and purchases from other collectors; some came from land sites. There is a great deal of traffic in Civil War mementos. Like stamp collecting, all of it is open and aboveboard.

The clammers traded with the collectors: items from tongs for items from digs. No money changed hands.

Williams also owned a brass works in which he forged replicas and reproductions. Stevens gave some brass fasteners to Williams, and asked him to melt them down and mold them into belt buckles. The fasteners allegedly came from the *Florida*, so the buckles were embossed with the vessel's name. Stevens offered these buckles for sale by advertising them in the North South Trader's Civil War magazine, for $125 each.

Kevin Foster spotted the ad. Foster was the director of a competing Civil War museum that was called the Confederate Naval Museum, in Columbus, Georgia. He brought the ad to the attention of John Townley, a compatriot and the publisher of a self-promotional newsletter that goes by the histrionic name of the Confederate Naval Historical Society. Together, Foster and Townley conspired to find some way to crucify their rivals.

Townley agreed with Cussler that the U.S. Navy did not own the *Florida*, but for reasons that differed from Cussler's. Nonetheless, because the Navy *believed* (or wished to dupe the public and the courts into believing) that the Navy owned the *Florida* and the *Cumberland*, Townley tried to get the Naval Criminal Investigative Service to prosecute the alleged offenders. The NCIS refused to be a cat's-paw for private interests.

Clutching at straws, Townley tried to make a case that the federal government owned the *Florida* because it assumed ownership of everything that was Confederate, on the premise that to the victor go the spoils. As noted in the previous section, according to his interpretation, after the South surrendered, the *Florida* became the property of the United States government (but not the Department of the Navy). Townley ignored the touchy legal issue with regard to Brazil. It was old and sordid history that no one was likely to uncover. He figured that, as the chief law enforcement agency of the federal government was the Federal Bureau of Investigation, it was worth a try at being a stool pigeon in order to get the FBI to prosecute his competitors.

As Townley put it, "I was on the phone the next morning to the Hampton Roads FBI office with the tale, and they had only one question for me: 'Is this stuff worth over $10,000?' You bet. 'Well that's ten years in prison and a $10,000 fine' came their reply, and all they needed were the details."

Shipwreck Case File - CSS Florida

It was a long stretch of the imagination for Townley the informer to declare categorically that the recovered artifacts exceeded $10,000 in value. He had never seen the artifacts and didn't know exactly what they were. Nor did he claim to be an appraiser. Absent an official appraisal by a bona fide appraiser, the monetary value of an item is not established until it is converted into cash on the open market, or when the item is sold at auction.

In addition, Townley claimed that the clammers "were busily raking the wrecks with oyster dredges and selling everything they could find." This statement was patently false. Oyster dredges are contrivances that are dragged from a boat much in the way in which draggers and trawlers tow weighted nets and trawl doors across the ocean bottom for scallops and bottom-feeding fish. Oyster dredges are not legal in Virginia waters (although they are legal in Maryland). Christman and Hastings collected clams with tongs.

Furthermore, the clammers never received any payment for the artifacts. Townley was writing through his hat. But much can be accomplished by means of lies and false accusations. Take the Salem witch trials for example . . .

The truth notwithstanding, these were the circumstances that prompted the FBI to confiscate the relevant items that were in Williams' and Stevens' possession. They interrogated Williams and Stevens on multiple occasions, and learned the names of their "suppliers." They placed a tap on Stevens' telephone. Then they charged Christman and Hastings as accomplices in the theft of government property. . . . that is, American government property, not Brazilian.

According to Townley's propaganda, the FBI arrested the gang that was trafficking in illegal Civil War relics, in the process "seizing so many artifacts they had to rent a hotel room to store them in until the Hampton Roads Naval Museum agreed to take charge of what had been confiscated."

The reality was not quite as dramatic as Townley

would have people believe. No one was arrested.

According to Williams, when the G-men appeared at the Cold Harbor Civil War Museum to make their confiscations, "The FBI was very professional and did not embarrass me at all. They did it as quiet as they could; they could have made a scene, but they didn't."

It is interesting to note how Townley characterized the FBI's quiet and inoffensive visits to Williams and Stevens: "FBI agents swooped down in simultaneous raids on multiple dealers, including the largest in Virginia." He made it seem as if a horde of G-men dressed in full combat gear and bulletproof vests broke up an interstate ring of gangsters and racketeers by kicking in the doors of a dozen criminal hangouts, and waved automatic weapons in their faces.

Williams went on to say, "Everything I got in this museum [from the *Cumberland* and *Florida*], I got over a period of three years. I got them from the clammers; they are commercial fishermen . . . [They] can't help but bring this stuff up out of the water . . . The clam buckets get into the mud and sometimes they pick up items. It's not like these guys go out and take things off the ships. . . . Maybe there should be a buoy or something out there and a restricted area marked. These guys are country fishermen; they're not out to make money off artifacts."

Hastings said, "I don't know that I've done anything wrong. . . . I had no idea the items were government property. I'm not sure that they are. Nobody has ever come to me and told me that a ship was sunk out there. I've found Civil War artifacts all over the river – some of them nowhere near where some of these items came from."

Hastings added that he had never sold anything to Williams or Stevens. "I've traded with them. I've gone relic hunting with Williams. He [Williams] finds things in the ground and I find things in the water. If he [Williams] thought he was doing something wrong he wouldn't have put those labels on [the artifacts] in his museum."

Shipwreck Case File - CSS *Florida*

I suppose some wag might say that ignorance of the law is no excuse. I take exception to that stupid but oft-quoted justification for prosecuting a person for breaking some trifling law that is so obscure that it takes the entire court system years to determine if a law was actually broken. The laws in the United States number into the millions. There are city laws, county laws, State laws, and federal laws. There are statutes, ordinances, regulations, and codes. Some laws contradict other laws. The laws regarding federal income tax alone fill 67,000 printed pages. It is absurd to suppose that a couple of hard working clammers with no legal expertise "should have known better."

It is even more absurd to assert that what Captain Brown did in 1875 (when he salvaged the *Cumberland*) constituted legitimate salvage, but what Christman and Hastings did more than a century later was considered looting and vandalism, as their self-indulgent naysayers would like to have had it perceived.

As a disgruntled competitor, Townley started a smear campaign when he told a reporter that the clammers had "totally trashed" the wrecks. In fact, government-hired archaeologists later concurred in observing that the wreck sites suffered from fast currents and tidal disturbances that "scoured-out depressions," and had been adversely impacted by accumulated spoil from dredging operations that deepened and widened the channel. Proximity to the shipping lanes was another cause for accelerating deterioration, due to the propeller wash from passing large ships.

The *Daily Press* of Hampton Roads took Townley's side and published other discrediting comments. The down and dirty rag accused Christman and Hastings of removing the bones of dead sailors. This was a bold-faced lie. The newspaper later retracted this false accusation.

The *Daily Press* then quoted Townley as their spokesperson: "Townley said he shares the Navy's anger that 'the bones of over 100 men were torn and scattered over the bottom' in pursuit of relics for profit. 'How do people feel about digging up bones from a cemetery?' he said."

The *Daily Press* also resorted to gross exaggeration by claiming that Christman and Hastings were "pillaging more than $40,000 in relics."

The FBI placed no value on the confiscated artifacts. They simply made an inventory: "One silver ladle; shadow box w/9 items; one block double shellacked dead-eye; 2 pc bucket; mustard bottle; brown bottle; iron bolt; glass umbrella ink stand; sq glass piece-salt; 9" powder measure shell; shellached [sic] block sm wood fm springfield stock; dead-eye; pistol butt & long piece; sabot; 2 pc blue china; gun site [sic] cover; sm carved head/pipe bowl; fuse; sm pc of wht china; shoe; doorknob; toothbrush; brush/broom partial; weight for marking depths; lock epavlette [sic]; pistol stock; double block shellached [sic]; ruler for brass; latch; epaulettes; hook w/plate; plate; clay pipe bowl; recast belt buckle; 3 pc wd; one pistol block; three bolts; 3 copper spikes w/wooden accretian [sic]; pistol butt plate; pistol trigger mount; wooden part of hand saw; 4 pcs wooden rigging wheels; flute; 9 pieces misc wood; plate & bolt; brass ring for rope; piece of wood-us/nyw; 3 bullet molds; lock-sq shape; cannon bell [sic]; lot of cloth and buttons; 9" bucket of cannister [sic]."

All these items fit comfortably in a large box, or perhaps in the trunk of a car. There was no item so large that it could not be held aloft easily in a person's hand. The FBI did not have to rent a hotel room as a storage facility, as Townley unjustly claimed.

The relics were certainly not worth a king's ransom. Most of the items were broken, damaged, or badly deteriorated. They were nothing like the artifacts that Cussler's group recovered and donated to The Mariners Museum. The real value of the items was intangible: historical rather than monetary. They were worth only what a collector would pay for them.

Even if it were proven that these items had been "stolen" – that is, if the courts adjudicated actual ownership – the charge could be no worse than petty theft.

Shipwreck Case File - CSS Florida

Furthermore, because the clammers collected these items from all over the James River, there was no way to prove that they came from the *Cumberland* or *Florida*; or from any wreck for that matter. This was another assumption that the prosecution made in light of the lack of adequate defense. There was no provenance because the clammers didn't know precisely where they were tonging when they brought up each individual relic. The only item whose provenance could be established with any certainty was the soup ladle, because the handle was stamped *Jacob Bell*, which was one of the vessels that the *Florida* captured and burned.

In the event, the issue of ownership was never raised. The court simply assumed that the Navy owned both the wrecks and their relics because the Navy said so. And perhaps the defendants could not afford the kind of attorney who knew enough to challenge that assumption. The Navy and the FBI had unlimited expense accounts. The defendants were struggling to earn a living and pay their monthly bills.

It was a travesty of justice that most of the evidence against the defendants was based on hearsay, unwarranted opinions, and false declarations, which an enlightened court would have ruled inadmissible.

The case dragged on for three years. Talk about making a mountain out of a molehill; this was more like going to the Supreme Court over a parking violation. The personal and financial backgrounds of all four defendants were thoroughly investigated. The newspapers in general – and the *Daily Press* in particular – hung them out to dry. The FBI found no evidence of any other wrongdoing in the lives of the clammers or collectors.

Townley and the *Daily Press* continued to harass the defendants with lies and libels. Townley went so far as to claim, "In the subsequent trial, two watermen were convicted of felonies." Once again Townley grossly exaggerated the truth.

There was no trial because the defendants freely acknowledged their deeds. A judge announced sentences. Williams and Stevens were fined $1,250. Christman and

Hastings were found guilty of a misdemeanor violation; neither one was fined or jailed or put on probation. Case closed.

Although Townley's conduct was questionable, the Department of the Interior paid him $500 for his role as a snitch.

Even though the Navy let the FBI prosecute the case, the Navy obtained the artifacts by falsely claiming ownership of the wreck. Brazil and the General Services Administration did not enter the case.

Considering how much the investigation and prosecution cost American taxpayers, the Navy could have saved an incredible amount of time, trouble, and money by simply offering to purchase the boxful of trinkets outright.

Instead, payment for the artifacts came out of the FBI's budget. What the Navy could have purchased for a few hundred dollars cost the American people a few hundred *thousand* dollars.

The prosecution of four defendants for conducting salvage work was in direct opposition to centuries-old Admiralty law. Admiralty law, alias maritime law, precedes the Constitution of the United States. The intent of the law with regard to shipwreck is to encourage salvage by guaranteeing a profit for the salvors, in order to return salvaged materials to the stream of commerce. Under Admiralty law, the defendants would have been plaintiffs instead of defendants, and would have received a substantial salvage award for their efforts. In other words, the Navy would have had to *pay* Christman and Hastings for recovering long lost property – assuming, of course, that the Navy could establish a valid claim to the property; the burden of proof would then have been the responsibility of the Navy.

Clammers cannot control what comes up in their tongs. It could be a handful of clams, it could be worthless shell hash, it could by modern refuse, and it could be products of America's heritage. In the past, these precious historical relics were saved and returned to the stream of commerce. After fluky salvors were persecuted

Shipwreck Case File - CSS Florida

for their efforts at preservation, and rescuing relics from oblivion, this is no longer the case. Fear of prosecution has now forced clammers to dump artifacts back into the water. The losers are the American people.

While the FBI was spending an enormous amount of time and prodigious resources to conduct an exhaustive investigation into the lives of four individuals who were little more than pawns in a game that Foster and Townley instigated, and that the Departments of the Navy and Interior grandiosely supported, I wonder how many stolen automobiles were not returned to their owners, how many car thieves went uncaptured, how many kidnapping cases received short shrift, how many serial killers were not apprehended, how many bombers and terrorists got away with murder, how much violent crime was allowed to proceed unhindered, how much fraudulent activity was put on the back burner, and how many crimes went undetected.

Navy Clambake

Although this case was not one of the FBI's shining moments, it represented a much darker moment for the Navy. In its eagerness to abscond with the booty, it never questioned the provenance of the artifacts.

It goes without saying that clammers are not archaeologists. By this I mean no disrespect for clammers, nor do I mean to impugn their integrity. But by their own admission they drifted all over Hampton Roads and the James River in their endless quest for clams. They were never sure when they were over or near a shipwreck. And they scooped up relics from all over the area, including places where no shipwrecks have ever been found.

Yet like clods, Navy museum personnel blindly accepted the clammers' word about the provenance of the artifacts. Curators simply took it for granted that the clammers knew what they were talking about, and that all the relics had been recovered from the *Florida* and the *Cumberland* – perhaps because that was where they wanted them to have been found: an arbitrary and inept attitude if there ever was one, and one that does not smack of professional archaeology.

These are the kind of mindless workers that the Navy employs to care for its collections – and for collectibles of questionable ownership and provenance.

Although this federal case is now part of the *Florida's* history, the Naval History and Heritage Command neglected to mention it in the DANF entry, thus keeping it concealed from public awareness.

It should come as no surprise that, on the DANF entry for the *Wachusett*, the Naval History and Heritage Command noted her capture of the *Florida*, but neglected to mention that the capture violated international neutrality laws.

Furthermore, although the *Wachusett* was a screw steamer, the illustration that accompanies the entry shows a square-rigged sailing vessel with no smokestack - at least, it did at the time of publication of the volume in hand.

Four vessels are depicted in this contemporary woodcut in the author's collection. From left to right: the USS *Kearsarge*; the *Deerhound*, a private vessel which rescued survivors of the CSS *Alabama* and transported them to shore (including Captain Raphael Semmes); one of the *Alabama's* boats; and the *Alabama* in her death throes.

Shipwreck Case File
CSS *Alabama*

Alabama Belle

The *Alabama* was the most famous (or notorious) Confederate commerce raider of the Civil War. Under the command of Captain Rafael Semmes, she roamed the world in search of Union-registered vessels to destroy. Her renown was justly deserved, not only for the number of vessels that she captured or sank, but by the vast number of Union warships that were diverted from other duties in their search for the dreaded raider. The *Alabama* grossly disrupted American commerce, and caused a huge increase in insurance rates.

On June 19, 1864, the Union warship *Kearsarge* engaged the *Alabama* in battle off the coast of France. The *Kearsarge* outmaneuvered and outgunned the *Alabama*. According to Semmes's autobiography:

"After the lapse of about one hour and ten minutes, our ship was ascertained to be in a sinking condition, the enemy's shell having exploded in our side, and between decks, opening large apertures through which the water rushed with great rapidity. For some few minutes I had hopes of being able to reach the French coast, for which purpose I gave the ship all steam, and set such of the fore-and-aft sails as were available. The ship filled so rapidly, however, that before we had made much progress, the fires were extinguished in the furnaces, and we were evidently on the point of sinking. I now hauled down my colors, to prevent further destruction of life, and dispatched a boat to inform the enemy of our condition. Although we were now but 400 yards from each other, the enemy fired upon me five times after my colors had been struck."

Striking colors (that is, hauling down the flag, or ensign) was the signal to cease firing. The *Alabama* did so but the *Kearsarge* did not.

By continuing to fire, the *Kearsarge* did not honor the *Alabama's* signal, but pretended that striking colors was a ruse that Semmes employed so as to enable the *Alabama* to reach the territorial waters of France, which lay only four miles away. The *Alabama* sank a few minutes later as a result of the *Kearsarge's* continued firing. Ten additional Confederate fatalities were attributed to the *Kearsarge's* refusal to cease firing.

Semmes stated explicitly that he "dispatched a boat to inform the enemy of our condition."

The U.S. Navy twisted actual events by rewriting Semmes's statement to suit its purposes. In the first edition of DANF: "After an hour's battle an officer of *Alabama* came alongside *Kearsarge* and surrendered his vessel." In the re-edited online version: "Semmes struck his colors and sent a boat to *Kearsarge* with a message of surrender and an appeal for help."

Semmes never said anything about surrendering. He stated only that he wanted "to prevent further destruction of life, and dispatched a boat to inform the enemy of our condition."

The false declaration of "surrender" was inserted by modern Navy historians as a way to bolster a faked claim of ownership.

For Whom the Bell Tolls . . .

According to court documents:

> In 1979 Mr. [Richard] Steinmetz participated in an antique gun show in London. A dealer informed him that he knew where the bell of the CSS *Alabama* was located, and Mr. Steinmetz asked to see it. The dealer took Mr. Steinmetz to Hastings on the English coast where an antique dealer, a Mr. Walker, showed him the bell and documentation concerning it. It purportedly came from the Isle of Guernsey off the French coast.

Shipwreck Case File - CSS Alabama

Mr. Steinmetz was skeptical, but he paid a deposit, took possession of the bell and proceeded to Guernsey to check it out.

Guernsey fishermen have a sideline – wreck stripping. Mr. Steinmetz visited a Guernsey friend and the friend introduced him to various persons who dealt in shipwrecks and salvage. When these persons were shown the bell they identified it as a bell which had hung in a Guernsey bar. It developed that a diver, William Lawson, had salvaged the bell in about 1936 and most likely had traded it at the bar for drinks. There it hung until World War II. The Germans captured Guernsey from the British. Thereafter, the bar was destroyed in a British bombing raid.

After the destruction of the bar the bell passed from hand to hand until it was acquired in 1978 by the Hastings antique dealer.

Satisfied with the authenticity of the bell, Mr. Steinmetz completed the purchase and brought it to the United States. He had given the dealer other antique items having a value of approximately $12,000 in exchange for the bell.

In 1979, after returning to the United States, Mr. Steinmetz offered the bell to the Naval Academy. The Academy was unwilling or unable to trade or purchase it. Mr. Steinmetz put the bell on a shelf until December 1990, at which time he placed it in the Marmer Rooke Gallery for auction.

The Bell was advertised in the Gallery's catalogue. Alert Naval authorities noticed the advertisement and claimed entitlement to the bell. Mr. Steinmetz resisted the claim, and this action ensued.

. . . It Tolls Not for Thee

Documents that were submitted to the court included quotes from the *Alabama's* executive officer, Lieutenant John Kell: "Captain Semmes said to me, 'Dispatch an officer to the *Kearsarge* and ask that they send boats to save our wounded – ours are disabled.' Our little dingey [sic] was not injured, so I sent Master's Mate Fulham with the request."

Again, there was no mention of the word "surrender." Furthermore, the *Alabama* was not captured because she sank before the enemy could board her.

Despite the undisputed facts regarding the *Alabama's* loss without surrendering or being captured, the modern Navy conspired to relieve Steinmetz of his hard-earned property by filing a civil action against him.

The judge in the case reluctantly – and I stress the word "reluctantly" – ruled: "The bell is the property of the United States both by the right of capture and by the virtue of the fact that the United States is successor to the rights and property of the Confederate States of America."

In the previous sections I dispelled the notion of "capture." In the previous chapter I dispelled the notion of the succession of Confederate property. While it is true that Confederate property may under certain circumstances succeed to the United States, the agency to which it is succeeded is the General Services Administration, not the U.S. Navy.

Clearly, the Navy had no right to sue Steinmetz over property that may have belonged to the General Services Administration. How the Navy persuaded the court that it (the Navy) should take possession of property that rightfully belonged to another (either Steinmetz or the General Services Administration), I cannot conceive. Perhaps Navy witnesses committed perjury. Perhaps Navy witnesses did not "tell the truth, the whole truth, and nothing but the truth," but told only that portion of the truth that advanced the Navy's case, and declined to mention that Confederate property succeeded to the General Services Administration, not to the Navy. Or perhaps Navy lawyers submitted false evidence to bolster their case. Or all of the above.

On the website of the Naval History and Heritage Command, the Navy holds that "Warships on the high seas have complete immunity from the jurisdiction of any state other than the flag states."

I cannot believe that no one has called attention to the obvious fact that shipwrecks are not "on" the high seas. Shipwrecks are "under" the high seas, and therefore do not conform to the article quoted above. This is just another case of the Navy stretching or misrepresenting the truth as a way to achieve personal advantage.

Based on the evidence that the Navy submitted to (or withheld from) the court, the judge held, "The bell is the property of the United States both by the right of capture and by virtue of the fact that the United States is successor to the rights and property of the Confederate States of America."

The Toll of Defeat

However, with regard to my use of the word "reluctant" in the previous section, the judge appended his ruling thus: "I expressed my view at the hearing that fairness and equity suggest that, regardless of the legal merits of the case, the United States should at least reimburse Mr. Steinmetz for his expenses in acquiring, shipping and preserving the bell, since through these efforts the bell has been returned to the American people. . . . One would think, however, that in the unusual circumstances of this case some way could have been devised to make Mr. Steinmetz whole. But that, apparently, was more than the bureaucratic mind could accomplish."

General sentiment also sided with Steinmetz. He was perceived as a maligned martyr whose good faith in his country had been suborned by the Navy. One headline read, "Less-than-ringing win for the 'Union' Navy."

The judge continued his disparaging criticism of the Navy in the public venue. One newspaper noted, "U.S. District Judge Dickinson Debevoise said in his ruling yesterday that 'fundamental fairness' dictated that the government compensate Steinmetz, but he said he could not order it to do so. . . . The Navy, for all its ingeniousness and ability, is unable to break the bureaucratic logjams,' Debevoise said. 'This isn't the can-do spirit I want to attribute to the Navy.' Steinmetz would have to savor the 'psychic compensation' of thanks from U.S. citizens for saving the artifact, the judge said."

Too bad, judge. What you see is what you get.

"That did not satisfy Steinmetz. 'You expect this to happen in a communist country, not in the United States,' he said outside court. 'This was an organized rip-off.' "

Steinmetz hit the Confederate nail on the Union head when he said, " 'Dealers were at risk of having items such as Confederate flags worth $40,000 seized by the government.' The government attorney would not comment outside court."

By extrapolation, with this unjust ruling on the books, the Navy could now effect wholesale slaughter by swooping down on Civil War conferences, conventions, museums, even re-enactments, and confiscate every item of putative Naval origin. Responsibility would then fall upon the victimized owners to prove their innocence by establishing non-Navy provenance, instead of the Navy having to prove guilt. The Navy would win most cases by default, because it had unlimited funding and legal resources, while each individual would have to hire attorneys to plead his case.

Collectors of Civil War relics and maritime memorability agreed about the catastrophic result of the Navy's arrogant attitude toward private ownership. The general consensus was that anyone now in possession of Civil War relics would go underground. They would no longer promote Navy history by displaying their relics in public, but would conceal them. Black market sales and auctions would become the wave of the future.

As defense attorney Peter Hess noted, "If it wasn't for Richard Steinmetz, an important piece of U.S. History would never have been on U.S. soil. It would still be in England."

Hess's co-counsel, David Bederman, said, "If I found a rebel bullet in my old oak tree, the U.S. would have a

Shipwreck Case File - CSS Alabama

good argument that that bullet belongs to it. . . . I'm not sure the court intended that, but I think that's where it is now."

The public outcry garnered column-inches or -feet in many newspapers. For another example, "A federal judge ruled that a legal loophole permits the U.S. Navy to lay claim to the historic Civil War artifact without any compensation to the dealer. . . . Steinmetz said he had been offered $40,000 for the bell, but that before it could be sold, government agents came to his home seeking to seize the item."

Steinmetz hammered another Confederate nail (or perhaps it was a stake) by calling the Navy's courtroom success "nothing but legalized theft." He also stated, "The government's attitude is that, 'We're going to take it and there's nothing you can do about it.'"

One reporter pondered, "Did the *Kearsarge* capture the *Alabama*, or simply send it to the bottom?" Hess tendered the facts, "The *Alabama* never came under U.S. command. Its offer to surrender was rebuffed and no Union sailor ever set foot on the deck." Hess went on to say, "The 'newly concocted theory' of 'constructive capture' . . . would create international confusion over the ownership and jurisdiction of sunken warships."

Hess: "The United States chose to treat the Confederate commerce raiders as pirates, not as lawfully commissioned vessels of an enemy, so it can't claim the wreck now."

Although it is true that the Union never recognized the Confederacy as a sovereign nation, the modern U.S. Navy now contended otherwise, in order to justify its rationale for subsuming its contrived legal position.

The appeals court agreed with Debevoise's sentiments: "It is not lost on us that this leaves uncompensated Steinmetz's considerable energy and creativity in retrieving and returning to the United States an irreplaceable artifact from its history."

New evidence may not be introduced when a case is appealed. Nor can fictitious evidence be withdrawn or stricken from the record. The introduction of evidence and the hearing of testimony are sealed by the trial court. An appeals court obtains its findings solely by reviewing the evidence and testimony that is already on record, to determine if the lower court misconstrued a point of law. Thus the appeals court was forced to side with the lower court's ruling, because, inter alia (among other things), the Navy neglected to mention that the true successor to Confederate property was the General Services Administration, and not the U.S. Navy.

The Navy remained obdurate (hardened against good or moral influence), and maintained its callous attitude toward bilking Steinmetz out of his just desserts.

A Bell of a Different Color

Meanwhile, the French navy discovered the *Alabama's* resting place, in French territorial waters off Cherbourg. French archaeologists surveyed the wreck, as they had every right to do, because it lay within the country's territorial borders. But they wanted to take souvenirs from the wreck which, in accordance with the U.S. court decision that conveyed ownership to the Navy, they were not permitted to do without the U.S. Navy's say-so.

So, the U.S. Navy allowed the French archaeologists to take souvenirs from the wreck as long as everything was eventually turned over to the U.S. Navy.

But wait! There's more! According to the directive of the Naval History and Heritage Command, "The Navy's policy towards these historic wrecks is to leave them undisturbed."

The Navy believes (or would like to make other people believe), "Sites that have reached chemical and physical equilibrium with their immediate underwater environment are subject to a substantially reduced deterioration rate. If disturbed, this deterioration rate accelerates."

Furthermore, the Navy contends, "Sunken military craft are often considered war graves and therefore must be respected."

No matter. What the Navy says has nothing to do

Shipwreck Case File - CSS Alabama

with what the Navy does. The Navy signed a formal agreement with the French government in which collecting souvenirs was permissible as long as the Navy got the goods.

Although the Navy was willing to spend hundreds of thousands of dollars on legal fees in order to steal a bell, it wouldn't spend a dime on archaeology of the *Alabama*. A non-profit organization was formed to work in coordination with volunteer French archaeologists.

Excavation and souvenir salvage continued throughout the 1990's and into the 2000's. The 2002 season was the most rewarding with respect to salvage and recovery operations. Hundreds of souvenirs and knickknacks were salvaged, including human bones, two large cannons, and the ship's bell.

You read that correctly but I will add emphasis. Salvors found and recovered *the* ship's bell. It was neither Blue nor Gray. It was brass.

The Ding Dong Navy

Now the Navy had two *Alabama* bells: one for the ding and one for the dong. Or did it?

How did the Navy know that the Steinmetz bell was authentic? What kind of metallurgical tests did the Navy conduct on the bell before it sued Steinmetz for possession? For that matter, did the Navy conduct *any* kind of test? The answers are all negative: it did not, none, and no.

Navy historians – the new powermongers who were taking over the Naval Historical Center – simply assumed that the bell was authentic because it was advertised as such; and perhaps because a bidder at the auction house was willing to pay $40,000 for it. And anyway, Steinmetz should know it was authentic because he was bona fide antiquities dealer, whereas the Navy historians were . . . not.

Perhaps the self-puffing Navy historians were so eager to exercise their newfound authority that they didn't look any farther than their collective noses to authenticate the bell. To their shame, they shot themselves in their collective foot with their own Naval gun. Those who smirked as they proudly put the Steinmetz bell on display in the Navy museum, were now grimacing at their cupidity.

Steinmetz must have had faith in the bell's authenticity, else he would not have spent so much money to retain it. In retrospect, it appears that he was hoodwinked by the Guernsey folks.

Now the Navy possessed a bell that had been taken under more than one false pretense.

Did the Navy apologize for its naivety? Did the Navy acknowledge its unpardonable sin? A glance at the *Alabama* entry on the Naval History and Heritage Command website reveals that the answer is a definite "no." There is no mention of the Steinmetz case, and no mention of the fake bell: as if years of legal wrangling never existed.

Like the Ministry of Truth in George Orwell's *1984*, Navy historians rewrote history so as to present themselves in a favorable light. Instead of telling the truth, the whole truth, and nothing but the truth about their blunder, Navy historians told only that part of the truth that fit the false image that they wanted to present to the public.

That is what the Navy *did*. What the Navy did *not* do was return the bell to Steinmetz. After all, if the Steinmetz bell did not come from the *Alabama*, then it was never the property of the Navy – *any* navy. But the Navy is not known for correcting the errors of its ways. Better to ignore its mistakes and hope they will be forgotten, or lost in the wisps of time.

In the Navy, honesty is not the best policy – or any part of its policy.

Shipwreck Case File
Hamilton and *Scourge*

Another Navy Scourge

One has to wonder what motivates the Navy when, on one hand it fought bitterly to wrest a small hunk of brass from an honest citizen, while on the other hand it literally gave away a pair of *the* most well preserved wooden warships in the entire underwater world, bar none (so far).

In the War of 1812, the *Hamilton* and *Scourge* were two components of a fleet of "thirteen sail" under the command of Commodore Isaac Chauncey. Chauncey's fleet was opposing the British fleet on Lake Ontario.

According to DANF, "A sudden squall caused two ships, *Hamilton* and *Scourge*, to capsize and sink." This single sentence about their fate contains two gross errors that Navy historians, of all people, should not have made.

First, the *Hamilton* and *Scourge* were two-masted-schooners (whose triangular sails were rigged fore-and-aft), not ships (whose quadrilateral sails were square-rigged on three or more masts).

Second, contemporary accounts do not declare that the vessels capsized. To "capsize" means "to turn a vessel upside down" so that the bottom of the hull faces upward, toward the sky. In fact, the *Hamilton* and *Scourge* swamped in a sudden squall. They may have rolled to one side so that water poured over the gunwale, but they did not turn upside down, else the wrecks would not have been found sitting bolt upright, with the cannons and other loose paraphernalia residing on the open decks.

I hope the rest of the Navy pays better attention to detail. I wouldn't want a nuclear submarine to launch a missile at Moscow, Idaho instead of Moscow, Russia.

Reductio ad Absurdum

Once again, a private citizen initiated the search and ultimately discovered both wreck sites: Daniel Nelson. The shipwrecks were a trove of old-time arms and ammunition: cutlasses and boarding axes, cannons and cannonballs. They were also a trove of human skulls and associated skeletal remains, which littered the decks and the adjacent lake bottom: grim reminders of the loss of approximately seventy American sailors.

Although the shipwrecks were located in Canadian territorial waters, the U.S. Navy wasted no time in asserting ownership. In this case, however, the Navy's ownership of the *Scourge* (ex-*Lord Nelson*) had already been adjudicated by Congress, and not in the Navy's favor.

Canadian Brothers James and William Crooks owned the *Lord Nelson*, which they used for commerce. On June 4, 1812, the U.S. Navy brig *Oneida* seized the *Lord Nelson* and confiscated her cargo, claiming the vessel as a prize of war. The fledgling U.S. Navy needed "bottoms." It assumed ownership of the vessel, sold the cargo, and distributed the proceeds to the officers and crew of the *Oneida*.

The Navy armed the confiscated vessel and renamed her *Scourge*. The U.S. government declared war on Great Britain on June 18, 1812.

It is apparent from the chronology of events that when the Navy seized the *Lord Nelson*, the U.S. government had not yet declared war. This begs the question: How can the *Lord Nelson* be considered a prize of war if no war existed at the time of her seizure? This was precisely the point that the Crooks brothers argued.

In 1817, the Court of the Northern District of New York found that the seizure was indeed illegal. The court decreed that the Crooks brothers should be reimbursed for the value of the vessel and her cargo – one thousand pounds in Halifax currency. Despite the decree, the Crooks brothers did not receive their settlement because the clerk of the New York court, Theron Rudd, embezzled all the court's money.

Shipwreck Case File - *Hamilton/Scourge*

The obverse and reverse of a commemorative coin that the City of Hamilton minted.

James Crooks was not without political connections. The settlement claim was pushed through a succession of assemblies and legislative bodies, including the Senate and the House of Representatives. In addition to Congressional acceptance, the Crooks brothers' claim was backed by the President of the United States, James Monroe, in 1819. Despite this awesome amount of political pressure and unanimous approval, payment was still not forthcoming – for reasons that were never adequately explained. Both Crooks brothers finally died without ever receiving compensation for their loss.

Although their descendants kept the case alive, the point under discussion here is that the federal courts ruled, and the U.S. Congress confirmed, and the President of the United States insisted, that the U.S. Navy did not possess title to the *Scourge*.

Nonetheless, the modern Navy ignored the law and documented history, and claimed ownership of both the *Hamilton* and the *Scourge*. Then, in an unprecedented turnabout, *gave* them away.

Navy Assignation

According to the Navy's official transfer of title, in 1979, "The Royal Ontario Museum (hereinafter referred to as the 'DONEE') or its duly constituted assigns shall carry out scientific studies to ascertain the condition of the said wrecks and develop feasibility studies on the

128 Shipwreck Case File - *Hamilton/Scourge*

basis of which the DONEE or its assign may raise one or both of the Vessels for use as a static display."

What happened to the Navy's adamant protocol of preservation in situ? Of non-disturbance? Of war graves?

A year later, the Royal Ontario Museum conveyed title to the City of Hamilton, with instructions to "observe and perform, all of the terms, conditions, obligations, liabilities, indemnities, and stipulations in the said [U.S. Navy] contract."

And there the matter remains. What scientific studies has the City of Hamilton conducted in the *thirty-six years* that have passed after the original transfer of title? Absolutely none.

In fact, the City's grand scheme was not about archaeology at all; it was about gross exploitation, to capitalize on the death of American sailors. "According to a city plan, the two preserved ships would be placed in a lakeside museum attracting hundreds of thousands of visitors each year." A *Hamilton/Scourge* Committee member stated, "It'll be the single biggest tourism boost in the history of the city." And the U.S. Navy went along with this scheme.

Today, the fate of both shipwrecks still lies in limbo. Or is the right word oblivion? For the unexpurgated answer to that question, see *Stolen Heritage*.

Another scheme to capitalize on dead American sailors was a stamp and cachet issue.

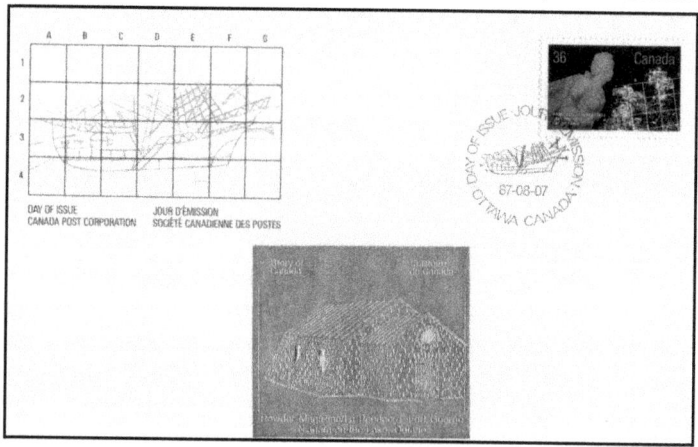

Shipwreck Case File
U-352

A Bone to Pick

The *U-352* was a German U-boat that was depth-charged and shelled by the U.S. Coast Guard cutter *Icarus*. The U-boat sustained so much damage that it was forced to surface. A majority of the crew managed to climb through the hatches and jump overboard, but thirteen men were left inside the pressure hull when the submarine sank a few minutes later.

The U-boat's precise location was lost until recreational scuba diver George Purifoy discovered it in 1975. The site quickly became a popular destination for recreational scuba divers who were fascinated by Nazi naval history.

The wreck's popularity drew the attention of Senator Lowell Weicker. He started a solo bandwagon that recreational scuba divers neither needed nor wanted, by claiming that unexploded ordnance – namely, 88-millimeter projectiles and live torpedoes with warheads supposedly intact – constituted a safety hazard. He ignored the fact that divers had been swimming past this ordnance for years without encountering any problems. After all, the long-forgotten explosive devices were stowed deep in the interior of the pressure hull or inside sealed torpedo tubes.

Weicker exerted his senatorial influence to enjoin the Navy to conduct a major salvage job whose purpose was to remove all ordnance from the interior. The Navy used the USS *Hoist* as a surface support vessel for an operation that lasted for six full weeks.

For two days and nights, working round the clock, the *Hoist* towed a side-scan sonar unit over four different positions that were annotated in Navy historical records. "However, no probable contacts were made."

In frustration at not being able to locate a shipwreck that was visited every weekend during the summer tourist season, the "decision was made to ask the Squadron to make arrangements for commercial assistance from Morehead City in locating the submarine."

Voila! What insight. Instead of wasting wages and enormous quantities of fuel, someone thought of the obvious: ask the skippers who ran their fishing and diving boats to the wreck on a daily basis. "Using loran charlie navigation, *Atlantis II* located and buoyed off *U-352* within 20 minutes."

Initial diving operations (on scuba) consisted of tying a series of radar buoys to the bow, conning tower, and stern of the hull, in order to determine the U-boat's heading (which was northeast), so that a six-point mooring could be established. This set-up job took two days.

Finally, the first underwater survey was conducted. Wearing MK 12 Surface Supplied Diving System with three hundred feet of hose, and taking photographs with a UDATS camera, it was ascertained that "the submarine is at rest on a sandy bottom, with a 65-75 degree starboard list. Divers reported soundings of 110 feet at the stern and amidship, and 116 feet at the bow. A variety of sea life linger in the vicinity of the submarine, including a school of barracuda. The forward 30 feet of the bow hull section is broken and down at an angle of 30 degrees. The entire submarine is heavily encrusted in barnacles, 75 percent of the decking is missing and only structural framing remains attached to the pressure hull. Approximately 20 per cent of the starboard hull is submerged in the sandy bottom, and an air lift or falcon nozzle could be used to remove this sand to gain access for a complete hull inspection. As previously mentioned, the submarine's outer shell is badly deteriorated and all that remains is the structural framing attached to the very accessible pressure hull which is in good shape. Because of the 65-75 degree starboard list, divers were unable to determine whether or not the two starboard forward torpedo tube outer doors are opened.

Shipwreck Case File - U-352

Number two torpedo tube (upper port tube) is broken in half and number four tube (lower port tube) is intact but divers were unable to confirm the presence of torpedoes. Although the external survey revealed that no torpedoes are stowed topside on the maindeck, a torpedo warhead was discovered wedged in the deck framing approximately 30 feet forward of the conning tower, above the forward torpedo room. The warhead is intact with exploder removed. The forward torpedo loading hatch is open and the hatch cover is missing. Divers passed survey of conning tower to continue looking aft. The messdecks hatch and after torpedo loading hatch are both open and both hatch covers are missing. Divers reported that after torpedo loading hatch is blocked by two six inch diameter pipes, possible vents. Divers moved further aft and determined stern torpedo outer door is opened and approximately 2.5 feet of a torpedo extends out the stern tube."

They also found a single 88-millimeter shell in the sand some twenty-five feet off the starboard side.

The next day, divers found that "the upper conning tower hatch is open and is lying on the bottom of the conning tower. The lower conning tower hatch, which allows access into the control room, is partially open. Divers reported that the ready service aft of the 88mm gun mount is completely deteriorated. Only the gun mount base remains intact . . . divers entered the forward torpedo room through the forward torpedo loading hatch and began the internal search. Divers reported the forward torpedo room contains a considerable amount of mud, sand and silt. The presence of unexploded ordnance could not be determined at this time. However, two horizontal HP [high pressure] air flasks were identified extending between frames 26 and 37 on the port side, partially covered by mud and sand. A violet colored Petroleum Oil Lubricant (POL) product is present in the overhead with a depth of approximately 8 inches. A square water tight door (door missing) provides access between petty officer's compartment and the forward torpedo room. At about frame 45 within the petty officer's compartment, an approximate rectangular shaped 18 inch by 24 inch hole passes through the pressure hull in the overhead and into the sea. Upon completion of the brief internal survey of the forward torpedo room and the petty officer's compartment, divers prepared for the X-ray of the stern torpedo. The radiation exposure device is heavy and required two divers to horse it around into position. . . . An exposure was taken and the preliminary picture indicated the torpedo is unarmed."

Divers commenced the removal of mud and sand from the forward torpedo room in order to "make the final determination as to the presence of unexploded ordnance" by implanting a jet. Bad weather, strong currents, and hard-packed mud conspired to make this a difficult and time-consuming job. Two weeks later they were they able to excavate down as far as the deck plates. Furthermore, it was possible that more torpedoes might be stowed below the deck plates. "Several divers attempted to release the inner torpedo tube locking device using a 36 inch aluminum pipe wrench, but were unsuccessful."

Then came a couple of days of bad weather, one day of good, a couple more days of bad. "Probing by hand in the bilges revealed no evidence of any torpedoes/unexploded ordnance in the excavation. Four air flasks, extended between frames 26 to 36, were positively identified within the forward torpedo room. Two lie end to end along the port side bulkhead and two lie end to end along the starboard side bulkhead."

Then, "The lower port torpedo tube was found to be cracked and the battery section of a torpedo was visible. The lower port torpedo tube is cracked approximately 3 to 4 feet outside of the pressure hull which would indicate the torpedo is broken in the center section."

Also, "Alongside the starboard quarter, approximately 10 feet from the submarines side, divers located the end of a torpedo center section. . . . Divers confirmed this torpedo was without an exploder."

Furthermore, "Two torpedoes were located in the

Shipwreck Case File - U-352   133

bilges and confirmed, one directly underneath the port side air flasks and a second approximately 8 inches to the right of the first (as facing the bow). Both torpedoes are without exploders." The next day they found two more torpedoes in the bilges.

"In the vicinity of the CO's cabin there is approximately 3 feet of clearance between the mud and sand level and the overhead. There is also a considerable amount of mud and sand in the mates compartment and the officers mess."

Also, "Tubes one and four were drilled and probing revealed the presence of a torpedo in each tube. The two new torpedoes bring the total to ten torpedoes located thus far. . . .

"Divers reported the galley is approximately 2/3 full of mud and debris. The galley hatch door leading forward is present and partially open. Divers proceeded forward into the mates compartment and reported the space is approximately half full of mud and noticeably clear of debris, and that there is approximately five feet of clearance between the mud level and the overhead. A circular watertight hatch opens into the mates compartment and provides access into the conning tower control room. Divers then back tracked and proceeded aft through the engine room. However, the extreme star-

The Navy left this and other unexploded torpedoes and warheads in place, apparently because it was beyond their ability to remove them.

board list, combined with the mud, debris and the port and starboard engines, made transit of the engine room very difficult. Divers continued through the engine room space and into the after torpedo room to investigate the two bars obstructing the after torpedo loading hatch. Investigation revealed the two bars appear to be securely in place and will probably require removal to allow easier access into the torpedo room. Like the forward torpedo room, the after torpedo room is full of a considerable amount of mud and debris. To complete a comprehensive survey all mud and debris will have to be excavated."

The next day they proceeded to torch through the bars, but then found that in MK II gear they could slip between them. After much excavation and time lost to bad weather, the determination was made that no torpedoes were stored in the after torpedo room. Then they partially excavated the galley, where they removed the deck plates, and the CO's cabin. No unexploded ordnance was disclosed.

"It was decided that any remote removal of the exploder from the torpedo in the stern tube is not considered a practical course of action." The next day, "divers completed external excavation of sand alongside the entire length of the starboard side of *U-352*. No additional unexploded ordnance was found. However, communications problems developed with MK12 hats and diving had to be secured."

Because replacement communication assemblies were unavailable, survey operations were terminated.

"Divers discovered all 88MM and loaded them on board. Divers then placed the torpedo warhead section into a cargo net lowered to the bottom . . . lifted approximately 3 feet off the ocean floor and towed to a point 1500 yards away from the ship and submarine." Divers then attached an Incendiary Torch Remote Opening Device. "The first sign of the warhead burning was a large amount of smoke and bubbles on the surface. Approximately 5 minutes after commencing the burn, the warhead became buoyant and ascended to the surface

Shipwreck Case File - U-352

engulfed in flames. The warhead was recovered and lifted onboard along with 5 lbs of raw explosive and 7 lbs of residual."

After a month and a half on site, the salvage operation had completed its objective. Navy divers had made 137 dives for a total bottom time of 361 hours. A summary report stated that they had found numerous rounds from the ship's gun and an unexploded torpedo outside the submarine, as well as eight torpedoes inside the hull (seven in the forward torpedo room and one in the stern torpedo tube.

Inexplicably, the report failed to mention the torpedo that was trapped outside under the starboard hull. "The torpedoes in the forward room do not pose a hazard as long as left undisturbed, i.e., if restricted from access they will not explode spontaneously but the torpedo in the aft tube does constitute a hazard as it can be approached from outside the hull."

The recommendation was made that the torpedo in the after tube be burned by ITROD, while gratings could "be welded on the entrances to the submarine to prevent access and accidental detonation of any of the torpedoes inside the hull or their associated exploders, six of which could not be located and could be anywhere inside the vessel."

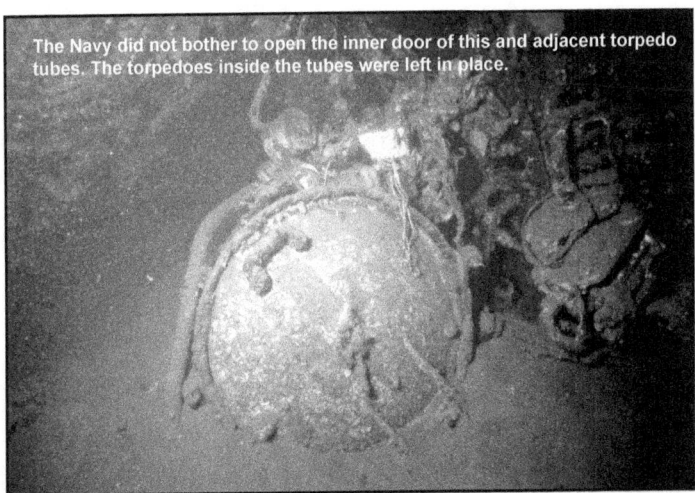

The Navy did not bother to open the inner door of this and adjacent torpedo tubes. The torpedoes inside the tubes were left in place.

The results of the survey were pondered for a year. Navy divers returned to the wreck the following year, stayed nine days, and made 67 dives. Using ITROD, they succeeded in burning the torpedo that was protruding from the stern tube as well as the one that was trapped under the starboard hull in the bow.

Then they proceeded to seal off the hatches. Instead of welding a grating across each opening, as recommended, they opted instead to emplace on each hatch a locking device that consisted of a steel T-bar that slipped inside the coaming and a smooth circular plate on the outside. The circular plate had a rounded hole in the middle, for the T-bar bolt, and two half-moon cutouts on opposite sides: so the T-bar could be held in place while the nut was run down the shaft from the outside. The nut was then welded in place.

Torpedoes that required too much work for Navy divers to reach were left in place.

Navy Speak with Forked Tongue

It is important to understand that this highly publicized salvage operation was not conducted in accordance with archaeological standards or guidelines. The Navy had no archaeologist on site to oversee the methodology (or lack of) that the divers employed. Digging was not done in the painstaking manner in which fossils were habitually unearthed, but with a water jet.

In order to clear the bilges under the main deck, and to reach the lower torpedo tubes on the starboard side, divers removed more than ten *feet* of mud, silt, and sand from four major compartments totaling one-third of the length of the hull, or 70 feet. These compartments measured some 15 feet across. The cubic footage of the sand that was removed approached 10,000 cubic feet (allowing for the curvature of the hull).

Sand weighs approximately 100 pounds per cubic foot. This means that more than 500 *tons* of thick overburden was spewed indiscriminately into the ocean outside the pressure hull, then spread by itinerant currents for miles in all directions.

Shipwreck Case File - U-352

There was no collection sieve to separate human remains from other debris: skeletal material and cultural objects were expelled along with the rest of the junk, with no thought given to sanctity in any form. The Navy didn't care about exhuming German bones and body parts, then spitting them into the water column.

This kind of "down and dirty" conduct not only received full Navy approval; it was authorized by the federal government, and for two years running. The only people who protested the wholesale devastation of the *U-352* were recreational scuba divers and the current German government (which had no connection to the Nazi regime).

Potsdam Agreement

Not that the German government had any say in the matter. It was never consulted. If it had been consulted, it may have registered an official complaint about the way the Navy was grossly disrupting a Nazi war grave. But making a diplomatic protest was as far as Germany could go.

In accordance with the terms of the Potsdam Agreement, Germany was completely stripped of its army and navy. It was not allowed to produce either arms or ammunition; indeed, Krupp (Germany's primary arms and armor manufacturer) was largely dismantled, and what remained of the company was converted to the manufacture of kitchen appliances. Germany's entire navy – its few remaining capital ships as well as hundreds of U-boats and even part of its merchant fleet – was seized by the Allies for reparations or disposal.

Each of the three major Allied powers (U.S., U.K. and U.S.S.R.) kept a number of U-boats "for technical assessment and experimental purposes." The remainder were scuttled at sea.

It was stipulated in the Potsdam Agreement that Germany was not allowed to possess instruments of war of any kind: tanks, cannons, artillery, rockets, surface warships, and particularly U-boats. Winston Churchill went as far as to *specify* that U-boats must be dismantled or destroyed.

What the Potsdam Agreement means in relation to the subject at hand is that Germany was not allowed to own U-boats: then or forever more. In turn, this means that the present-day German government does not and never has owned the Nazi U-boats that were sunk off the American eastern seaboard – or anywhere else in the world, for that matter.

Because the provisions of the Potsdam Agreement specifically forbid Germany from ever again possessing U-boats, the German government has no claim to sunken U-boats.

I will mention only one instance that relates to this particular issue. In 1993, Danish millionaire Karsten Lee funded the salvage of Nazi U-boat *U-534*. The hull was raised intact, and is now on public display in Birkenhead, England.

The German government neither protested the salvage nor had any say in how or where the U-boat should be exhibited.

The same legal rationale applies to U-boats off the coast of the U.S. eastern seaboard. This means that the Navy had the right and the might to do as it pleased with the *U-352* – except that what it did violated one of the Navy's own policies: to wit, "Sunken military craft are often considered war graves and therefore must be respected."

That was precisely the point made by Captain Dieter Ehrhardt, the Naval Liaison for the German Embassy in Washington, DC, when media hype alerted him about Weicker's proposal: "My government prefers to leave wreckage from World War II at the bottom of the sea, to give the dead sailors rest." He elaborated, "Generally speaking, the boat is a cemetery, and nobody wants to disturb a cemetery. It is not good, if you are in a cemetery, to pull dead bodies out of the earth."

The U.S. Navy pooh-poohed Ehrhardt's sentiment. It seems that what is good for the Navy goose isn't good for the German gander.

Shipwreck Case File
U-85

Grab and Bag

The *U-85* was shelled and depth-charged by the USS *Roper*. There were no survivors.

The site has been a popular dive destination since the 1970's.

In the late 1980's or early 1990's (the precise date has been concealed), the U.S. Navy conducted a clandestine souvenir collecting operation on the *U-85*. The goal was to recover a torpedo that was stowed inside the outer skin but outside the pressure hull. The torpedo in question – a G7a T1 compressed air model – weighed 3,369 pounds. A salvage vessel with heavy-duty lift capacity was needed to raise an object that weighed nearly two tons, (including slings, hardware, and miscellaneous lifting apparatus).

I remember seeing this torpedo in place in the 1970's. I photographed it in the 1980's. I noticed its absence in the 1990's. According to word of mouth, the salvaged torpedo was placed on display for Navy personnel to see: a place that is not readily accessible by the non-uniformed public. I have been unable to ascertain this torpedo's current location.

This large-scale salvage operation did considerable damage to the hull structure in the vicinity of the torpedo's stowage location. Metal plates were either torn and shredded or missing. A previously covered section of the pressure hull was exposed to the ravages of the sea.

If recreational scuba divers had taken this torpedo, the Navy would have been the first to point the finger and call the act looting, and desecrating a war grave: a holier-than-thou attitude that the Navy adopts whenever it is to its advantage to do so.

There is no way to determine how many less obvious souvenirs the Navy divers took when they absconded with the torpedo.

This is the torpedo that went missing: an easy snatch for the Navy with its heavy-lift equipment, although the lift required tearing apart some of the outer skin. This clandestine operation amply demonstrated the Janus-faced Navy's attitude toward the recovery of artifacts from wrecks: It is okay for the Navy but not for ordinary citizens.

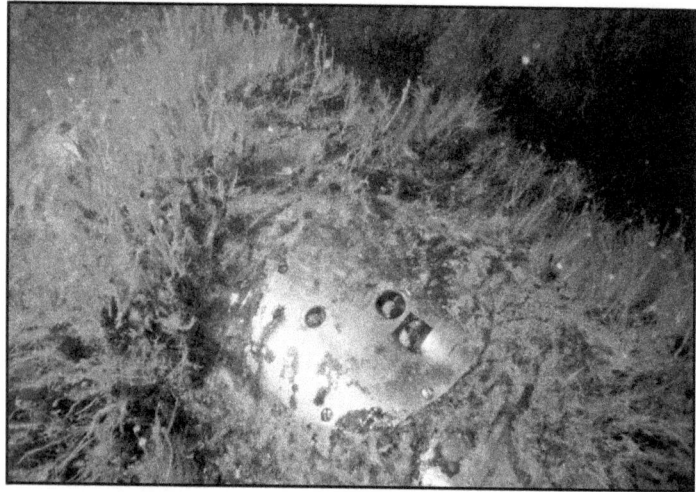

Shipwreck Case File
USS *Murphy*

Strangers in the Night

On the dark night of October 21, 1943, eastbound convoy UT-4 was on route to the United Kingdom. This convoy consisted of seventeen merchant vessels and ten U.S. warships: the battleship *Texas*, the refueling vessel *Enoree*, and eight destroyers. In accordance with standard anti-submarine warfare protocol, none of these vessels was displaying any lights, navigational or otherwise. When the *Murphy*'s radar unit detected the approach of an unidentified vessel, the Screen Commander on the USS *Nelson* was notified. The Screen Commander directed the *Murphy* to investigate the radar contact, and to force it away from the path of the convoy.

Meanwhile, southbound convoy CU-6 was proceeding to Curacao. The tanker *Bulkoil* became disabled, necessitating a reduction in speed and preventing her from keeping up with the convoy. The escort commander directed the *Bulkoil* to return to port unescorted at her best possible speed while complying with zigzag regulations. The tanker reversed direction. She was proceeding under blackout conditions when her torpedo detector sounded. The *Bulkoil* was not equipped with radar. Nor had the officers of the tanker been informed that the torpedo detector could not discriminate between a torpedo and a high-speed surface craft. The *Bulkoil* initiated a hard turn to starboard.

The men on the *Murphy* could not see the unlighted tanker because of the moonless sky. As the convoy was ordered onto the right leg of the zigzag – in order to avoid the oncoming vessel – the *Murphy* turned to starboard to herd the stranger away from the convoy. The tanker's radical course change caught the *Murphy* off guard. The

USS *Murphy*. (Courtesy of the National Archives.)

Murphy's commander ordered "all engines ahead emergency flank," but before the order could be executed, the stem and starboard bow of the tanker struck the port side of the destroyer.

The *Bulkoil* cut the *Murphy* completely in two. The stern section of the *Murphy* remained upright and afloat, and was in no immediate danger of sinking. But the forward section rolled onto its starboard side and commenced to flood; with the loss of electrical power, all interior lights were extinguished. Men who were topside either leaped overboard or slid down the slanted hull into the water. Gunners in the forward turrets escaped through the side hatches. Men in the fire director atop the navigating bridge crawled out of the overhead hatches. Officers in the wheelhouse climbed through the doorway onto the port side of the superstructure, thence to the hull. A number of men were trapped below deck in suddenly blackened compartments; a few lucky ones squeezed through a porthole.

Of the 255 men onboard the destroyer, thirty-five perished. (The Naval History and Heritage Command claims that thirty-eight men died, but the Court of Inquiry – which contained more than one thousand pages of testimony and factual findings – gave the number of fatalities as thirty-five.)

The floating stern section was towed to New York where – after seven months and the expenditure of $2.5

Shipwreck Case File - USS *Murphy*

million – a new forward section was fabricated and welded to the undamaged portion of the stern section. The destroyer then resumed operations till the end of the war. See *Shipwreck Heresies* for the full and dramatic story of escape from the sinking vessel.

The Naval History and Heritage Command claims that the *Murphy* was decommissioned on March 9, 1946, "and joined the Charleston Group, Atlantic Reserve Fleet, where she remains into 1969."

In fact, the *Murphy* was sold for scrap in 1972.

Strangers When We Meet

A group of recreational divers discovered the wreckage of the forward section in 2000. At first, the dive-boat skipper (whose name I withhold in order to protect the guilty; I shall call him Skippy) believed that the truncated shipwreck was part of a Liberty ship. Christina Young knew otherwise, for she videotaped an object that was clearly a gun turret. Liberty ships were outfitted with gun *tubs*, but only warships were equipped with guns that were mounted in rotating turrets.

Two of Skippy's customers ultimately identified the wreck by contributing different pieces to the puzzle: the aforementioned Christina Young, and Richie Kohler.

Young started by studying the offshore nautical chart and following the depth contour until she found a wreck symbol at the appropriate depth. The symbol corresponded to Record 1401 on NOAA's Automated Wreck and Obstruction Information System. The AWOIS annotation was based on the Wreck Information List of 1945, and the Navy Wreck List of 1957. The second source was an outgrowth of the first. Both sources concurred in citing the originating source: the cryptic acronym ESF. The Eastern Sea Frontier reported the sinking of a vessel on October 22, 1943, and established the position.

In the meantime, while diving from Skippy's boat, Kohler recovered a steam pressure gauge from the debris field. A tag that was mounted on the face of the gauge read "LAUNDRY STEAM". Beneath the tag was an inspection stamp that was inscribed with a date

("6.17.42") and an alphanumeric designation ("JG 603").

Young called Kohler and told him what her research had unearthed. She also told him where to find additional information about the casualty: the Eastern Sea Frontier War Diary. During World War Two, the ESF kept a diary in which all reported incidents were logged on a daily basis. She knew that the ESF War Diary was archived at the National Archives. This was a problem for her because the Archives was open only during weekday business hours. She had obligations to her employer and was unable to take off a day at a moment's notice.

Kohler was self-employed, so he could play hooky without fear of angering the boss. He headed for the Archives the very next day, looked where Young told him to look, and learned about the collision on the date in question between the *Bulkoil* and the U.S. destroyer *Murphy* (DD 603). The number "603" was the same number as the one on the steam gauge tag.

This kind of dedicated research and detective work is standard operating procedure for recreational scuba divers who go out of their way to document shipwrecks.

Kohler told Skippy the name of the wreck and the circumstances that accounted for its existence. Skippy fumed because he had been outgunned by a turret in place of a tub.

Kohler also informed the Naval Historical Center of the find, and provided an account of how the wreck had been identified. The Naval Historical Center replied with a letter of congratulations, then let the matter drop. It had no interest in the *Murphy*.

Young wanted to document the wreck further, but Skippy was in no hurry to return to the site. Additionally, Skippy was so possessive about the wreck's location that he refused to share it with anyone. So, armed with the coordinates from the ESF War Diary, Young chartered another dive boat to conduct a search pattern in the vicinity. The boat was the *Independence*, and the captain was Dan Bartone. They found the wreck in a couple of hours.

Skippy was infuriated when he learned that he had

Shipwreck Case File - USS *Murphy*

been outwitted. He gave the impression that the *Murphy* was his exclusive domain; that only *he* should be allowed to take customers to the site; that only *he* was allowed to make money off the wreck. So *he* called the Naval Historical Center and lodged a complaint against the so-called claim jumpers, charging them with the recovery of artifacts from the wreck. He neglected to mention that Kohler had recovered the steam gauge while diving off his (Skippy's) boat, and that he had not objected to the recovery at the time of its occurrence.

Skippy posted this vitriolic diatribe on the Internet: "It has been reported to me by an extremely reliable source that over Labor Day weekend divers, Richard Kohler and Christina Young, aboard the boat *Independence* owned by Dan Bartone, ventured out to the wreck sight [sic] of a US Naval war grave USS *Murphy* where on October 21, 1943, 35 sailors lost there [sic] lives after a collision with the US tanker *Bulkoil* sending the bow of the ship to the bottom. The trip was cloaked in secrecy as their intentions where [sic] to steal artifacts from the war grave. The report is that Richard Kohler removed the ship's binnacle as well as any artifacts that could be carried away while Christina Young photographed the event. The theft is being reported to several agencies in hopes of recovering the artifacts as well as the possibility of prosecution if applicable."

As noted above, the Naval Historical Center professed no interest in the *Murphy*. Now, the Center chose not to be used as the cat's-paw in the vendetta of a disgruntled dive boat competitor. The Center ignored Skippy's entreaties. But Skippy continued to call – again, and again, and again, and again. Eventually, and seemingly as an appeasement, the Center alerted the Naval Criminal Investigative Service.

The NCIS was reluctant to get involved on two counts: no crime had been committed, and the participants were civilians. After some foot dragging, the NCIS sent a Navy investigator to Bartone's house. Although Bartone had a couple of souvenirs from another shipwreck, which the investigator took with him, he did not have any from the *Murphy*. The investigator frankly told Bartone that he had better things to do than to retrieve lost trinkets and knick-knacks. Nor did he think that the *Murphy* situation was NCIS business. Nor did the *Murphy* or shipwreck souvenirs have anything to do with national defense or homeland security: the Navy's congressionally mandated functions.

The investigator wanted to close the case and get back to investigating real Navy crime. But he was ordered to interview both Young and Kohler.

The investigator parked in Young's driveway for two days straight while she was away at work. Apparently, NCIS investigators worked banking hours, for each day the investigator departed before Young returned home from her company office. After the investigator left a message, Young called and spoke with him. He wanted to know if she had removed any junk from the wreck. She told him that the only thing she took was video footage. He was satisfied with this, and let the matter drop.

The investigator then called Kohler on the phone. Kohler suggested that they schedule a meeting at the investigator's office. The investigator agreed. Kohler arrived with the artifact that he had used to help in identifying the *Murphy* – the very artifact that was pictured in the report that he and Young had submitted to the Naval Historical Center: the steam gauge with the tag. He gave a copy of the report to the investigator, and showed him copies of correspondence between him and the Center. The report informed the Center how the identification had been made.

Kohler also showed the investigator the letter of commendation that the Center had sent to him, thanking him and Young for their efforts in researching and identifying the *Murphy*. Thus the staff at the Center was well aware that Kohler had recovered a gauge from the wreck before the wreck was identified as the *Murphy*.

It is ironic that the Navy commended Kohler and Young out of one side of its collective mouth, then castigated them out of the other side.

Shipwreck Case File - USS Murphy

The investigator took the gauge and tag. The case was closed.

Strange Case of the Barking Dog

The above *Murphy* incident is ironic in a number of ways.

The Navy abandoned the sunken forward section where it lay on the bottom after colliding with the *Bulkoil*, and made no attempt to recover the bodies or to salvage any part of the wreck. The Navy later struck the *Murphy* from the Navy Register, and sold the reconstructed destroyer for scrap. It never expressed any interest in searching for the sunken forward section. Thus a case can be made that the Navy sold its right to own or control any parts of the *Murphy* that might still exist.

After recreational scuba divers found the lost wreckage, and then identified it, the Navy was blasé about the discovery. The Navy's sole response was a typewritten letter of acknowledgment.

In a prime display of capriciousness toward recreational scuba divers, the Navy did not ask Kohler for the gauge when he submitted his report, along with the photographic and documentary evidence that confirmed the wreck's identity. The Navy did not want the item, and was content to let him keep it. Yet the Navy later took the gauge when the NCIS conducted interviews at the insistence of a civilian whose motive was purely personal and mercenary.

From the Navy perspective, none of this case makes any sense at all. Go, Navy!

Shipwreck Case File
H.L. Hunley

Submarine Torpedo Boat

Next to Jules Verne's *Nautilus*, the *H.L. Hunley* is probably the most celebrated submarine in the world today. This wasn't always the case. Its renown used to be limited to Civil War buffs and armchair historians. It took a great deal of promotion to create its aura of well-deserved fame.

The *Hunley* (as she is nicknamed) had some unusual characteristics and distinctions: she was a privately-built and -owned submarine; her propeller was operated by a hand crank instead of an engine; she sank accidentally three times; she went into battle manned by a volunteer crew of inexperienced sailors; and she was the first submarine in history to sink a warship.

The *Hunley* was the brainchild of Horace Lawson Hunley (after whom the submarine was named). Together with James R. McClintock and Baxter Watson, they fabricated the hull in the machine shop of Park and Lyons, in Mobile, Alabama.

The Naval History and Heritage Command misinforms the public that the hull "was fashioned from a cylindrical iron steam boiler as the main center section, with tapered ends added." This is nowhere near the truth. The Command ridicules the vessel's construction as if it were patched together from discarded spare parts, like a diving helmet that was made from an upside-down bucket.

In actuality, the frame was custom built from curved iron beams, or ribs, to which iron plates were riveted. Deadlights in the overhead allowed light to enter the hull. Two hatchways with extended coamings (equivalent to conning towers on modern subs) were installed

Shipwreck Case File - H.L. Hunley

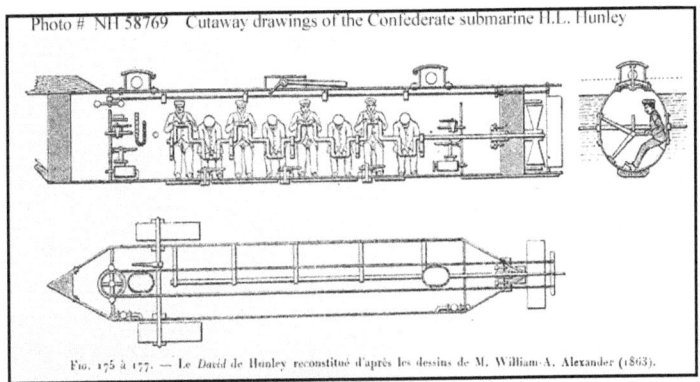

This contemporary illustration and cutaway diagram of the *Hunley* is from the Naval Photographic Center. Considering the secrecy that surrounded the submarine's construction, it is remarkably accurate. The most obvious deviation from the actual layout is the number of manned positions on the crankshaft: it shows eight when in fact there were seven.

for access from either end.

The propeller was not turned by an engine, but by hand: by means of an offset crankshaft that was operated by seven men who sat hunched-over in a space that stood only four and a half feet high. An eighth man stood in the forward hatchway, where he could look through a glass port and steer by means of a tiller whose linkage was connected to the rudder.

Death and Destruction

The *Hunley* was transported by train to Charleston, South Carolina, where her career started inauspiciously. According to the Naval History and Heritage Command, the submarine was "moored by lines fastened to steamer *Etiwan* at the dock at Fort Johnson. The steamer unexpectedly moved away from the dock, drawing *H.L. Hunley* on her side and she filled and went down."

In reality, the *Hunley* was preparing to shove off from the dock for a trial run when the *Etiwan* steamed past her. The steamer's wake caused large waves that rolled the *Hunley* so violently that she shipped massive quantities of water through the still-open hatches. The submarine sank in six fathoms of water. There were two survivors: one escaped through the forward hatch while the other escaped through the after hatch. Five other men drowned inside the hull.

The submarine was raised, repaired, and returned to service.

For the next trial, Horace Hunley decided to conn the submarine himself, to demonstrate how she could be used effectively against enemy vessels. The plan was to tow a floating barrel of explosives at the end of a long line, submerge, pass under a vessel, let the barrel strike the enemy hull, and detonate on contact. No explosives were carried when the *Hunley* prosecuted a mock attack against the *Indian Chief*.

According to the Naval History and Heritage Command, "After several successful dives, the submarine again went under *Indian Chief* but air bubbles traced the downward course of the submarine which failed to surface."

That isn't the way it happened at all. Witnesses watched the *Hunley* poke her bow beneath the surface as she approached the *Indian Chief*. Instead of submerging on an even keel, the submarine nosedived into the muddy bottom. The hull hung at an angle with its stern elevated as water poured into the bow through an open seacock. The angle decreased somewhat until flooding was complete. The hull settled on the bottom in ten fathoms of water. All eight crewmembers drowned.

Again the hull was raised, repaired, and returned to service.

Finally, on the night of February 17, 1864, the *Hunley* departed for the event that made worldwide history. This time she was armed with a spar torpedo: an explosive charge mounted on the end of long pole that extended forward from the bow: much like a carrot on a stick, or the lance of a charging knight. Instead of submerging completely, she slunk across the harbor barely awash, with the hull hidden under water but with the "conning towers" protruding far enough above the surface that Lieutenant George Dixon, at the conn, could peer through the glass ports. Seven men cranked the long offset shaft that rotated the propeller.

Shipwreck Case File - *H.L. Hunley* 151

The *Hunley*'s target was the USS *Housatonic*: an armed screw steamer that measured 207 feet in length, against the submarine's 40 feet: a David and Goliath battle fought with an explosive charge instead of a slingshot.

At the last minute, alert lookouts on the *Housatonic* spotted what at first appeared to be a drifting log – until they noticed that the log was moving across the current instead of with it. They sounded the alarm . . .

. . . too late. Before the *Housatonic* could slip her anchor and get up steam from banked boiler fires, the barbed spar torpedo (as the explosive charge was called in those days) struck her hull below the waterline, sticking like a dart in a cork board; or, to switch similes, like the barbed stinger of a honey bee. The *Hunley* backed away, unreeling the pull cord that would trigger the explosive device that was snagged in the hull.

Union sailors discharged hand-held weapons, pinging the iron "log" but doing no noticeable damage.

Suddenly a tremendous explosion erupted. The *Housatonic*'s wooden hull was blown in from the outside. The force of the explosion rocked the vessel as if it were a toy boat in a bathtub. It took only five minutes for the *Housatonic* to settle to the bottom in twenty-five feet of water. Most of the crew scrambled up the ratlines and spread out on the rigging. Hastily launched lifeboats

This cachet painting shows how the spar torpedo was secured to the *Hunley*'s stem.

The destruction of the *Housatonic*, as depicted in *Frank Leslie's Illustrated Newspaper*.

searched the dark sea for survivors who had fallen overboard.

Five Union sailors died. One hundred fifty-five survived to tell the tale of a phantom in the night.

The *Hunley* disappeared. Somewhere under water, eight men drowned or suffocated in a riveted iron coffin.

Who's on First

According to Ecclesiastes, chapter 3, verse 1, "To every thing there is a season, and a time to every purpose under the heaven."

In relation to shipwrecks, there is a time for their discovery, and a time when their discovery shall be noticed by the world. America was discovered more than a dozen times before Columbus made his famous voyage, yet none of those prior discoveries was recognized as a great event, until European countries were in the right frame of mind to celebrate the discovery, due to growing ambitions to expand their control over occupied territory, and to acquire valuable property that could turn a profit. As stated in the *Bible*, timing is everything.

By the end of the Civil War, Charleston Harbor was a disaster zone that was filled with sunken vessels: block ships, blockade runners, and warships. These hulks had to be cleared because they presented hazards to navigation. Extensive salvage operations resulted in many of them, including the *Housatonic*, being blasted

Shipwreck Case File - H.L. Hunley

apart as a way to reduce their vertical profile. The two primary salvors were Benjamin Maillefert and Angus Smith.

According to the correspondence file of Confederate General Pierre Beauregard:

> Charleston, S.C., May 18th, 1876
> Mr. E. Willis:
>
> Dear Sir,—In answer to your request, and also that it will be a pleasure to do anything in my power for General Beauregard, to give my old general the particulars of the fish torpedo-boat that struck the *Housatonic*. After the evacuation I took the contract of removing all the Confederate wrecks and obstructions. I claimed that the fish torpedo-boat was in my contract. Professor Mallefeil [sic] claimed that it was in his contract, and that he had the contract of lifting all the United States wrecks that were in Charleston Harbor. And I went to work to save the torpedo-boat, and I got on the top of her, and found out the cause of her sinking. The boat is outside or alongside of the *Housatonic*. She can be lifted any time our people wish. Mallefeil [sic] is bursted [sic] and out of the way. I have no more to say than that she can be saved, and my opinion is she is as good as the day she was sunk.
>
> Yours truly,
> Angus Smith, Sullivan's Island.

Nothing came of Smith's observation. His timing was wrong.

What's on Second

Lee Spence was a local boy (local to South Carolina, that is) who started diving on local shipwrecks in the 1960's, when he was still a teenager. His primary interest was Civil War wrecks, of which he discovered and

The caption for this woodcut from *Frank Leslie's Illustrated Newspaper* reads: "SOUTH CAROLINA.--THE WRECKS OF THE GREAT REBELLION IN THE BAY OF CHARLESTON--DIVERS EXAMINING THE BOTTOM OF THE HARBOR." The concentration of shipwrecks is obviously exaggerated. The wreck depicted in the foreground is either the *Weehawken* or the *Patapsco*, both of which were *Passaic*-class monitors. The *Housatonic* was mentioned in passing in the accompanying article. The *Hunley* was not mentioned.

Shipwreck Case File - H.L. Hunley

salvaged quite a few. One of those discoveries was the *H.L Hunley*, which he found when he dived in Charleston Harbor to free some fish traps.

According to letter that he wrote to State archaeologist Robert Stephenson on November 25, 1970, "It was about 18 feet long and 3 1/2 feet in diameter. It appeared to be intact. I was only on it for a matter of seconds because the guys on the boat pulled the trap free and I was afraid to push my luck around an unexplored area. What I saw could have been a boiler of some kind or possibly a smokestack, and it was nowhere near the size of the model on display in Charleston. We tossed a buoy over the side as soon as we could make one up. But we had already drifted at least a hundred yards at that time. The weather has prevented us from returning to the spot since that time. We have the general bearings. . . . The site, whatever it is, is definitely outside of the 3 mile State jurisdiction."

Despite having the general bearings, Spence was unable to relocate the wreck. The sandy bottom in Charleston Harbor moves with every tidal change. One day's troughs become the next day's dunes, and vice versa. Storm damage is even worse.

Over the next few years, Spence wrote more than eighty letters to "to various government officials and public figures . . . advising them that I believed I had found the *Hunley* and seeking their help in getting permission to salvage the wreck."

The overall response was a big yawn accompanied by advice that W.C. Fields made famous: "Go away kid. Ya bother me."

Even the U.S. Navy didn't give a hoot.

He first broke the news to the media on June 13, 1975. The *Orangeburg Times & Democrat* wrote, "After four years of attempts to gain permission from the federal government to undertake search and salvage operations near Charleston, Lee Spence, an underwater archeologist, has decided to make public his claim to having discovered what he thinks are the long-lost remains of the Confederate submarine *H.L. Hunley*."

Spence plotted the location on a chart in order to obtain permission from the Army Corps of Engineers to excavate the wreck site. Permission was granted, but the General Services Administration was lackadaisical about giving the go ahead to his planned salvage of the wreck. Furthermore, the South Carolina Institute of Archaeology and Anthropology was openly antagonistic to Spence and all his endeavors, apparently due to envy on the part of the director, who tried his utmost to hamper Spence in any way he could, not only with regard to the *Hunley* but to all of Spence's shipwreck projects.

On July 7, 1981, Spence filed papers with the Federal Court asking that his title to the "unidentified, wrecked and abandoned vessel or vessels, (believed to be the Steamer *Housatonic* and/or the Submarine *H.L. Hunley*, both sunk in 1864) her tackle, armament, apparel and cargo" be confirmed "against all claimants and all the world," and that he be awarded a "full and liberal salvage award."

And there the matter rested. Throughout the years, Spence's accidental discovery met with indifference, hostility, tangential acknowledgment, but never enthusiasm. The timing was wrong.

I Don't Know's on Third

Clive Cussler has spent more time and money in search of historic shipwrecks than the U.S. Navy has spent in its entire existence for the same purpose. For decades, Cussler has scoured the world's oceans for elusive targets for no better reason than his interest in maritime history. He does this by donating money to the non-profit organization known as the National Underwater and Marine Agency, or NUMA, which he created for the express purpose of locating lost wrecks of all descriptions.

His first search for the *Hunley* took place in July 1980.

The detection instruments of choice were side-scan sonar, proton magnetometer, and sub-bottom profiler. Each of these delicate devices utilized a towed electronic

Shipwreck Case File - H.L. Hunley

package that was commonly called a "fish," or "tow fish," which was shaped like a torpedo. This initial expedition was unsuccessful.

Cussler was persistent, so he returned for another try in June 1981. Once again he and his stalwart crew dragged (or towed) underwater detection gear back and forth across Charleston Harbor, making invisible tracks on the bottom but drawing them on a plotter the way a lawnmower cuts grass in a yard. This expedition located several Civil War shipwrecks but not the sought-for *Hunley*.

After circumnavigating the world several times over, Cussler returned once again, in July 1994. Instead of an all-out all-aboard expedition, this one ran sporadically for almost a year, despite fierce opposition from the South Carolina Institute of Archaeology and Anthropology.

Wrote Cussler: "Determined to find *Hunley* and her crew before my final deathbed gasp, I made a decision that assured success. I contracted with Ralph Wilbanks and Wes Hall to keep the search alive during their free time. . . . Ralph and Wes went out rain or shine and searched the grids I faxed them through the fall and winter of '94 and into the spring of '95."

The third time was the charm. Wilbanks and Hall found the wreck, which was totally buried, in May of 1995. To confirm that their electronic target was the real thing, they "dug through the silt and came in contact with the forward hatch tower. Then we uncovered the snorkel box and the port dive fin."

At last the timing was right.

Raised from Obscurity

As expected, the Navy jumped in with both left feet. By this time in the corruption of the Naval Historical Center – from a bona fide if incompetent and obstructionist Navy archive to a group of egotistical control freaks – the staff consisted of power-hungry civilians who were bent on domination of the underwater world. They were beginning to believe that they owned every wreck that lay on the bottom of the world's oceans, and that they had inherited the divine right to control access to those wrecks.

The Navy wasted no time in aggressively seeking to assert its ownership of the *Hunley* by convincing (or coercing) the General Services Administration to transfer title to the Navy. There the Navy ran into a snag – not with private citizens who could be cajoled and bamboozled with threats of prosecution and costly litigation, and who could be tricked and cheated of their rightful property by the submission of false evidence and the testimony of perjuring witnesses – but with other government agencies that were just as determined to take possession of the Confederate submarine.

Like the old phrase, "There's gold in them thar hills," government agencies were beginning to realize that shipwrecks were valuable commercial commodities that could be exploited as tourist attractions. You can see this today with wrecks such as the *Arizona* and *Monitor*. The National Park Service makes a mint off deceased sailors whose bodies are interred inside the hallowed hull of the *Arizona*. The Mariners Museum and the National Oceanic and Atmospheric Administration charge hefty fees to visitors who want to see the disassembled parts of the *Monitor*, and the skeletal remains that were exhumed from the turret.

Government agencies no longer ascribed to President Abraham Lincoln's philosophy, which he articulated in his Gettysburg Address, that "government of the people, by the people, for the people, shall not perish from the earth." Lincoln's "new birth of freedom" has degenerated to "ripping off the public whenever and wherever possible."

And the U.S. Navy was the leader of the pack. In many respects all government agencies are equal, but the Navy ardently believed that the Navy was more equal than others.

Yet the Navy took a knockout punch in the first round of the fight to procure title to the *Hunley*. The General Services Administration could not establish

Shipwreck Case File - H.L. Hunley

ownership by means of succession because the *Hunley* did not belong to the Confederate navy. She was never commissioned as a Confederate States Ship, or CSS *Hunley*. She was privately owned.

I wish I knew the name of the pundit who founded the Luters Nautical Antiques Emporium. I would like to commend him or her for creating the single-sheet gag sale brochure of nautical memorabilia. Under the boldface headline, "But Wait, There's More!" was written:

> Coming in 1996, or at least by 2026, the milking stools used by the South Carolina Institute of Archaeology, the National Park Service Submerged Cultural Resource Unit, and the Advisory Council on Underwater Archaeology. They, of course, were used to milk the *Hunley* for all it was worth.

That paragraph sums up the situation perfectly.

The *Hunley* proprietorship bandwagon was so overburdened that its axles were creaking to the point of breaking. Although the General Services Administration and the U.S. Navy had been knocked out of the ring, the host of other contenders included the Smithsonian Institution; the city of Mobile, Alabama; the aforementioned three musketeers, and the State of South Carolina.

Creeping Jurisdiction

The only competing entity that came close to having any legal justification for assuming title to the *Hunley* was the State of South Carolina. As Spence noted above, the *Hunley* lay beyond the territorial waters of federal and State governments: more than four miles from shore. But the simple matter of international law did not stop South Carolina from pursuing the path toward ownership. The governor established a *Hunley* Commission to further the State's goal of procuring the submarine as a money-making tourist attraction.

The once Confederate State already had an unsavory

history with regard to claiming ownership of shipwrecks. Its primary cat's-paw was the State sponsored South Carolina Institute of Archaeology and Anthropology (SCIAA): the same agency that gave Cussler such grief throughout his search for the *Hunley*, and which had waged a life-long battle against Spence about Civil War shipwrecks that he discovered, documented, and salvaged without any help from State archaeologists.

In the case of the *William Lawrence*, the State submitted false evidence to the court in order to wrest control of the wreck from salvors who were rescuing the freighter's cargo and returning it to the stream of commerce. Witnesses for the State committed perjury. As a final straw to ensure State dominion, the State conjured a bogus mechanism to extend its jurisdiction into international waters.

According to federal law, United States territorial seas extended three miles from shore. Beyond three miles was international water, which was not subject to federal or State jurisdiction. The *William Lawrence* lay more than four miles from shore. By conspiring with the National Oceanic and Atmospheric Administration, and the Wildlife and Marine Resources Department, the State "found" a submerged shoal that, under extraordinary conditions of extreme low tide in conjunction with certain seasonal phases of the Moon, became intermittently awash in the troughs of storm-generated waves. For the purpose of its case, the State claimed that this impermanent and shifting sandbar constituted a "land mass" from which its territorial jurisdiction should be measured.

The federal government neither commits nor condones gerrymandering the coast line as a way to serve private interests. By doing so, the State's nonce hypothetical border extended beyond the federal border: a legal impossibility and an unapproved and unlawful encroachment on international waters.

But this was a local matter, and the judge hearing the case was prejudiced on the side of the State. Thus for actions that were illegal, illogical, and without reason or common sense, and for purposes that were politically motivated, the court bought the State's scenario despite international law to the contrary. For the full gruesome story, see *Shipwrecks of South Carolina and Georgia.*

Now the State invoked a similar stratagem: one that was even more patently absurd than the 1989 rationalization. Gerrymandering worked before, why not again? In this instance the State made the ridiculous claim that manmade rock jetties – which stretched outward from shore perpendicular to the beach – could be used to extend its jurisdiction that much farther into international waters, by using the far end of the jetty as the starting point for measuring the three-mile territorial limit. In other words, the State proposed that an artificial jetty extended the State's territorial jurisdiction by the length of the jetty.

By extrapolation of this spurious mechanism, the construction of longer and longer jetties could be employed to extend a State's jurisdiction all the way to another country's beachhead – and beyond.

Be that as it may, after years of Machiavellian political maneuvering and legal wrangling among competing State and federal agencies, the *Hunley* ended up in the hands of South Carolina, which profiteers on the demise of dedicated Confederate sailors by charging visitors a fee to view the *Hunley's* remains that were put on exhibit in Charleston.

Falsifying History

So what does the Naval History and Heritage Command write about the discovery, recovery, preservation, and display of the *Hunley*? Not a word. Grapes were never more sour.

Instead of promoting naval history and heritage, the Command still insists that the *Hunley* was knocked together amateurishly from a cast away steam boiler and a few spare parts – and expresses nothing about the newly revealed nature of the submarine's construction. Examination of the wreck, after it was raised and after removal of the mud that was packed inside the hull, revealed mechanisms and design innovations of incredible ingenuity far in advance for the time: designs that became standard submarine technological features fifty years later:

1 – The curved hull was supported internally by iron ribs that resisted the outside pressure that was exerted by the water.

2 – The rivets that were used to secure the hull plates to the ribs were filed flat so as to decrease the hydrodynamic drag of the moving vessel.

3 – Bulkheads at either end created compartments or ballast tanks in which water could be collected and ejected as an aid in submerging and surfacing. Water was collected by means of a seacock, and ejected by means of a hand-operated pump.

4 – A pipe connected the two ballast tanks so that water could be pumped from one tank to the other in order to maintain the trim of the vessel.

5 – A pair of hydroplanes was located in the forward part of the vessel. The angle of these hydroplanes could be changed from inside the hull, so as to assist or hasten descent and ascent, and to help control depth under water. (*Hunley* archaeologists referred to these hydroplanes as "diving planes," a misnomer that gives the impression that they helped or enabled the submarine only to dive, and were not used to surface the vessel or to control depth under water.)

6 – The vessel was steered by means of a vertical rod or tiller that was located under the forward hatch where it was handy for the helmsman or skipper. This tiller rod and connecting linkage was equivalent to a joystick that is now employed to steer modern vessels and aircraft.

7 – The forward hull was tapered inward from the sides until they met to form a slender edge, forming a sharp bow that could cleave through water with reduced resistance. The top and bottom of the bow were curved backward, mimicking the axelike blade of a halberd: another means of creating hydrodynamic efficiency.

8 – The hatches protruded above the hull much like the modern conning tower.

Shipwreck Case File - H.L. Hunley

9 – The hatches were fitted with cutwaters as an enhancement to hydrodynamics.

10 – The forward hatch was fitted with a pair of glass ports or deadlights, which enabled the helmsmen to see forward without having to open the hatch. An overhead deadlight allowed light to enter from above. Other deadlights (portholes that didn't open) were arranged in the overhead above the crank handle for the convenience of the crew.

11 – The interior of the hull was painted white in order to reflect and increase candle light.

12 – An iron shroud encircled the propeller so as to prevent entanglement from drifting or dangling ropes, similar in shape to a modern Kort nozzle.

12 – Perhaps the most amazing – and amazingly prescient – feature was an air-circulation system that modern naval engineers have termed a "snorkel box" (although the word "snorkel" did not exist in Civil War times). This boxlike contrivance was located atop the hull immediately abaft the forward hatch. A pair of iron pipes extended aft from the box, where they lay flat

The *Hunley* is currently stored in a wet environment. The liquid is drained periodically so that archaeologists can remove exterior encrustation and excavate the interior. The skeletal remains and personal possessions of all eight sailors were embedded in mud.

against the upper hull. These "breathing" pipes could be raised to a vertical position so that the inlet ends stood some ten feet above the hull. A bellows was connected to the inlet pipe so that fresh air could be drawn into the hull; stale air was automatically expelled through the outlet pipe.

The submarine snorkel was thought to have first been used on Dutch submarines in the 1930's. It came into prominence after Germany invaded the Netherlands, and adopted the design for incorporation in its later-built U-boats.

In short, the *Hunley* was nothing like the patchwork submarine that the Naval History and Heritage Command portrays on its website. The Command persists in sticking to pre-recovery descriptions that are belied by archaeological examinations that have been ongoing for nearly twenty years. It continues to misinform the reading public that the crew consisted of nine men instead of eight. (Examination has established that there are seven crank positions and one seat for the skipper.) It continues to theorize that the *Hunley* "may have gone down beneath *Housatonic*," when it is a known fact – to the world at large if not to Navy historians – that the submarine was found nearly a quarter mile away.

This begs the question: What is the Naval History and Heritage Command doing in place of correcting its historical errors and conducting genuine historical studies about Navy vessels? The answer is obvious: the Command has no time to do the work for which it was established because it is wholly consumed by political machinations toward expanding its control over more and more wrecks – when it can't even serve those over which it already claims jurisdiction.

The Naval History and Heritage Command has forsaken history for possession: demonic as well as territorial.

At least Hitler got the trains to run on time.

Into the Deep Blue Yonder

Reverse Robin Hood

An entire subculture exists for the express purpose of locating, recovering, restoring, and displaying lost aircraft. Dedicated individuals scour the world and spend enormous amounts of their own time and money to find crashed and ditched planes from yesteryear: in mountain aeries, in desert wastelands, in remote forests, in primeval jungles, under water, and even deep down in Arctic ice.

Entire books have been written about the endeavors of these hearty adventurers: modern day equivalents of Roy Chapman Andrews, who unearthed fossilized dinosaur eggs in his lifelong quest on the trail of ancient man. I must annotate some of these aircraft discoveries in order to establish the background for the Navy's illicit encroachment.

Whereas the legendary Robin Hood stole from the rich and gave to the poor, the Navy steals from the poor as a way to enrich itself – or to boost the egos of the control freaks that run the circus at the Naval History and Heritage Command.

The Navy would rather let downed aircraft rot into nonexistence than have them saved for posterity. Because of this absurd Navy attitude, future generations will lose much of their military heritage.

Warbirds

During the war, American manufacturers cranked out airplanes by the tens of thousands – literally. More than 12,000 Corsair fighter planes alone were mass-produced in four war-torn years. And that's to say nothing of countless other models that were built and flown in the fight for global freedom.

So many aircraft crashed or were shot down during

World War Two that these lost military planes have come to be known as "warbirds." Hundreds of them have been recovered from all over the world. The irony in the modern day hunt for downed aircraft is that the American armed services discarded thousands of them after the Japanese surrender.

There is archival footage of airplanes being shoved off the decks of carriers because their post-war value was less than the cost of the fuel that would be expended to return them to the States. Hundreds or thousands of others were abandoned on remote Pacific islands or on European fields of battle. While this mass disposal of fighters and bombers may sound like an enormous waste of money, bear in mind that there was little or no use for military aircraft in peacetime.

I personally witnessed one disposal site on the island of Espiritu Santo, in an archipelago that was known during the war as the New Hebrides but which is now called Vanuatu. When the military base was abandoned, American forces drove or pushed masses of construction equipment off the end of a pier. Today they lie in a huge vehicular pile that is reminiscent of a child's game of Pick-Up Sticks.

Despite post-war dumping and discarding, military aircraft graveyards still litter little known areas of the country. These unmonitored sites are crammed with planes that won the war and are now forgotten. All have deteriorated as a result of summer heat and winter cold, rain and snow, wind, rust, and more than half a century of disownership and lack of care.

Submerged aircraft are more at risk than those that lay on land, due to the corrosive environment in which they reside. These are the ones that should be recovered before there is nothing recognizable to recover, and the remains deteriorate to little more than a few salvageable parts.

Spectacular Recovery

Perhaps *the* most spectacular aircraft recovery in the history of recoveries took place in Greenland in 1989.

Into the Deep Blue Yonder

After America's entry into World War Two, combined U.S. military forces started shipping men, machines, and materiel to staging areas in the British Isles, thence to the fighting front in Europe. High on the priority list were aircraft with trained crews. The particular flight under consideration here consisted of two bombers and six fighters. The bombers were B-17 Flying Fortresses; the fighters were P-38 Lightnings, known as Forked-Tail Devils because of their distinctive dual fuselage design.

Due to inadequate fuel storage capacities, nonstop flights across the Atlantic Ocean were problematical if not impossible. Therefore, plane and crew deliveries were conducted by island hopping from the American continent to Greenland to Iceland to England, using Greenland and Iceland as refueling stations.

Soon after departing from western Greenland, the eight-plane flight ran into foul weather that forced their return to land. But the raging storm also affected Greenland. Fuel reserves were reduced by bucking winds. The crews calculated that they could not reach base, so, precariously low on aviation fuel, the pilots ditched (or crash-landed) their planes on the ice in an uninhabited area near the east coast of Greenland. The date was July 15, 1942.

Everyone survived. All were rescued. The aircraft were abandoned. The eight planes achieved fame (or notoriety) as the Lost Squadron.

Skip to 1981, when Pat Epps and Richard Taylor began their years-long search for the crash site. By this time, nearly four decades of falling snow had completely buried the aircraft. Magnetometers failed to record the precise location of any of the eight planes. Annual expeditions did not make the big strike until 1988, this time by means of sled-drawn sub-surface radar.

The news was bad. The first plane they found lay under 260 feet of ice. It would have been a monumental task to dig or blast through that much compacted snow, which had nearly the consistency of ice – or steel. So they and their cohorts put their heads together, and hatched an ingenious and grandiose plan to extricate at least one plane by melting a hole through the snowpack.

A full-scale expedition returned in 1989. A boiler was used to generate steam that was directed through a mammoth homemade nozzle into the ice above the plane. The device bored a tunnel straight down to the depth of the plane: a P-38. Then steam was used to hollow out a cave that exceeded the dimensions of the aircraft, which had a length of 38 feet and a wingspan of 52 feet. Finally, the plane was partially disassembled and extracted through the vertical tunnel.

Another P-38 was recovered by the same remarkable method in 1992.

The planes were transported to the United States, where they were painstakingly rebuilt. Parts that had been damaged or crushed by glacial drift were replaced by newly fabricated components.

These remarkable discovery and recovery operations cost hundreds of thousands of dollars, all of which was provided by private contributions. Scores of volunteers were involved in the project; their only payment was the satisfaction of bringing home a part of American history.

Official Abandonment

I chose to describe the extreme example above because it so aptly demonstrates the incredible lengths to which individuals have gone – and continue to go – to rescue and restore extinct warbirds of yesteryear. They do it on their own hitch without government funding. And if private citizens didn't do it, those lost and missing aircraft would remain lost and missing forever.

The U.S. Army makes no claims of ownership over lost or missing Army aircraft. The U.S. Air Force went one better by formally declaring that all Air Force aircraft that were lost or missing prior to November 19, 1961, were officially abandoned; such timeworn aircraft contained no instruments, mechanisms, or structural components that were classified, and that needed to be kept from scrutiny by hostile foreign governments or terrorist organizations.

Only the U.S. Navy, via its appointed witch-hunters

Into the Deep Blue Yonder

in the Naval History and Heritage Command, tries to exert control over downed Navy aircraft – not by searching for and salvaging crashed planes at the Navy's expense, but by lurking in the sidelines and reading newspapers and magazines, by scouring the Internet, then prosecuting devoted individuals in a dastardly attempt to take what those individuals found and recovered at their own expense.

Case in Point

In 1984, teenager scuba divers Jeffrey Hummel and Matthew McCauley discovered a Curtis Helldiver in Lake Washington (in the State of Washington). They succeeded in raising the World War Two dive bomber – or rather, what was left of it after its destruction and long immersion.

The Navy filed a lawsuit against the duo in hopes of confiscating the badly scarred aircraft. However, the court ruled that the Navy had abandoned the plane, and could not at this stage "unabandon" it.

Undeterred by Navy harassment, the young pair subsequently discovered and raised four more combat planes from the lake: two additional Curtiss Helldivers and two Grumman Wildcat fighters.

At no time did the Navy ever take the initiative to search for and recover these ex-Navy aircraft. Navy policy was to let others spend their money and do the dirty work, then step in and roll up the sleeves of cackling Navy lawyers. Stealing is more cost effective than honest labor.

Down and Dirty

In another case, the U.S. Navy's National Museum of Naval Aviation (now called the National Naval Aviation Museum) contacted one Peter Theophanis – a successful aircraft recovery expert – and asked him to search for Navy plane wrecks in Lake Michigan. He agreed, and the Museum awarded him a "no cure, no pay" contract. He would receive reimbursement only if he found a plane that the Museum wanted for its collection.

Sunken airplanes are seldom found intact. They are battered apart by tides, current, and storm-driven swells, then spread across the seabed in disarticulated pieces. The top photo shows the nose and propeller. The middle photo shows the engine. The bottom photo shows a battery that has broken apart so that the plates and leaves have spilled into the debris field. The Navy promotes an image of ditched aircraft as if they were perfectly preserved and ready to fly after a simple turn-up, instead of images like these.

Into the Deep Blue Yonder

Theophanis spent the summer of 1993 towing a side-scan sonar unit over the area where pilots trained by taking-off from and landing on aircraft carriers during the war, and where scores if not hundreds of planes were known to have crashed or been dumped.

Scuba divers shot video footage of the first plane he found – a Dauntless dive bomber – but the Museum representative viewed the footage and claimed that the wreck was not in good enough condition for display. The representative authorized Theophanis to recover the wreck for himself as payment for his services, as long as the Navy was not held liable for any of the recovery costs.

After Theophanis "landed" the badly damaged plane on a U.S. Coast Guard parking lot, where coastguardsmen protected the wreckage from curiosity seekers, he sold it for parts to Kevin Hooey: the person who subsidized the recovery operation by hiring the barge and crane that were used to raise the hulk from the bottom.

Despite the contract and the official go-ahead from the Museum representative, the Navy decided to prosecute Theophanis for theft of government property – *two years later.*

The Navy's first step was to wiretap his phone. Then the Navy sat back and waited for the most inappropriate time to strike.

Attorney for the defense Peter Hess summarized what he called the Navy's Gestapo tactics: "Dawn, October 24, 1995: Clad head to toe in black, an elite SWAT team, including the U.S. Marshal's Service, the FBI, the N[S]IS and the Department of Justice burst through a door in Jupiter, Florida. Peter Theophanis, 36, is pinned to the wall, handcuffed, and dragged away. His wife, Peyton, hearing the commotion as she steps from the shower, stands in shock, dripping wet and wrapped in a towel. She is nine months pregnant and due to give birth that very day. She soon learns that her husband is being held without bail as a flight risk and a threat to the community."

If anything, Hess understated the situation.

Into the Deep Blue Yonder

More parts of the aircraft that is shown two pages previous. The top photo shows fuel tanks in a disarticulated wing, of which most of the exterior metal sheeting has been dissolved by seawater. The middle photo shows an oil cooler. The bottom photo shows a coolant radiator. These photos demonstrate the fate of aircraft that are not recovered. The Navy would rather doom abandoned aircraft to perdition than have recovery and restoration experts prepare them for public display. Navy control equals heritage lost.

Into the Deep Blue Yonder

Jumping the Gun

The subsequent trial swiftly turned into a comedy of Navy errors. After swooping down on the authorized recovery expert, and keeping him incommunicado for a day, the court instructed the Navy to release Theophanis on $5,000 bail. The judge thought that the charges were ridiculous.

As usual in such situations, the Navy did no investigative work on the circumstances surrounding the case. Thus it was caught off guard when the Museum representative committed perjury in order to bolster an indefensible case. The Museum rep stated that he had never made a deal with Theophanis, and that he had never received videotape footage of the aircraft.

To quote again from Hess: "Over the ensuing year, the NMNA' Buddy Macon would change his story to the investigator three times. He first told NIS agent Larry Fuentes that he had misplaced the Theophanis video of the salvaged Dauntless; a month later he couldn't recall if a video had ever been sent; and finally, Macon denied that the sunken aircraft had ever been videotaped at all.

"When the Grand Jury was later convened to decide whether to charge Theophanis with the felony theft of government property, Fuentes was specifically thrice asked by the jurors about the existence of any videotape of the Dauntless. In spite of his own notes stating that the tape had been lost by the NMNA, Fuentes perjured himself and steadfastly maintained that Theophanis had never fulfilled his contractual obligation to provide footage of the sunken plane to the Museum."

Keep in mind that this was a criminal case, and that lives and reputations were at stake.

In order to protect innocent people from being ruined by spurious and unsubstantiated allegations, American jurisprudence adheres to a strict set of guidelines for pursuing criminal prosecution. First, prosecutors must determine that a law has been broken. If one has, then – and only then – investigators must obtain a preponderance of evidence to establish the likelihood that a person or group of persons has broken that law.

The Naval Criminal Investigative Service operated in reverse order. First, the Navy picked the individual it wished to persecute. Then, as in the case of the *Murphy* (which see), the Service used word-of-mouth evidence from a disgruntled and competing salvor to establish its case. The Navy had never seen the recovered aircraft, and had no way of knowing if it had ever flown for the Navy. In legalese, the Navy did not have a corpus delecti. It had only a goal, but one with no lawful path that led to that goal.

In order to compensate for the lack of evidence, the Navy arrested Theophanis in the hope that the evidence would turn up in court. This is like the old-fashioned methods of proving witchcraft: by throwing a woman in the water to see if she sank or floated. If she sank and drowned, she was innocent; if she floated, she was guilty of being a witch, and was duly put to the death that she escaped in the water by means of witchcraft. Or, to use a similar analogy, the Navy tried to burn Theophanis at the stake to see if the flames would bring forth evidence against him. It was no concern of the Navy's if he died in the process.

In other words, the Navy used the courtroom as a mechanism of evidentiary discovery, claiming that Theophanis was guilty until he proved himself innocent beyond the Navy's doubt.

The subsequent trial made a new depth record in the annals of Navy litigation.

Hess: "The prosecutor, obviously a neophyte to maritime matters, was unable to decipher the Longitude and Latitude coordinates of the Dauntless' crash report and hence, was unable to even place the wreckage at the location from which it was recovered. When asked by District Judge Rudy Lozano what the terms degrees and seconds meant – units of distance on the water – she guessed miles, feet and inches, missing the mark by the proverbial nautical mile and arousing the ire of the judge."

To elaborate on this point for my Navy and non-nautical readers, let's say that the coordinates were 76° 59'

Into the Deep Blue Yonder

40" west and 38° 52' 29' north. That translates as seventy-six degrees, fifty-nine minutes, forty seconds west longitude, and thirty-eight degrees, fifty-two minutes, twenty-nine seconds north latitude. It does *not* translate as seventy-six miles, fifty-nine feet, forty inches, and thirty-eight miles, fifty-two feet, twenty-nine inches: measures of length or distance whose only relationships to location are the symbols ' and ". Depending on the context, the symbol ' can mean either minutes of a degree or feet; the symbol " can mean either seconds of a minute or inches. (They are also used as quote marks.)

By the bye, the coordinates in the example above do not refer to the location of my home. If the Navy launches a missile to that target in an assassination attempt, the resulting explosion will destroy the Naval Historical Center – which might not necessarily be a bad thing.

After the prosecutor's initial fiasco, she had NCIS agent Fuentes repeat his perjured testimony that no videotape footage had ever been shot, "and was duly impeached with his own written reports to the contrary." The defense produced Kevin Hooey as a rebuttal witness. In addition to his oral rebuttal, he showed the videotape footage that he had in his possession.

The Museum rep persisted in repudiating that he had ever made a deal with Theophanis. Because of his ever-changing testimony with regard to the videotape, the judge doubted his credibility.

Furthermore, Gary Larkins, an expert witness for the defense, pointed out that both the Air Force and the Navy flew Dauntless dive bombers during the war. How had the Navy determined that the recovered aircraft was a Navy plane and not an Air Force plane? In fact, how had the Navy determined that the recovered aircraft was a Dauntless? Neither the Navy nor its witnesses claimed to have ever seen the plane.

At this point the trial ended abruptly. "Larkins was still testifying when Judge Lozano called a halt to the travesty of justice. Granting a defense motion for a directed verdict, the court ruled that the prosecution's evidence was so weak that no reasonable jury could find Theophanis guilty. Most of the defense witnesses had not even been called, nor had Peter yet taken the stand."

Case closed.

What does the Naval History and Heritage Command post about this case on its website? "During the trial it was discovered that the identifying bureau number of the aircraft was misidentified and the case was dismissed on this technicality." I found nothing in the record to support this declaration.

Worse, the Command neglected to mention that Navy witnesses knowingly submitted false evidence and committed perjury multiple times. Instead, the Command concocted a cover story to explain away why the Navy lost the case.

Museum Wars

Because Americans are attracted to military aircraft, aircraft museums have been established to satisfy the demand. Among these burgeoning specialty museums is the Quonset Air Museum in Rhode Island. This nonprofit museum is staffed by volunteers who are devoted to expanding their exhibits.

In 1993, the U.S. Coast Guard discovered a hazard to navigation that turned out to be a Hellcat fighter plane that was planted nose down under water near Martha's Vineyard. The plane's attitude placed its tail barely fifteen feet beneath the surface.

To stop the endangered aircraft from being wire-dragged or dredged out of existence, members of the Quonset Air Museum organized an ad hoc recovery operation that consisted of scuba divers, cranes, and barges. Their tremendous effort proved successful. The badly corroded and disarticulated plane was rescued from oblivion, and placed in the museum where volunteers commenced the long-term and expensive process of restoring the abandoned wartime relic.

But Navy snipers had their sights set on the plane almost as soon as it was recovered. They claimed that it was the one that had been ditched by Navy Ensign Vincent Frankwitz in 1943. Frankwitz swam away from the plane before it sank, but drowned before he could be rescued. How the Navy determined that this was Frankwitz's plane was unexplained. The Navy simply said that it was so, and demanded that the Museum ship the aircraft to the National Museum of Naval Aviation in Pensacola, Florida – at the expense of the Quonset Air Museum.

Frankwitz's relatives were ecstatic about the recovery and restoration of the plane, if the recovered aircraft was truly the one that he flew. They viewed the physical remains of the aircraft as an embodiment of his efforts for the war. They lauded the Quonset Air Museum's labors on behalf of their relative.

To affirm and defend its rights, the Quonset Air Museum invoked Admiralty law by "arresting" the wreck. In Admiralty law, "arresting" is a legal mechanism by which a salvor stakes a claim on a wreck and is granted protection from competing salvors. The Navy, a competitor, contested the claim. The Quonset Air Museum then sought contributions to defray the cost of litigation.

According to Peter Hess, attorney for the Quonset Air Museum, "United States Magistrate Donald Lovegreen asked about the fate of the Frankwitz Hellcat were either part to prevail. QAM detailed the thousands of hours to that date spent disassembling, desalinating, and restoring each piece of the aircraft prior to its reassembly and the tens of thousands of additional hours still to come over the course of the multi-year project. As one of the only surviving planes that had flown out of the 'Ocean State' during the War, Quonset wanted the Hellcat to become the museum's centerpiece and a memorial not only to Frankwitz, but to the thousands of other undecorated and unsung heroes lost in training behind friendly lines.

"The Navy, on the other hand, was adamant about taking possession of the Hellcat. They openly admitted that they had neither the funds nor the inclination to restore the Warbird. As a matter of law and principle, the Navy intended to confiscate the aircraft and simply warehouse the unconserved wreckage until whenever – if at all – it would undertake preservation measures. Yet without immediate and appropriate treatment, the aircraft would be rapidly consumed by corrosion. The Magistrate was astonished that the Navy could take such a cavalier attitude toward the Hellcat while prohibiting a not-for-profit museum from restoring it for public display.

"The court made it clear that were the issue pressed to judgment, it intended to find that as a Coast Guard-designated hazard to navigation, Hellcat would be deemed abandoned, the Navy was strongly urged to consider settlement."

At the risk of losing face, the case, and the Hellcat, the Navy conceded by negotiating a truce in which the Museum could keep the aircraft as long as the Museum acknowledged that it was a Navy plane.

The irony of the situation was exacerbated by the fact that the National Museum of Naval Aviation already had several Hellcats in its inventory. The Navy didn't really want another Hellcat; it just didn't want a competing museum to have one. This unsporting attitude and vindictive nature are harmful to the preservation of military aircraft history.

Navy Corsair

On December 14, 1944, Lieutenant Robin Pennington took off from the Marine air station at Cherry Point, North Carolina for a standard training exercise. It will never be known what difficulty he had with his Corsair fighter. He was killed either when he bailed out of the aircraft or when he struck the trees where his body was found. The plane crashed in a nearby swamp.

Investigation revealed that the plane had suffered severe damage in the crash. One wing was torn off, and the engine was dislodged from its housing. The Navy claimed that the plane was "demolished," removed reusable instruments and other components, then left it to corrode in the swamp.

As everyone knows, everything rots in swamps, and

Into the Deep Blue Yonder

this plane was no exception. Time, weather, and other natural forces took their toll on the already demolished aircraft. Eventually the plane was discovered by aviation buffs. There was no great rush to recover the plane because of its undesirable location: the middle of a swamp with no nearby roads. To reach the crash site, civilian recovery specialists had to trudge or wade through water-filled bogs and decaying vegetation where thick rank mud could suck boots off feet if the laces were not tied extra tight.

This was not a job for soft Navy desk-holders.

Enter Lex Cralley: airplane mechanic and restoration expert. He traveled from his home in Minnesota to examine the plane in the North Carolina swamp, in order to ascertain the feasibility of recovery: a tall order because vehicles could not get anywhere near the site. In 1991, Cralley spent three days in the swamp, packaging the aircraft's disarticulated parts. He then hired a Sikorsky helicopter to lift the plane and fly it to a waiting flatbed truck, which subsequently transported the parts to Minnesota.

It is a well-established fact that the cost of reconstruction of demolished aircraft is many times the cost of original manufacture. Over subsequent years, Cralley worked part-time on restoring the aircraft: not to make it flyable but to make it displayable. To replace missing or badly damaged parts, he bought, bartered, traded, and – when all else failed – ordered specially machined members and fabricated framework components, in order to make the plane presentable.

The Navy did not disturb him, but hovered in the background until the restoration process neared completion. Then, modern Navy legal corsairs sought to dispossess him of his hard-earned reward for his prodigious and expensive effort. The Navy not only wanted him to give the restored plane to the Navy, but expected him to pay for transporting it to a location of the Navy's choice. Plus, the Navy wanted to be paid for "any damage to or alteration of" the plane that Cralley had done over the years. In other words, the Navy wanted Cralley to pay twice for his services: first for the replacement parts that he purchased, then again for having installed those parts in the aircraft. Furthermore, the Navy did not expect to compensate him for the time and loving care that he had spent on restoration.

Threats and the lawsuit lingered for years, with Cralley suffering under a cloud of emotional turmoil and potential bankruptcy – until Congress got a whiff of the gross injustice that the Navy was trying to perpetrate.

After six years of Navy harassment – which included an intensive examination by Navy-appointed lawyers, appraisers, and historians – Congress intervened by passing a special Act.

Under the provisions of Public Law 108-375, Section 1083, dated October 28, 2004, and titled "Transfer of Historic F3A-1 Brewster Corsair Aircraft," the U.S. government granted the authority to convey title in the following manner: "The Secretary of the Navy may convey, without consideration, to Lex Cralley of Princeton, Minnesota (in this section referred to as 'transferee'), all right, title, and interest of the United States in and to a F3A-1 Brewster Corsair aircraft (Bureau Number 04634). The conveyance shall be made by means of a deed of gift."

Representative Walter B. Jones – whose district included the swamp where the aircraft had rested for so many decades, and who introduced the private bill – raved about big government run amok, when he stated, "Here was a good solid American citizen who wants to preserve naval air history at his own expense and the Big Brother Navy comes down and says, 'No you can't.' To me this was just ridiculous."

This special Act of Congress clearly shows where the federal government's sentiments lie.

Fabricating the Future
Part 1

Quicksand Foundation

On November 19, 1999, the Navy proposed new rules under the title "Application Guidelines for Underwater Archeological Research Permits." The preamble to the proposed rules contained a number of false assumptions and misleading statements that were needed to grant control over abandoned resources to the Navy.

To wit: "Navy custody of its wrecks is based on the property clause of the U.S. Constitution and international maritime law, and is consistent with Articles 95 and 96 of the Law of the Sea Convention. These laws establish that right, title, or ownership of Federal property is not lost to the government due to the passage of time. Navy ships and aircraft cannot be abandoned without formal action as authorized by Congress. Aircraft and ships stricken from the active inventory list are not considered formally disposed of or abandoned."

Making a statement is not the same as establishing a fact.

I will parse the previous paragraph in order to show how the Navy used lies and deceptive wording to trick the public and its representatives into accepting falsehoods as truisms.

The property clause to which the Navy refers is Article IV, Section 3, Clause 2, which reads: "The Congress shall have the power to dispose of and make all needful rules and regulations respecting the territory and other property belonging to the United States."

This sentence does not mean that every time the ink runs out of a pen, or a worn desk needs to be replaced, or a vehicle is too old and decrepit to be repaired, a federal employee must submit a formal request to Congress, which Congress must then review and accept, before the property can be discarded – the way the Navy makes it sound. The mechanisms for disposal devolve upon to the various government departments, and each department handles disposal in sundry ways that depend upon the condition of the property to be disposed. Property may be sold, trashed, or simply abandoned by Departments without intervening Congressional consent.

Crashed Navy aircraft that are not worth repairing are generally abandoned where they lay: in a continental swamp, on foreign land, or under water. Such abandonment saves the cost of recovery and some other form of disposal. Abandonment *is* disposal.

Floating vessels that have outlived their usefulness may be sold to private individuals or to third-world nations for continued use, or to salvage companies for dismantlement and scrapping, or scuttled as an inexpensive way to get rid of them.

Vessels that are sunk by accident or as a casualty of war may be sold to salvage companies, or may be abandoned if the cost of salvage and either reconstruction or disposal exceeds the cost of building a replacement vessel.

In every instance of the disposal of a commissioned vessel, the vessel is said to have been "stricken from the Register," or "stricken from the Navy list." These phrases have long been defined as the mechanism or "formal action" that the Navy uses – in compliance with the delegation of Congressional authority – to divest itself of unwanted property, and to dissociate itself from liability that may be connected (or become connected) with the property.

Navy records contain hundreds, perhaps thousands of documents that clearly establish this protocol, that the above named phrases were equivalent to abandonment. Two examples that are covered in the present volume are the *G-1* and the *Texas*.

Official Navy documents proclaim that the *G-1* was "abandoned." The Navy did not object when private

Fabricating the Future - Part 1

salvors later raised portions of the hull in front of the Naval Station at Newport, Rhode Island.

The *Texas* "was struck from the Navy list" before being scuttled. Later, when lawsuits were initiated against the wreck, the Navy declared that by this means it had affirmatively renounced ownership.

These proofs and numerous others are contained in Naval historical documents, but the Naval History and Heritage Command overlooks or conceals them in its quest to perpetrate the illusion that lost and sunken Naval vessels and aircraft were never really abandoned, despite hard evidence to the contrary. Many others examples can be found in primary documents that are held in the Ships History branch.

It is absurd to believe that sunken vessels and aircraft were merely docked or stored under water for future deployment, or that crashed planes on land were being held in reserve status.

When the Naval History and Heritage Command declared, "Aircraft and ships stricken from the active inventory list are not considered formally disposed of or abandoned," it was declaring its newfound ambition to change the definition of a term in its favor: a definition that had been recognized for its original intent for more than two hundred years.

One cannot help but wonder how the Command would like the phrase "stricken from the Navy list" to mean, if not abandonment. The Command avoids this sticky issue altogether, and offers no alternative definition. Wish fulfillment cannot be exploited to manipulate history.

The facts speak for themselves because the phrase is used in connection with vessels that were scuttled or abandoned.

False Lead

In the preamble to "Application Guidelines for Underwater Archeological Research Permits," the Navy pretends that "Navy custody of its wrecks is based" also on "international maritime law."

In fact, international maritime law states absolutely nothing about custody of wrecks of any kind.

It appears that the Navy cited international maritime law as a way to add credibility to a fatuous claim.

Gratuitous Misdirection

The preamble to "Application Guidelines for Underwater Archeological Research Permits" notes that it "is consistent with Articles 95 and 96 of the Law of the Sea Convention. These laws establish that right, title, or ownership of Federal property is not lost to the government due to the passage of time."

In fact, the Law of the Sea Convention makes no such declaration.

In the first place, Article 29 of the Law of the Sea Convention defines warships as "a ship belonging to the armed forces of a State bearing the external marks distinguishing such ships of its nationality, under the command of an officer duly commissioned by the government of the State and whose name appears in the appropriate service list or its equivalent, and manned by a crew which is under regular armed forces discipline."

Shipwrecks hardly fit this definition, which definition the Naval History and Heritage Command neglected to mention in its Guidelines. Collapsed and deteriorating shipwrecks have lost the external markings that designate them as one-time warships.

Article 95, titled "Immunity of warships on the high seas," states (*in full*), "Warships on the high seas have complete immunity from the jurisdiction of any State other than the flag State."

Article 96, titled "Immunity of ships used only on government non-commercial service," states (*in full*), "Ships owned or operated by a State and used only on government non-commercial service shall, on the high seas, have complete immunity from the jurisdiction of any State other than the flat State."

Neither of these two Articles has anything to do with shipwrecks, or with abandoned property, or with the passage of time. It is clearly stated that they refer to

Fabricating the Future - Part 1

"warships on the high seas." Shipwrecks on the other hand reside *under* the high seas, on the *seabed*, and they are not under the command of anyone much less a duly commissioned officer and crew.

Furthermore, the Law of the Sea Convention has nothing to do with downed aircraft.

Thus the Law of the Sea Convention is totally irrelevant to the issue at hand. It is a pure red herring: an official sounding but meaningless contrivance. It appears, therefore, that the Naval History and Heritage Command invoked the Law of the Sea Convention as a means to lend legitimacy to its proposal. Anyone who did not bother to read the Convention might be impressed by the Command's conjuration.

In any case, the United States has found so many problems with the Law of the Sea Convention, that it has refused to sign or ratify it even today (16 years after the Command used it to mislead readers of the Guidelines), so that conformance or consistency is not only immaterial in the presented context, but contrary to the best interests of the country.

False Premises

Elsewhere in the Guidelines it is noted that the "National Historic Preservation Act of 1966 as amended (NHPA), 16 U.S.C. 470 (1999), DON [Department of the Navy] is obligated to protect historic properties, including ship and aircraft wrecks, for which it has custodial responsibilities. The NHPA directs federal agencies to manage their cultural resource properties in a way that emphasizes preservation and minimizes the impact of undertakings that might adversely affect such properties."

This is another instance in which the Naval History and Heritage Command has misrepresented the truth as a way to deceive the public into believing (first) that the Navy has custodial responsibilities, and (second) that it is "obligated" to protect historic properties. The word "obligated" (in any form) is nowhere mentioned in the Act or in its amendments. There is no affirmative duty to nominate historic property; nomination of historic properties is purely voluntary. Any such obligation would place an undue burden on a government agency's financial resources.

Additionally, nowhere does the Act mention ship and aircraft wrecks, as the Guideline framers would have their readers believe. This is only one more deception among a legion of deceptive practices.

Eligibility for inclusion on the National Register of Historic Places is specific in a number of ways. A property must be culturally significant. The property must be accurately described. The location of the property must be precisely given. The property must be fully evaluated before it can be accepted.

The Navy cannot submit a list of 17,000 named or numbered properties for gross nomination. Every property must be nominated individually, and must meet the criteria given in the previous paragraph. Some important issues that must be addressed are:

> "Property is associated with events that have made a significant contribution to the broad patterns of our history.
>
> "Property is associated with the lives of persons significant in our past.
>
> "Property embodies the distinctive characteristics of a type, period, or method of construction or represents the work of a master, or possesses high artistic value, or represents a significant and distinguishable entity whose components lack individual distinction.
>
> "Property has yielded, or is likely to yield information important in prehistory or history."

A lengthy Statement of Significance must be appended, complete with a detailed description of the property, plus photographs of the property.

As the Navy doesn't have any idea about the location of the vast majority of the names and numbers on its list, it is unable to furnish the required data.

Fabricating the Future - Part 1

Furthermore, most Navy wrecks fail the eligibility requirements. For example, the National Naval Aviation Museum already has a Dauntless aircraft identical to the one that the Navy litigated so hard to procure; another one lacks uniqueness and would be redundant. In the same vein, the Navy lost hundreds or thousands of Hellcats during the war, so it cannot claim that every submerged Hellcat is distinctive or significant.

Then there is the clause that the Navy overlooked or concealed: it proclaims that nominations can be accepted "only if such property is located in a State where there is no program approved under subsection (b) of this section." The relevant wording is "located in a State." Properties may be nominated for inclusion on the list of historic places only if they are located on land or in waters in States of the Union. This rule excludes shipwrecks or aircraft that are located in international waters or on the soil (or under the ice) of foreign nations.

Furthermore, once a nomination is accepted, the nominating party is required to maintain the property in its current condition. This means that every wreck must be stabilized so that it does not deteriorate more than it already has, then maintained in stable condition.

For properties that have fallen into a state of disrepair by the time of nomination, the nominating party may be required to repair or restore the property to its original condition, in order to achieve its historic appearance, and then continue upkeep in perpetuity. Most properties on the list are buildings; these buildings must be constantly maintained. Buildings that have been modified or reconstructed since their construction must be restored to their historic appearance (except for modern occupancy safety standards such as fire alarms, smoke detectors, and so on).

Everyone over the age of puberty knows that buildings require constant maintenance, else they fall apart from neglect: from leaky roofs, faulty plumbing, peeling paint, rotting wood, broken glass, and so on.

It is incumbent upon the Navy to maintain all the properties in its holdings: vessels in its fleet afloat, ready aircraft, vehicles in its motor pool, administrative buildings, lodging, museums, offices, clothing, and so on. The Navy is not permitted to neglect hull maintenance and to let its vessels sink; it may not allow its aircraft to fly without constant operational checks; it may not let its vehicles fail to run through negligence; it may not let its administrative buildings and lodgings and museums fall apart through lack of proper care.

Similarly, before the Navy can lay claim to a shipwreck or wrecked plane, it must pledge to conserve these craft in their current state of collapse, and eventually to restore them to their operational condition.

Instead, the Navy is content to let them rust away on the bottom of the sea.

By law, the Navy cannot assume ownership or control of wrecks without also assuming the responsibility to conserve them. By this I mean *real* responsibility, not the hypocritical "custodial responsibility" that the Navy terms its dictatorial relationship to wrecks. The National Historic and Preservation Act mandates professional standards for the preservation of historical properties that are federally owned or controlled.

So far, the Navy has not demonstrated a conservation ethic toward wrecks. It has demonstrated only its craving to control them.

Navy Swill

Nowhere in Naval documents does the Navy pledge to actively conserve the shipwrecks or wrecked aircraft over which it seeks dominion.

In fact, it affirms just the opposite, in what may be called a "lack of conservation ethic." To wit: "Submerged Navy cultural resources will be left in place unless artifact removal or site disturbance is justified and necessary to protect Navy cultural resources, to conduct research, or provide public education and information that is otherwise inaccessible."

This attitude ensures that all those shipwrecks and wrecked aircraft will deteriorate through Navy neglect. Eventually, nothing will remain of them but a rust spot

Fabricating the Future - Part 1

on the ocean floor or scattered scraps in an unnamed swamp.

With regard to manmade structures, "in situ preservation" is either a horse-blinder attitude or a political stance that ignores the natural processes of decay. We're not talking about fossilized dinosaur bones that have been turned into rock. Ships and aircraft are constructed of materials that rust, rot, and deteriorate until nothing remains of the original form.

Wrecks that are not properly conserved and maintained will break down and disintegrate the same as abandoned buildings that are left to their own devices.

To accomplish the territorial demands of the Naval History and Heritage Command, the preamble to the "Application Guidelines for Underwater Archeological Research Permits" presents a number of wish-fulfillments as if they were established facts, when instead they are outright lies that are designed to fool a naïve public and easily-swayed representatives.

Anyone who believes that this farmhouse can be "preserved" in situ, without major restoration and constant upkeep, is an idiot. Mankind's constructs - whether they be buildings, shipwrecks, or aircraft - start to deteriorate as soon as maintenance ceases. Yet the Navy contends that manmade structures can be preserved by not disturbing them, by ignoring them, by leaving them alone in the elements under water or in open air.

Fabricating the Future
Part 2

In the Eating

Although the Navy fiercely lusted after control of abandoned warships and aircraft, it must have known all along that its protocol of striking them from the Navy list constituted affirmative action of abandonment that was consistent with the delegation of authority of the Constitution of the United States.

Yet the Naval History and Heritage Command did not want to accept the truth of the matter. Its appetite for conquest and possessive authority exceeded its sense of duty to American citizens that the Navy was sworn to protect from all enemies, both foreign and domestic. In this case the enemy was domestic: in the form of the Naval History and Heritage Command, a cancer that was metastasizing exponentially.

In reality, there was no Constitutional law that granted overall stewardship of abandoned Navy craft to the Navy. Sunken warships and downed aircraft had been legally abandoned in accordance with the Constitutional delegation of authority, by "striking" them from the Navy Register. So the Navy decided to write a new law that could overrule existing law in favor of the Navy's aggrandizing mission to control abandoned property under water.

The fictitious tenets and self-indulgent assumptions that were set forth in the preamble to the "Application Guidelines for Underwater Archaeological Research Permits" laid the groundwork for this legislation. Forever after, the Navy could point back to the Application Guidelines as if its falsehoods and artifices carried the weight of truth and law.

Logically, if the Navy's basic premises were factual,

Fabricating the Future - Part 2

there would be no need for new legislation. The proof that the Navy didn't believe its own hype came in the form of a tiny piece of self-written and self-serving legislation that was known as Title XIV, or the "Sunken Military Craft" rider of 2005.

Machiavellian Sneak Attack

The fault with this crafty piece of legislation was that it was never vetted by the American people. Neither the voters nor their Congressional representatives suspected the existence of the Navy's magic act until after it was passed.

This stage performance of prestidigitation was neither announced or published in the *Federal Register*. It was not discussed by members of Congress. It was not put on the Senate floor. In fact, it wasn't an Act at all. It was an invisible rider that was slipped at the last minute into the "Ronald W. Reagan National Defense Authorization Act for Fiscal Year 2005," where it was buried among some 3,000 pages of funding appropriations that were absolutely essential to the defense of the United States.

The folks at the Naval History and Heritage Command must have hoped that the bill would get passed even if anyone knew about the rider's insertion. In the event, when Congress and the Senate passed the "National Defense Authorization Act" that year, they didn't even know that they were voting for "Sunken Military Craft."

This makes it law but it doesn't make it right. Law is more than a moral philosophy, to be discarded when it gets in the way of personal ambition. Laws are supposed to be passed by common consent, not chicanery.

Now the American people were stuck with a rider that could not have been passed by honest means. The false pretenses in the rider were promulgated by a Department that had forsworn its honor so a handful of civilian employees could wield a big stick against their own country: an action that smacks of treason.

America was torpedoed in the stern by its own Navy.

Damn the Ethics, Full Speed Ahead.

The basic propositions of the Act were twofold: "Right, title, and interest of the United States in and to any United States sunken military craft (1) shall not be extinguished except by an express divestiture of title by the United States; and (2) shall not be extinguished by the passage of time, regardless of when the sunken military craft sank."

Superficially the wording sounded straightforward, yet a moment of reflection reveals that it was anything but simple and clear-cut. The two propositions gave the appearance of having been hastily drafted for last minute insertion. The above quote and several others were confusing and open to interpretation.

The "Sunken Military Craft" rider failed to address the issue of "striking" from the Register or the Navy list. As I have already noted, the Congressionally intended purpose of "striking" a commissioned Navy vessel was to officially abandon a warship that had sunk or that the Navy no longer wanted to maintain for active service. The term had been defined this way for more than two hundred years. Only recently had the control freaks at the Naval History and Heritage Command attempted to redefine the phrase to their own advantage, and to the disadvantage of the American people.

Therefore, proposition (1) changed nothing; or perhaps very little. By original definition, historically stricken vessels had already been abandoned, as courts often ruled when given the opportunity to do so. They could not be "unabandoned" retroactively after they had fallen into the public domain. Like the miner's daughter, they were lost and gone forever from the Navy's control.

So while proposition (1) appeared to be all-encompassing, in reality it referred only to shipwrecks and sunken aircraft that were lost or scuttled *after* the date of rider's passage.

The Navy depressed its guns too far and shot itself in the foot by writing proposition (2). In one sense proposition (2) was redundant, with regard to U.S. military vessels that had already been abandoned. Proposition

Fabricating the Future - Part 2

(2) appears to have been included as a result of court cases in which judgments went against the Navy. (See previous sections for instances in this regard.)

Yet proposition (2) limited the effectiveness of proposition (1) by specifying *sunken* military craft. By doing so, the rider excluded Navy aircraft that crashed or were otherwise abandoned on land.

The "Sunken Military Craft" rider had definite shortcomings with regard to the hood that the Navy was attempting to pull over the public's eyes. It also contained other incongruities and adverse side effects which may or may not have been intentional, or which resulted from "reckless" last-minute assembly or poor premeditation.

Absurdity

The "Sunken Military Craft" rider did not apply to "foreign persons," or to "a person who is not a citizen, national, or resident alien of the United States."

This meant that illegal aliens and citizens of foreign countries "may possess, disturb, remove, or injure any sunken military craft" (the Navy's words), or may salvage, recover, damage, destroy, or demolish (my words) sunken military craft without interference by the U.S. government.

So, patriotic American citizens, to whom Naval heritage was of paramount importance, were prohibited from conducting activities which foreign nationals were permitted to conduct – not only with impunity but with the blessing of the Navy.

This makes no sense whatsoever. Why should American taxpayers be penalized for their loyalty and citizenship?

Conflicts with Admiralty Law

Parts of the "Sunken Military Craft" rider were illegitimate because they conflicted with existing centuries-old laws to which the Navy did not wish to be bound. In other words, by means of this rider the Navy sought to be above the law.

With regard to the Law of Finds, "The law of finds shall not apply to (1) any United States sunken military craft, wherever located; or (2) any foreign sunken military craft located in United States waters."

According to the Law of Finds, "to the finder go the spoils;" or in lay language, "finders, keepers." The Navy wanted to recast this international law to read, "to the Navy go the spoils, no matter who spent his own time and money to find and recover the spoils." Not a very noble attitude.

With regard to the Law of Salvage, "No salvage rights or awards shall be granted with respect to (1) any United States sunken military craft without the express permission of the United States; or (2) any foreign sunken military craft located in United States waters without the express permission of the relevant foreign state."

Historically, centuries-old international Admiralty Law provided a monetary incentive for salvors to save vessels on the high seas, to raise sunken hulls and their contents, and to collect wreckage that had washed ashore, in order for salvaged merchandise to be "returned to the stream of commerce."

The Law of Salvage disfavored the Navy's newly ordained ambition. The renunciation of this law seemed to be the direct result of an Admiralty case that the Navy lost to Robert Cervoni, who not only prevailed with regard to recovery of a ditched aircraft, but who was awarded reimbursement of his legal fees in defending himself against Navy aggression: a double-barreled loss to Navy gunnery whose first shell missed its target and whose second shell exploded in the breech.

The Navy's new legislation was aimed at forestalling a repetition of such an adverse ruling: a pre-emptive strike against future litigants.

Truth Will Out

The Naval History and Heritage Command harps on the concept of the preservation of sunken warships and aircraft, but has never done anything to actually preserve them in the commonly accepted meaning of the

Fabricating the Future - Part 2

word: to prevent ultimate destruction by the natural processes of decay and deterioration. Now, the Navy has finally admitted what it means by "preservation."

One of the subtitles of the "Sunken Military Craft" rider is "Preservation of Title to Sunken Military Craft and Associated Contents."

The Navy has at last made it clear that it is not concerned at all with preserving wrecks from collapse and disintegration, but only with maintaining ownership of their remains – for as long as they remain.

Parting Shots

The Navy persists in referring to the "Sunken Military Craft" legislation as an Act, as in "Sunken Military Craft Act." It is not and never was an Act of Congress; it was an unannounced and dishonestly attached rider and nothing more. I reiterate: neither the American people nor their duly elected representatives were given the opportunity to review the rider as an individual piece of legislation. Thus the Navy cheated the voters by not letting them decide for themselves whether they wanted to grant such self-serving and totalitarian authority to a few civilians who work in the Naval History and Heritage Command.

The American people were blindsided by an unscrupulous Navy broadside that did not have the best interests of the country at heart.

Worse yet, by phrasing the rider to encompass abandoned "military craft" instead of abandoned Navy warships, the minions at the Naval History and Heritage Command sought to seize not only sunken Navy craft which at one time belonged to the Navy, but sought to take over *all* military craft no matter to which war department they belonged (or used to belong, or perhaps still belonged).

By this cunning "act" of treachery, the Navy sought to take control of abandoned Army and Air Force wrecks, which the Navy never owned in the first place, and which the Navy never had the right or authority to possess.

But this was not the Command's last territorial demand . . .

Upping the Ante
Now for the worst part. The offensive rider defines "sunken military craft" as "all or any portion of (A) any sunken warship, naval auxiliary, or other vessel that was owned or operated by a government on military noncommercial service when it sank; (B) any sunken military aircraft or military spacecraft that was owned or operated by a government when it sank; and (C) the associated contents of a craft referred to in subparagraph (A) or (B), if title thereto has not been abandoned or transferred by the government concerned."

One operative phrase here is "military noncommercial service." If you're wondering what this obtuse phrase means – or rather, what the Navy intended it to mean but didn't want to telegraph its punch by defining it – I will interpret it for you.

At the beginning of World War Two, the U.S. government established the War Shipping Administration. One of the many functions of the WSA was to coordinate the movement of commercial transport vessels that operated in war zones (both the European and Pacific theaters) by forming transoceanic convoys that were escorted by warships of the U.S. and British navies.

Escort vessels provided a measure of protection from Axis submarines and aircraft. Nonetheless, thousands of tankers and freighters were sunk as a result of enemy torpedoes, submarine gunfire, and aircraft bombing and strafing attacks. Some of the freighters were transporting valuable cargoes of precious metals which today are being located and harvested by enterprising venture capitalists who are dedicated to returning these lost shipments to the stream of commerce.

I strongly suspect that the Navy inserted the seemingly innocuous and gratuitous phrase "military noncommercial service" as a way to assert ownership of rich cargoes (but not until *after* they have been recovered). The Navy will do this by claiming that commercial trans-

Fabricating the Future - Part 2

port vessels that operated under the aegis of the WSA were performing a *military* service instead of a purely commercial service, by transporting what the Navy will contend was war materiel: that is, freight that was needed for the prosecution of the war.

By stretching the imagination, freight that helped to prosecute the war might be construed as more than arms and ammunition and other actual military products, but also clothing that kept the troops warm, medical supplies that kept the troops healthy and treated their wounds, and – by stretching the imagination beyond the breaking point, but well within the parameters that the Navy would like to apply – canned goods and groceries that fed the civilians who provided miscellaneous services for the fighting forces.

In short, every commonly grown or manufactured item can be construed as serving the war effort as long as you don't mind passing the point of absurdity.

Now consider the other operative phrase – "operated by a government" – and the stage is set for the Navy to contrive to take possession and control of every company-owned vessel that ever plied the seven seas while under charter to the WSA. In other words, the Navy would like "charter" to be defined as "operated by a government," even though the word "charter" does not have such a meaning in peacetime, when a freight-forwarding company charters a shipping line vessel to deliver goods to foreign shores.

Whether this contrivance will prove valid in court is quite another matter. There is no doubt that salvors, shipping companies, and underwriters will object to the Navy's presumption of ownership.

There is also no doubt that when the situation arises, the Navy will litigate ad nauseam for absolute possession, because it has unlimited funding to do so and no moral compunction against thwarting property laws. If the taxpayers complain about the way their money is being spent to gratify Navy control freaks, raise the taxes to hire more lawyers to quell the complaints of the unwashed masses.

198 Fabricating the Future - Part 2

I state "no doubt" without doubt that it will occur because – as I have clearly established in previous chapters – the Navy has a steadfast history of suing everyone over everything that has or may have anything to do with abandoned wrecks: whether those wrecks were ever Navy wrecks or wrecks that were abandoned by other war departments. The Navy's policy is to sue, sue, sue so it might either win by default (in cases in which the defendants are not rich enough to defend themselves in court) or by the submission of false evidence and untrue testimony.

The Navy has never tried to win a case on its merits when unscrupulous means were more efficient to employ. The subject of this chapter is a case in point. The Navy can use the obscure phraseology to mean anything it wants it to mean, until proven otherwise in a court of law - after which it can ignore the court's ruling and initiate another case, and so on ad infinitum.

The sea giveth, and the sea taketh away. But the Navy only taketh.

This engine is one of the few remaining components of a World War Two warbird that lies in pieces on the bottom of the sea amid a widely scattered debris field. If the Navy gets its way, all wrecks will keep decomposing until even this small remnant disappears.

Fabricating the Future
Part 3

Hidden Agenda

The Navy legislation that was proposed in 2014 prevents diving and bans fishing on all sunken wrecks to which the Navy would like to claim ownership. It accomplishes this with such devious subterfuge that most readers of the proposal won't notice the craftily written disinformation that is split apart and buried in more than 12,000 words of text.

Consider this parable. Let's say that the Navy advertises a museum that is open to the public. The museum is located on the tenth floor of a building that is owned or controlled by the Navy. A visitor arrives and inquires about seeing the exhibit. He is told that the exhibits are open to all comers and that he is welcome to view the items on display. Except that . . .

. . . the elevators and stairwells are closed to the public, and visitors are not allowed to touch the floor of the museum or to breathe in the exhibit area. Visitors are allowed to view the exhibits only from outside the museum windows.

Thus the visitor can see the exhibits only if he can find some other way to reach the tenth floor. Perhaps he can scale the outer wall of the building, or parachute down to a window ledge, or erect a hundred feet of scaffolding, or build a bridge from an adjacent building, or . . . but you get you point. Unless he has super powers, reaching the tenth floor is impossible for the average visitor to accomplish. This museum isn't just wheelchair inaccessible; it is totally inaccessible.

I know this analogy sounds ridiculous and far-fetched, but hear me out, and you will understand how shrewdly the Navy has contrived the proposal so that it gives the impression that scuba diving and fishing will not be adversely affected, but has in fact constructed prohibitive language in such a cunning way, and in such widely separated locations within the text, that it disguises the Navy's true imperative to prevent scuba diving and ban fishing on Navy-claimed wrecks.

Look how the Navy worded access to wrecks in the 2014 proposal: "Non-intrusive activities including diving adjacent to or remotely documenting sites do not require a permit or authorization from the NHHC [Naval History and Heritage Command]."

At first glance this sentence appears to give consent to uninhibited scuba diving as a recreational activity. However, closer scrutiny and word-by-word analysis reveals that it states nothing of the kind. In fact, the statement is purposely designed to deceive people into thinking that the Navy intends to allow recreational scuba diving, so that they and their Congressional representatives won't object to passage of the legislation.

Access Denied

Nowhere in the proposal is the word "non-intrusive" defined. This means that, after passage of the proposal, the Navy can define the term any way it likes.

On the other hand, eight pages after statement of the phrase "non-intrusive activities," the proposal defines the oft-used word "disturbance" thus: "Disturb or Disturbance means directly or indirectly affecting the physical condition of any portion of a sunken military craft or terrestrial military craft, altering the position or arrangement of any portion of a sunken military craft or terrestrial military craft, or influencing the wrecksite or its immediate environment in such a way that any portion of a craft's physical condition is affected or its position or arrangement is altered."

This definition is analogous to my museum access parable above. Here's how.

The standard procedure for diving on a wreck is for a dive boat to drop a grapnel into or next to the wreck, then drift with the current until the grapnel snags firmly

Fabricating the Future - Part 3

The standard safety procedure for recreational scuba diving is to "hook" the wreck, then secure the grapnel to the wreckage. The proposed legislation prohibits this safeguard.

in the wreckage. The anchor line provides a direct line of descent from the boat to the wreck, much like a firehouse pole enables fire fighters to slide from the waiting room to the garage. This means of descent is critically important in the open ocean, where rough seas and strong current would otherwise prevent a diver from reaching a wreck that can't be seen from the surface because of limited underwater visibility.

The anchor line is even more important for returning to the dive boat. A diver needs to hold onto the anchor line during his ascent so he doesn't get swept away and lost in the wide, wide sea. Moreover, he also needs to hang onto the anchor line in order to control the rate of ascent, then spend minutes or hours at prescribed depths to make decompression stops, in order to conduct his required decompression. Otherwise, he might suffer decompression injury (the bends) and either die or be paralyzed for life.

The anchor line is a crucial safety device for recreational divers.

The proposed ban on "disturbance" effectively prevents recreational divers from reaching a wreck, because the use of a grapnel might "disturb" the site according to the Navy's strict definition of the word. In other words, the separation of "non-intrusive activities" from the definition of "disturbance" by eight pages of unrelated text, is an underhanded way to achieve a goal that the Navy does not want known to the public or their elected representatives.

I have no doubt that, if the proposal is ever passed, the Navy will invoke this "non-intrusive" measure as a way to prevent access to Navy-claimed wrecks.

Divers decompressing at prescribed depths or stops to prevent decompression injury (the bends).

Smoke and Mirrors

The Navy's definition of "disturbance" is so broad that it encompasses every kind of recreational activity that could possibly occur on a wreck.

To go another step further, consider the adjective and preposition that the proposal employs to describe activity that is authorized: "Non-intrusive activities including diving *adjacent to* or remotely documenting sites . . ."

The sentence states "diving adjacent to," as opposed to "diving on" or "diving inside of" Navy-claimed wrecks. This carefully worded expression cannot be shrugged off as unintentional or accidental usage, or as a simple case of semantics. The proposal *explicitly* states "diving adjacent to" because that is precisely how the Navy intends

Fabricating the Future - Part 3

to limit recreational scuba diving on Navy-claimed wrecks.

As in my museum access parable in the previous section, not only does the proposal's wording deny the use of a grapnel (elevators and stairwells), but it also compels recreational scuba divers to stay outside the periphery of Navy-claimed wrecks. In other words, recreational scuba divers may swim around the perimeter – not just the perimeter of a wreck but the perimeter of its associated debris field – but they won't be allowed to get close enough to the wreck itself to see it in reduced visibility.

My non-diving readers – whose sole experience with scuba diving is the Hollywood presentation of crystal clear visibility – may be astonished to learn that outside the Caribbean Sea, average visibility in northern coastal waters rarely exceeds ten to twenty feet, and is sometimes less. For example, visibility on the *YMS-14* (which see) averaged two to five feet, with ten feet an uncommon occurrence. On other wrecks, I have dived to 250 feet and found only eight feet of visibility on the bottom. Sometimes visibility is less than two feet; this is what recreational scuba divers call a braille dive.

Now imagine rolling off a dive boat into turbid water in which you can barely see your hand in front of your face, sinking down blindly through the water column, to a point on the seabed beyond the periphery of a wreck, and trying the *find* the wreck, much less explore it. Then think about ascending to the surface without any point of reference, and drifting at specified depths in order to conduct an hour's decompression, and then hoping that the skipper of the dive boat can find you after you have drifted a mile or more away from the wreck site.

Keep in mind that I am talking about recreational scuba divers, not Navy SEALS.

If you still don't believe my interpretation, or if you think that I am reaching for something that isn't there, know that other government agencies have already employed identical measures to restrict or make it impossible to access shipwrecks.

When I first dived on the *Monitor* – which lies at a depth of 230 feet in the Monitor National Marine Sanctuary – NOAA did not permit the dive boat to grapple the wreck, and did not permit divers to touch the encrustation that coated the iron hull. The fine for doing so was $50,000. A NOAA representative inspected the wetsuits of returning divers to determine if they had accidentally brushed or otherwise contacted encrusted wreckage, or had knelt on the seabed that comprised the debris field.

NOAA ignored the fact that trigger fish feed on coral that grows on wreck surfaces. No trigger fish were arrested or fined. In fact, no coral colonies were prohibited from growing on wreck surfaces. Natural destruction of the wreck was never remediated.

In California, National Park rangers arrested and prosecuted a group of divers for fanning the sand over the buried portions of the wreck of the *Winfield Scott*, which is located in the Channel Islands National Marine Sanctuary. The crux of the case rested on whether "fanning" sand or "alteration of the seabed" constituted damage to the site. The court found that it did, and fined the divers between $50,000 and $100,000.

How so? Because archaeologists surmised that moving a tiny bit of sand might uncover bits of wreckage that were previously buried, the undocumented supposition being that the resulting exposure of wood and metal to the sea might increase the ongoing rate of decay and rust due to exposure to higher levels of oxygen.

Every diver knows that, in swimming over the seabed, his fins kick up sand, which then swirls in the water column until it settles back down onto the bottom. The amount of disturbance that this action causes to a wreck is about the same as the disturbance that a homeowner causes to dust-laden furniture when he walks past it, and his passing causes air to move and dislodge dust motes.

Hand-fanning and fin-kicking are nothing compared to the disturbance that deep ground swells cause to the seabed when a fierce storm passes over a wreck site. I've seen as much as two feet of sand moved off a wreck after an ordinary northeaster struck the area, and hurricanes have been known to cause wrecks to collapse and scatter the pieces like leaves blown off trees in autumn – but those are acts of God, and God cannot be sued or prosecuted (so far).

The erosion and deposition of sand on shipwrecks is an ongoing natural process and an acknowledged fact of life . . . but that doesn't stop government agencies from using sand-fanning – by hand or by fin – as an excuse to prohibit scuba diving: especially the Naval History and Heritage Command, in light of its adversarial posture toward non-Navy activities on wrecks, and its zealous attitude of possessiveness that is amply demonstrated in the present proposal.

The Navy's proposed regulations have nothing to do with rationality or intelligent thinking. They have to do with bureaucratic territoriality. Government agencies have and will continue to hold that the infinitesimal manmade movement of sand constitutes destructive "disturbance," as long as it is in their best interests to do so.

A Navy Fish Story

So far I have concluded that the "non-intrusive" and "no disturbance" clauses will prevent recreational scuba divers from accessing wrecks by traditional means, and that if they do manage to reach a wreck by some other method, they will be permitted only to circle the wreck and view it from afar but not to explore it the way they have always done, such as by swimming over top of it or ducking under protruding hull plates or entering intact compartments.

The rationalization for the latter two circumstances is as bogus as that of sand-fanning. As ridiculous as it sounds, when it suits their purposes, archaeologists claim that exhaled bubbles may cause damage to wood or metal structures. This is the Navy's version of the fairytale about the Three Little Pigs, in which the big bad wolf exclaims, "I'll huff and I'll puff and I'll blow your house down."

It stands to reason that no recreational scuba diver can exhale hard enough to blow down a wreck, especially when human respiration is compared to the extraordinary power of natural forces – diurnal tidal changes, shifting high-speed currents, and storm-driven ground swells – all of which pummel wrecks constantly and unmercifully, and aerate them all the time.

But there you have it. The Navy will claim anything that will prevent recreational scuba divers from exploring wrecks.

By Hook or by Crook

With regard to "disturbance," the prohibitions that pertain to recreational scuba divers also hold true for recreational anglers.

The grappling deterrent can be overcome by dropping a sand-anchor upcurrent of a wreck, then letting out enough anchor line for the boat to drift downcurrent into position over top of the hull and debris field. But the prohibition against "disturbance" still isn't met, for in order to catch fish, recreational anglers must cast their rigs into the water and let the fishhooks and lead sinkers land in the wreckage. That is where fish thrive and congregate.

Every recreational angler has at one time or another snagged a hook or sinker in wreckage, and either lost the rig when the line broke, or managed to yank it free. Either eventuality constitutes "disturbance" in the eyes of the Navy. A lead weight that strikes wreckage is regarded by Navy naysayers as a cause of terrible damage; a hook that snags a small piece of iron scale may dislodge it or move it incrementally; or a hook that nicks wreckage may stab a pinhole in wood or metal structure.

As absurd as it sounds, these are some of the weak justifications that the Navy will make in order to prohibit fishing on Navy-claimed wrecks. NOAA and the National Park Service already prohibit fishing on many wrecks that are under their dominion, as a way to reduce what they call "impact." On the other hand, natural "impact" and destruction by oceanic forces are unavoidable, and therefore are never declared.

Note that recreational fishing is not mentioned anywhere in the 2014 proposal. The issue was avoided so as not to draw attention to the planned prohibition against fishing on wrecks, because recreational fishing advocates have a huge lobby in Washington. The Navy doesn't want to tip its hand in this regard, lest the ban on fishing incur more bad press on a proposal that is already unpopular.

Caveat piscator. Let the angler beware. The 2014 proposal does not specifically state that the Navy will ban recreational fishing on wrecks, but the definition of "disturbance" is explicit and intentionally obfuscating. Circuitous language is the Navy's forte.

If you compare the lack of precision with regard to recreational diving and fishing, to the obvious precision that is inherent in the rest of the proposal, you will see that the imprecision is deliberate, so as not to give away the Navy's hidden agenda to prevent diving and ban fishing on Navy-claimed wrecks.

Plugging the Loopholes

The Naval History and Heritage Command also proposes to control access to foreign military craft that reside in American coastal waters, even if those craft lie beyond the U.S. territorial limit, in international waters.

Furthermore, the 2014 proposal seeks to mend a Navy-perceived oversight or deficiency in the 2005 rider, by now asserting control over "terrestrial military craft." If only the Navy had done it right the first time . . .

Haste makes waste.

So, with regard to the Navy's all-inclusive and encyclopedic definition of so-called military craft – floating and flying, submerged or crash-landed, anywhere and anytime – what freedoms remain for the American people who fought so hard to preserve their country, their way of life, and their national heritage?

None. The Navy wants it all.

Point and Counterpoint

The Measure of Incompetence

On its website, the Naval History and Heritage Command has posted thousands of so-called warship "histories" that more rightly fit the category of historical fiction than nonfiction or textbook entries.

In the volume in hand I have gone to great lengths to dispute the Command's novelized versions of Navy history in order to demonstrate the ineptitude of the Command's staff members. With all the resources at their disposal, and right at their fingertips, one would think that they could have done a better job. Not only do errors of omission run rife throughout warship entries, but all too often the published information is either inaccurate, misleading, contradictory, whitewashed, or dead wrong.

And I have shown only the tip of the proverbial iceberg. I realized a couple of decades ago how the civilian employees (I cannot in all sincerity refer to them as historians) at the Naval History Center conspired to misinform the public – when it deemed to inform the public at all – about warships in general and shipwrecks in particular.

Time after time I found minor mistakes – hundreds of them – which obliged me to delve into primary sources in order to correct them in my own writings. I am talking about warships that were incidental to the wreck that I was covering. I would not go as far as to call the warship entries drivel; rather they were approximations of the facts with little or no thought given to accuracy.

The Naval History and Heritage Command has failed miserably as purveyors of Navy history.

Staff Infection

Yet this same bungling and ineffectual Command

Point and Counterpoint

now wants to take control of 17,000 wrecks, not so it can preserve them from the destructive forces of nature, but so it can deny and dictate terms of access; so it can prevent recreational scuba divers from exploring their Navy heritage; so it can stop recreational anglers from fishing on rotting and rusting wreckage; so it can halt and prosecute serious-minded aircraft recovery and restoration experts from raising and displaying historic aircraft so that the public can benefit from their efforts.

The goal of the Command is in no way *constructive*; it is *destructive*.

The Navy has no intention of preserving these wrecks. Its intention is to let them disintegrate through neglect.

Twenty-six years ago, in *U.S.S. San Diego: the Last Armored Cruiser*, I wrote: "To preserve a flag one does not hang it on a pole during a full gale: it is folded and packed away safely. One does not store precious china on an exposed mountain ridge where it is subject to rock falls, summer sun, and winter snow: it is kept in a glass case under controlled conditions. An artifact must be preserved *from* the elements of nature, not consigned to its capriciousness; the longer it is constrained to these wild forces the less likely it is to survive intact, to be found and appreciated by future generations."

Throughout the years I have personally witnessed these wild forces at work. Wrecks that I photographed decades ago when already they were only partially intact, have collapsed to the point at which the hull configuration is no longer recognizable. A wreck that used to look like a vessel is now nothing more than a junk pile of Pick-Up Sticks, or like a building that has collapsed due to lack of proper maintenance.

To deny that these wild forces continue to destroy wrecks is to repudiate reality. Wrecks cannot be preserved by bureaucratic fiat. They can be preserved only by stabilizing their constituent parts under water – a nearly impossible task – or by raising them, or parts of them, and then treating them with preservative chemical solutions.

Anyone who believes that wrecks can be preserved under water in situ (Latin for "in place") must reject empirical evidence. Anyone who tries to foster this belief upon less knowledgeable people is either a deluded ideologist or an outright liar. The Navy is the latter.

The folks at the oxymoronic Naval History and Heritage Command have ignored altogether the inevitable processes of decay. Nowhere on their website or in past or proposed legislation have they touched upon this issue. Never have they explained how leaving a wreck exposed to constantly changing weather on land, or immersed in a corrosive chemical bath, constitutes preservation.

Such an attitude smacks of faith healing and patent medicine. They are selling snake oil to the public.

Incompetence coupled with dishonesty and corruption make a bad combination. Putting such a group in charge of all of America's abandoned military craft, so that the little that remains of those craft can be allowed to crumble and collapse, is unconscionable. Their grand scheme is not to preserve these wrecks in any way, shape, or form, but to prevent more endeavoring and conscientious people from doing so.

The end result of their nostrums and political machinations will be museums that are overfilled with Army and Air Force artifacts, but a paucity of Navy relics and the consequential loss of Navy heritage.

The Command employees are so far behind in their work that, by their own admission, they cannot even keep up with FOIA requests, and are presently several years in arrears in the fulfillment of their duties. This despite the fact that they have closed their doors to civilian researchers and have nothing else to do but write self-serving legislation, and grin with false pride about how many wrecks they control.

Even if they were inclined to do so, where are they going to find the time and money to conduct archaeological surveys on 17,000 wrecks before those wrecks are completely decomposed? In the 1990's, there were only fifty marine archaeologists in the entire country.

Point and Counterpoint

The Navy professes that wrecks are preserved under water. If that were true, the *Hesperides* (pictured above, courtesy of the Steamship Historical Society of America) would still look exactly the same in underwater photographs (below left, stern, showing the steering quadrant and propeller; below right, amidships, showing the steam engine). The Navy is either stupid, fooling itself, or trying to dupe people who have never seen a shipwreck.

That number may have doubled by now, but how many of them work for the Navy; and how many are already consumed by their own underwater projects?

Even if every one of them worked on nothing but Navy wrecks, it would take thousands of years to locate and survey them all – by which time most of them would long since have reverted to their constituent atoms.

What Command employees should be doing is correcting all the errors in their previous work; revising warships' histories; helping civilian researchers do research; and minding the business that the Command was established to mind, instead of going on an unscrupulous power trip of their own.

Reality Check

To support its political ambitions, the Naval History and Heritage Command constantly harps upon issues that are either undocumented, highly opinionated, illogical, or contrary to observable evidence. Some of the

All that remains of a P-39 Airacobra (pictured above, courtesy of the Naval Photographic Center) is the engine (shown below). Other remnants may lie scattered around the area. The lower image represents the reality of so-called in situ preservation - which is not preservation at all but the path to ultimate destruction.

Point and Counterpoint

Command's published material reads more like a supermarket tabloid than a historical text.

For example, take the Navy's centuries-old administrative discipline for ridding itself of sunken, aged, and unwanted warships by striking them from the Navy Register. This was (and still is) standard practice. When the Command's goal orientation switched from documenting Navy history for public consumption, to exercising control over abandoned military and commercial craft, the Command decided that the process of "striking" had to be given a different meaning: one that conferred title to the civilians who run the Command, in order to justify their power ploy.

Yet the Command has never furnished documentation to support its prejudiced imposition. It merely *contends* that "striking" does not mean abandonment, without providing evidence to establish proof: a clear case of self-serving hearsay. In other words, the Command claims that that's the way it is because that's the way it wants it to be.

At the same time that the Command refutes the accepted meaning of "striking," it doesn't bother to give an alternative definition. "Striking" must mean something, yet the Command doesn't state what it wants the word to mean, or to have meant.

The fallacy of the Command's presumption is proven beyond a doubt by the 2005 "Sunken Military Craft" rider. If the Command truly believed that its ownership position was defensible, it would not have felt the need to pass redundant legislation.

Inherent in the rider is the Command's confession of the truth of the matter.

Staring Down Medusa

The Naval History and Heritage Command contends that wrecks are a limited resource and will be depleted if, for example, salvors are permitted to recover ditched and crashed aircraft; that instead these aircraft should be preserved in situ.

I have already demolished the pretense that wrecks

can be preserved under water or in open air, but because the Navy persists in deceiving the public and their congressional representatives with bureaucratic sophistry, it is necessary to remind my readers of the difference between wrecks and fossils.

Fossilization is a process in which organic material is gradually replaced by minerals so that the form of the original structure is preserved. In other words, under certain conditions, and over the course of tens of thousands or millions of years, bones that are buried before they decompose may turn into stone or rock. This stone or rock possesses none of the original organic material.

Preserved fossils. The Eocene fish (in sandstone above) is more than 33 million years old. The Devonian ammonite (below left) is more than 350 million years old. The Cambrian trilobite (below right) is half a billion years old. These fossils contain no original organic material. The Navy is trying to bamboozle the public with the illusion that, because the shapes of these prehistoric animals have been preserved in rock, manmade wrecks can also be preserved in situ: a make-believe analogy of incredible imbicility.

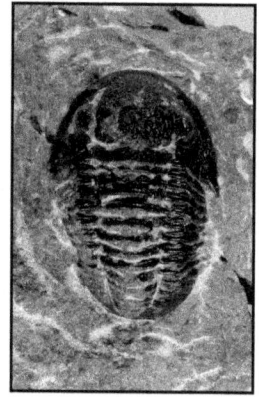

Point and Counterpoint

A fossil can endure forever in a sedimentary matrix because it is no longer organic tissue but, to state the obvious, stone or rock.

It is theoretically possible for a wooden hulled shipwreck to become fossilized, but only if it is buried immediately (before the onset of decomposition), and only under extraordinary circumstances that favor mineralization, and only after millions of years. In reality, wooden hulls decay until little or nothing remains but metal fasteners and other metallic parts. The proof of this is evident in Greek and Roman wreck sites, in which the only remains consist of ceramic cargoes. The timbers have long since been eaten by teredos (wood-boring mollusks) and seaborne bacteria.

Metal-hulled wrecks, both vessel and aircraft, start deteriorating immediately after abandonment due to the lack of protective maintenance. Everyone, even Navy historians, should know that floating vessels must be dry-docked periodically so as to have their hulls scraped clean of rust and scale, else the corrosion will eat through the steel plates. Then the hulls must be coated with one or more coats of heavy-duty marine paint.

Unless this ordinary maintenance is performed on wrecks, they rust away and collapse the same as abandoned buildings. The situation is worse for aircraft because they are constructed of much thinner material than armored steel, usually sheet aluminum, which soon becomes pockmarked by corrosion.

Land wrecks *can* be preserved in situ, but only by building a temperature-controlled structure around them. The only other way to preserve them is to move them into a building where they can receive constant care . . . such as a museum.

The Navy has no plans to rescue the thousands of land-locked aircraft that it wants to keep out of the hands of civilian museums which compete with the National Naval Aviation Museum for the tourist trade. The Navy would rather let abandoned aircraft rot and rust in place than allow recovery and restoration experts save them for posterity.

The same goes for shipwrecks and submerged aircraft. Again, submerged craft *can* be preserved in situ under water to a certain extent, but only if extraordinary measures are taken to care for them. Neglecting them serves only to ensure their ultimate destruction.

The best way to preserve a submerged wreck is to build a cofferdam around it. A cofferdam is an enclosure from which the water can be pumped in order to keep the wreck dry so that conservators can treat the remains with preservative chemicals. Cofferdams can be constructed of interlocking steel plates or large vertical tanks so placed as to completely encircle the wreck.

This is an expensive proposition. To build cofferdams around every wreck to which the Navy would like to claim ownership would cost more than the gross national product of the whole world for mankind's entire history, and take many times mankind's entire history to complete the project.

In any event, an evacuated cofferdam is only a stop-

The USS *Maine* sank in Havana Harbor, Cuba, in 1898, after a magazine exploded. A cofferdam was built around the battleship so that the hull could be examined. Note the cylindrical caissons that were butted together to create a watertight enclosure for the vessel.

Navy engineers determined that salvage was not worth the cost of repairs. The most intact portion of the wreck was patched temporarily, then towed offshore and scuttled.

(From a picture postcard.)

Point and Counterpoint

gap solution because it protects a wreck only from gross physical damage such as storm surge and deep ocean swells. To be fully protected from the ongoing processes of decay, a wreck must be completely enclosed from *all* the forces of nature, including the weather to which it will otherwise be exposed.

Cathodic protection can be implemented on iron- or steel-hulled wrecks and aluminum aircraft by the installation of sacrificial anodes. This method requires the emplacement of galvanic anodes (blocks of zinc, magnesium, or aluminum) in numerous places on the body of the wreck. Every small-boat owner knows about this process because every small boat is protected in this manner from the destructive process of galvanic action.

Protecting 17,000 wrecks might be possible – if only the Navy knew their locations and if the majority of the wrecks didn't lie hundreds or thousands of feet beneath the wave-ridden surface. If every diver in the world worked solely on this project, they might get the job completed in several thousand years.

Wooden-hulled wrecks can be partially preserved or protected by coating them with several layers of antifouling paint. Once again there is the problem of locating the wrecks to be painted, then employing divers and remotely operated vehicles to do the work. Plus, painting a wreck is much like painting a bridge: by the time the bridge is completely painted, it's time to start applying a new coat.

Lest my readers think that I am being facetious, compare the methods above with the Navy's sole approach to "preserving" wrecks by passing legislation. This is as stupid as repealing the law of gravity. Neither a shameless rider nor an Act of Congress can preserve wrecks of any kind from the brutal forces of nature.

When all is said and done, the Navy doesn't really want to preserve military craft; it just wants to prevent other people from preserving them. Rather than recover these priceless relics of the past, the Navy would have them left in situ until nature takes its course and utterly destroys them.

I reiterate: wrecks left unattended under water or on land are neither preserved nor protected for future generations to appreciate.

Nonetheless, in order to sell the product, the Navy keeps yapping about wrecks constituting a limited and irreplaceable resource: a resource that is depleted when, for example, recovery and restoration experts raise an aircraft, conserve it, and display it to the public.

This preservative action does not qualify as depleting a resource. Quite the opposite: the resource is depleted when it is left on the bottom or in a swamp or on a remote desert island, exposed to the destructive forces of nature, until nothing remains but particles of rust or aluminum powder.

The Navy's attitude is contrary to reason.

While it *may* be true that lost and sunken military craft constitute a non-renewable cultural resource, it is *definitely* true that those craft are a deteriorating resource when they are left to the caprices of nature and the Navy, and that soon they will not exist in any recognizable form, if they exist at all.

In reality, these resources are saved and preserved for future generations only when shipwrecks and aircraft (in whole or in part) are recovered and maintained in a controlled environment.

Before and after pictures of the *Tarpon's* conning tower: photographic proof that wrecks collapse. Restrictive legislation cannot prevent collapse and deterioration from occurring.

Point and Counterpoint

Grave Concerns

Another way in which the Navy attempts to sell its product is by sanctifying wrecked and sunken military craft as war graves. The Navy claims that "disturbing" a wreck is the same as disturbing a grave. This grievance is absurd. Furthermore, the Navy agrees that its own pronouncement is absurd.

Keep in mind that fatalities are not associated with every wreck. The dictionary defines "grave" as "any place of burial or final disposition." A wreck in which no fatalities occurred is therefore not a grave. Furthermore, a wreck in which the crew escaped but later perished is also not a grave. Yet Navy rhetoric poses this fallacious notion as a way to sway public sentiment toward its crusade for total control of abandoned military craft: as if every wreck were a shrine to be exalted for American fighting forces.

To put war graves in perspective, soldiers also died in tanks, jeeps, and deuce-and-a-halves; in trenches and foxholes; in houses and farm fields; in jungles and rice paddies. Not every place a soldier died becomes hallowed ground.

Damaged military vehicles may be scavenged for parts; or they may pushed aside in order to clear the way for traffic, or they may be towed to improvised junk yards where they are abandoned and forgotten.

The bodies of sailors who died aboard a warship that didn't sink after an attack were dumped overboard: a military expedience that is called burial at sea.

Marines who died during Pacific beach assaults were interred in unmarked jungle reaches.

My purpose is not to denigrate war graves, or soldiers and sailors and marines and pilots who died in the service of their country, but to illustrate that the Navy's argument in this regard is specious and self-serving.

Understand, too, that I make these correlations with the reverence of a disabled veteran who earned three Purple Hearts in Vietnam.

Now note that inherent in the guidelines that are promulgated by the Naval History and Heritage Command, the Navy has no objection to disturbing so-called sunken war graves . . . as long as permission to do is granted by the Command, and that the wreck is disturbed in accordance with archaeological procedure – which has nothing to do with reverence for the dead.

This double standard is made more ridiculous when the Navy's perception of wreck access and disturbance is compared with landside war graves, such as Arlington National Cemetery.

Fanning the sand or otherwise "disturbing" a wreck is equivalent only to crushing grass underfoot as visitors wander among grave sites in Arlington.

Moving or otherwise "disturbing" bits of wreckage is equivalent to picking up windblown trash at Arlington. It is not, as the Navy would like people to believe, the same as smashing headstones.

The Navy has twisted innocuous or productive activities, and redefined words and phrases to its advantage, yet willingly permits those same activities whenever the Navy benefits: such as when a recovered aircraft is donated to the National Naval Aviation Museum instead of to any other public or private museum.

In order to acquire a controlling interest in abandoned military craft, the Navy wants people to believe that when an American citizen raises an aircraft from incredibly deep water – where no one can ever see or appreciate it, or become aware of its existence – the action constitutes a destructive activity, even though the aircraft is restored, conserved, and displayed to the public. The Navy likens this patriotic activity to burning down a dying tree instead of leaving it in the forest to die and rot, when in reality the activity is equivalent to transplanting that tree to a place where it can be nurtured back to health.

According to the Navy's double standard, a civilian recovery is consecration, but a Navy recovery is preservation. If this makes it sound as if Captain Wrong Way Peachfuzz is at the helm of the Naval History and Heritage Command, so be it.

Navy Scams Recapitulated

I have never gone out of my way to research or investigate Navy improprieties. Everything that I have written about shipwrecks in this book has come about incidentally, during the course of ordinary historical research. I was tangentially aware of the Navy's lost aircraft persecutions because they were reported by the media.

The Navy aircraft debacles that I recorded, originated on the website of the Naval History and Heritage Command, where the facts were intentionally distorted so that circulated misinformation presented a false image of events to the public.

This wealth of accidental revelation makes me wonder – and should make my readers wonder – how many other gratuitous errors are embedded in published information that the Naval History and Heritage Command disseminates, and how many more Navy shenanigans are occurring behind the backs of the American people.

When I set out to ascertain the whereabouts of the *YMS-14*, I hoped to add an interesting piece of American history to the official record of events. I thought that the Naval History and Heritage Command would be ecstatic over my discovery. It never crossed my mind that the Navy would go to such extremes as to totally destroy this historic shipwreck: an unconscionable act of violence that violated the very cornerstone of historic preservation: the Command's avowed but tainted commitment.

Navy divers could easily have moved the decayed remains of the handful of depth charges to a distant location for disposal: the way the Navy moved and disposed of external torpedoes from the *U-352* nearly thirty years earlier.

Other contradictions abound. For example, the *G-1* was abandoned, stricken from the Navy Register, and – without being sold – raised by commercial salvors right in front of the Navy base in Newport, Rhode Island: literally under the eyes of Navy personnel. The Navy did not object.

The wreck of the *Cumberland* was filled with the

bodies of dead sailors, yet it was sold to a salvage outfit and commercially salvaged for treasure. In the twentieth century, the Navy was so eager to take possession of a handful of badly decayed trinkets and knick-knacks that had been recovered from the wreck in clam tongs and donated to a competing nautical museum, that a Navy admiral willingly committed perjury so as to swing judgment in favor of the Navy museum.

The *Florida* was captured illegally, then was scuttled as a way to avert repercussions from violating international law, and to avoid having to return the vessel to Brazil. Thereafter the wreck was abandoned. In the twentieth century, the Navy supported the prosecution of two clammers whose tongs accidentally brought up pieces of the wreck, and two memorabilia collectors who traded with the clammers. Either deliberately or otherwise, the Navy misidentified the wreck as a Union warship instead of a Confederate raider or privateer, the result of which circumvented the *Florida's* clouded history so that the Navy could claim ownership of the decomposed relics.

The Navy's case against the *Alabama's* bell was so immoral that both judges – the lower court judge and the appeals court judge – were incensed enough to vociferously denounce the Navy in their legal opinions and in the media, for preying upon a patriotic citizen who was solely responsible for obtaining the bell overseas and bringing it back the country. Later, when it was determined that the bell was a fake, the Navy refused to return the bell to the owner.

Although the Navy fought hard to win the *Alabama* bell case – going as far as to fabricate historical evidence and to introduce witnesses to give false testimony about it – after the *Hamilton* and *Scourge* were discovered, the Navy claimed ownership and then literally *gave away* the most well preserved and most historic warships that have ever been discovered: despite the fact that skulls and other skeletal remains lay scattered around the sites, as shown on underwater video footage.

Worse yet, the Navy never possessed title to the

Point and Counterpoint

Scourge: a fact that was clearly established in court. So the Navy gave away a wreck that it did not and never owned in the first place.

The Naval History and Heritage Command likes to claim that wrecks can be preserved in situ (in place). Yet Navy divers openly described how badly deteriorated they found the *U-352* after only thirty-eight years under water. For that matter, Navy divers observed even worse deterioration to the hull of the *San Diego*. Had it not been for gaping holes in the hull, and hull plates that had fallen off and were missing, Navy divers would not have had such easy access to the immediate interior where munitions were stored.

On a number of occasions, the Naval History and Heritage Command has written voluminous and exacting instructions regarding the survey of submerged wrecks. The Command demands that non-Navy archaeologists adhere strictly to these itemized archaeological guidelines. Yet when Navy divers excavated the *San Diego*, the *U-352*, and the *U-85* – to say nothing of totaling demolishing the *YMS-14* with explosives – these guidelines were completely ignored, and no Navy archaeologist was stationed on-site to oversee these destructive operations.

What is the point of the Navy writing reams and reams of archaeological guidelines if the Navy itself doesn't follow those guidelines? This is a clear case of "do as I say, not as I do."

Nor did anyone pay respect to the sailors whose skeletal remains were disturbed – even destroyed – by these massive intrusive activities.

The Command harps on the possibility that wrecks *may* – and I stress the word "may" – be war graves that should not be desecrated. Yet the worst wreck war grave desecration of all time was conducted by the Navy, on the *U-352*.

There is no difference between recreational scuba divers swimming across a shipwreck, and tourists walking on top of the *Arizona* memorial or through Arlington National Cemetery. The war-grave desecration pretense is a lame contrivance that the Navy invokes when it is to its advantage to do so.

If you ask an archaeologist – that is, a real working archaeologist, not a deskbound Navy quasi-historian – about the purpose of archaeology, you will be told that it is to obtain information that is unknown and otherwise unobtainable. The operative word here is "information."

What possible new information can the Navy hope to obtain from thousands of abandoned aircraft, when numerous aircraft of the same makes and models already grace aeronautical museums? The Navy's history of prosecution against aircraft recovery and restoration experts provides ample proof that archaeology is not the name of the Navy's game. The Navy is all about possession.

The Navy automatically claims title to every wreck that may have had some connection with the Navy before it sank, no matter how tenuous that connection may have been, then uses its unlimited funding and legal resources to prosecute discoverers and restoration and recovery experts who often do not have the money to defend their rights. The Navy seldom wins lawsuits on the merits of a case, but by concealing evidence, giving false testimony, browbeating defendants, hounding them unmercifully, wearing them down financially, or all of the above.

In civilian jurisprudence, a lawyer is considered to be an "officer of the court." As such, a civilian lawyer is pledged to uphold the law in a fair and honest manner. This doesn't appear to be the case with Navy lawyers.

The Naval History and Heritage Command is a juggernaut that is way out of control.

Denouement

Throughout this book I have repeatedly objected to the Naval History and Heritage Command's new but ingenuous, incorrect, and, under the circumstances, fraudulent interpretation of "striking or stricken from the Navy list" and "striking or stricken from the Register."

I repeatedly noted that the phrase signified official abandonment of vessels for which the Navy had no further use, in accordance with Congressional delegation of authority.

When the Navy is uncertain about the further use of a vessel, and wants to keep the vessel in case it might be needed in the future, that vessel is not – I repeat, *not* – stricken from the Navy list or Register

Such a vessel is decommissioned, taken out of service, and put into reserve. Vessels in the reserve fleet are "mothballed;" that is, they are laid up in an out-of-the-way location, sealed, and properly maintained. If the vessel is ever needed again, it is taken out of reserve, put back into service, and recommissioned.

The operative phrases are "decommissioned," "taken out of service," "put into reserve," "taken out of reserve," "put back into service," and "recommissioned."

Wrecked vessels and downed aircraft were never decommissioned and put into reserve, as the folks at the Naval History and Heritage Command would like the American people and their elected representatives to believe. They were abandoned.

The only confusion between these two official Navy actions is that which has been infused by the Command, in order to make it appear that the Navy never abandoned waterborne and airborne craft: a self-serving fiction that has no basis in fact or in Navy history.

The Lady or the Tiger?

Navy indifference to wreck preservation has contributed more to the collapse and ultimate disappearance of abandoned military craft than all the activities of recreational scuba divers, recreational anglers, and recovery and restoration experts in the world.

Continued Navy authoritarian rule and legislative hogwash will ensure that, instead of wrecks being discovered, recovered, restored, and displayed, they will remain lost, untreated, and destroyed by lack of attention.

Navy control freaks will be the winners. The American people will be the losers.

The Navy should get out of the business of wreck possession, and get back to the business of homeland security.

Congress should vote against the legislation that the Navy proposed in 2014.

Congress should repeal the rider that the Navy sneaked into the 2005 appropriations bill.

The Navy should replace the entire staff of the Naval History and Heritage Command with honest and competent historians who are untainted by the controlling disease of their predecessors, who will share public records with the public, and who will correct the multitudinous factual errors that are presently being foisted upon an unsuspecting public with regard to warship and Navy history.

A crossroad lies ahead. One path leads to Navy totalitarianism and the eventual loss of abandoned military craft. The other path leads to freedom for Americans to fish and explore, and to the preservation of military craft for future generations to honor and appreciate.

America must not hesitate to take the right path . . .

Shown below is a graphic image of how all sunken wrecks will look if they are left on the bottom for another hundred years. Remains do not remain forever, only temporarily.

Appendices

The Appendices in the following pages are reproduced verbatim in their entirety. I have deleted nothing: not a word, not a character. The only difference between the original publications and the following reprints is the formatting: this was necessitated by line width.

I copied the Navy's wish-list of restrictive regulations from the Internet, where line width was not limited by the printed page. The shorter line width on the following pages caused consecutive words in the original lines to break in different places. Thus printed paragraphs may occupy more lines than paragraphs on the Internet.

By the same token, page breaks are placed between different lines.

I did not alter the paragraph formatting: that is, I neither added nor deleted paragraphs. Any run-on paragraphs appeared that way in the original publication.

Occasionally there are lines that read "Back to Top." These words were printed in the original Internet publication. They refer to an Internet formatting protocol in which a link enabled the reader to go straight to the top of a screen page without passing Go and without collecting $200.

I let the phrase "Back to Top" remain in place so I could state categorically that I did not alter any of the original text.

In this regard, I copied and pasted all the text so as not to introduce any typographical errors. Any misspellings or grammatical misconstructions in the following Appendices are inherent in the original text.

The Appendices are not indexed.

As they say about romance novels, read it and weep.

[Federal Register Volume 64, Number 223 (Friday, November 19, 1999)]
[Proposed Rules]
[Pages 63263-63266]
From the Federal Register Online via the Government Printing Office [www.gpo.gov]
[FR Doc No: 99-30079]

[[Page 63263]]

==

DEPARTMENT OF DEFENSE
Department of the Navy
32 CFR Part 767
RIN 0703-AA57

Application Guidelines for Underwater Archeological Research Permits on Submerged Cultural Resources Under the Jurisdiction of the Department of the Navy

AGENCY: Department of the Navy, DOD.

ACTION: Notice of proposed rulemaking.

SUMMARY: The Department of the Navy (DON) proposes to issue underwater archeological research permits to those applying for permission to recover and/or conduct research on any submerged cultural resource, ship or aircraft wreck, under the jurisdiction of the DON. This action will assist the Navy in managing and protecting its historic underwater cultural resources. This rule will provide clear guidance on the permit application requirements to recover and/or conduct research on submerged Navy properties.

DATES: Submit comments on or before January 18, 2000.

ADDRESSES: Address all comments concerning this rule to

Appendix 1

Department of the Navy
U.S. Naval Historical Center
Office of the Underwater Archeologist
Building 1, Washington Navy Yard
805 Kidderbreese Ave. SE
Washington DC 20374-5060
Telefax number: 202-433-2729.
Please cite ``Application Guidelines for Underwater Archeological Research Permits."

FOR FURTHER INFORMATION CONTACT
Dr. Robert S. Neyland, Underwater Archeologist, or Barbara A. Voulgaris, 202-433-2210.

SUPPLEMENTARY INFORMATION:

Background

a. In 1993, DON initiated an archeological management program for its historic ship and aircraft wreck sites. This was aided in part by the U.S. Department of Defense (DoD) Legacy Resource Management Program that was established by Congress in 1991, 10 U.S.C. 114, to provide DoD with an opportunity to enhance the management of DoD stewardship resources. The U.S. Naval Historical Center's (NHC) Office of Underwater Archeology is the Navy command responsible for managing the Navy's submerged cultural resource properties under the guidelines of the Federal Archeological Program.

b. Under the National Historic Preservation Act of 1966 as amended (NHPA), 16 U.S.C. 470 (1999), DON is obligated to protect historic properties, including ship and aircraft wrecks, for which it has custodial responsibilities. The NHPA directs federal agencies to manage their cultural resource properties in a way that emphasizes preservation and minimizes the impact of undertakings that might adversely affect such properties. Management of DON cultural resources such as ship and aircraft wrecks is not simply a matter of preservation. The issues of gravesites, unexploded ordnance, and potential military usage of recovered weapons systems must also be addressed in wrecksite management.

Appendix 1

Custody and Management of Navy Shipwrecks and Aircraft Wrecksites

a. DON submerged shipwrecks and aircraft wrecks are government property in the custody of the Navy. These seemingly abandoned wrecks remain government property until specific formal action is taken to dispose of them. Navy custody of its wrecks is based on the property clause of the U.S. Constitution and international maritime law, and is consistent with Articles 95 and 96 of the Law of the Sea Convention. These laws establish that right, title, or ownership of Federal property is not lost to the government due to the passage of time. Navy ships and aircraft cannot be abandoned without formal action as authorized by Congress. Aircraft and ships stricken from the active inventory list are not considered formally disposed of or abandoned. Through the sovereign immunity provisions of admiralty law, DON retains custody of all its naval vessels and aircraft, whether lost in U.S., foreign, or international boundaries.

b. Divers may dive on Navy wrecks at their own risk; however, Federal property law dictates that no portion of a government wreck may be disturbed or removed. The Navy strongly encourages cooperation with other agencies and individuals interested in preserving our maritime and aviation heritage. Diving on sunken Navy ships and aircraft located in units of the national park system or the national marine sanctuary system may be prohibited unless authorized by a Federal land manager.

c. The diving public is encouraged to report the location of underwater ship and aircraft wrecksites to the NHC. Documentation of these wreck locations allows the Navy to evaluate and preserve important sites for the future. Under no circumstances will salvage of Navy aircraft or shipwrecks be undertaken without prior and specific written approval by the NHC.

d. Wrecksites that are not entire aircraft or ships, but are parts strewn in a debris field, are considered potential archeological sites. Such sites still contain Navy property and must be managed by the Navy in accordance with the NHPA, the Secretary of the Interior's Standards and Guidelines on Archeology and Historic Preservation, 48 FR 44716 (1983), and de-

Appendix 1

partmental regulations. Permits for recovery of submerged Navy ship or aircraft wrecks will be considered only for educational or scientific reasons. It is unlikely DON will recommend the disposal and sale of a Navy ship or aircraft wreck that is eligible for listing on the National Register of Historic Places. The Navy maintains a policy of not disposing wrecked ships and aircraft for the following reasons:

1. Congress has mandated through the NHPA that the DON make every effort to preserve its historic cultural resources;

2. The remains of crewmembers, if any, deserve to be treated with honor and dignity and to be properly retrieved for burial if possible;

3. There is a possibility that live explosives or ordnance may still be associated with the vessel or aircraft;

4. The arbitrary disposal and sale of wrecks may foster commercial exploitation of cultural resources and;

5. The abandonment of wrecks could deplete a finite inventory of significant cultural resources.

e. Because of the large number of aircraft wrecks and because they are generally easier to recover and conserve than shipwrecks, DON does consider and encourage requests for loans of historic aircraft. Museums or other private parties interested in the recovery of Navy aircraft for educational or scientific purposes should contact the NHC for guidance.

List of Subjects in 32 CFR Part 767

Aircraft, Archeology, Educational research, Government property, Government property management, Historic preservation, Permit, Research, Scientific research, Vessel.

For the reasons stated in the preamble, the Department of the Navy proposes to add 32 CFR part 767 to read as follows:

[[Page 63264]]

PART 767--APPLICATION GUIDELINES FOR UNDERWATER ARCHEOLOGICAL RESEARCH PERMITS ON SUBMERGED CULTURAL RESOURCES UNDER THE JURISDICATION OF THE DEPARTMENT OF THE NAVY

Subpart A--Regulations and Obligations

Sec.
767.1 Purpose.
767.2 Definitions.
767.3 Policy.

Subpart B--Permit Guidelines

767.4 Application for permit.
767.5 Evaluation of permit application.
767.6 Credentials of principal investigator.
767.7 Conditions of permits.
767.8 Requests for amendments or extensions of active permits.
767.9 Content of permit holder's final report.
767.10 Monitoring of performance.
767.11 Violations of permit conditions.
767.12 References for submission of permit application to conduct archeological research.

Authority: 5 U.S.C. 301; 16 U.S.C. 470.

Subpart A--Regulations and Obligations

Sec. 767.1 Purpose.

(a) The purpose of this part is to establish the requirement and procedural guidelines for permits to recover and/or conduct research on Department of the Navy (DON) submerged cultural resources.

(b) The U.S. Naval Historical Center's (NHC) Office of Underwater Archeology is the Navy command responsible for managing Navy submerged cultural resource properties under the guidelines of the Federal Archeological Program. In order for the NHC's management policy to be consistent with the Federal Archeology Program, and the goals of the NHPA, the Navy has implemented a permitting process applicable to Navy property consistent with and applying the Archeological Resources Protection Act of 1979 (ARPA), 16 U.S.C. 470aa-

Appendix 1

470ll (1999), permitting criteria. Navy policies regarding its submerged cultural resources, to include ship and aircraft wrecks are consistent with ARPA permitting requirements. Navy application of ARPA permitting criteria promotes consistency among federal agencies and meets the Navy's responsibilities under the NHPA, while allowing qualified non-federal and private individuals and entities access to Navy historic vessel and aircraft wrecks.

(c) To assist NHC in managing, protecting, and preserving DON submerged cultural resources.

Sec. 767.2 Definitions.

Aircraft wrecksite means the location where an aircraft has been crashed, ditched, damaged, or stranded. The wreck may be intact or scattered, may be on land or in water, and may be a structure or a site.

Archeological site means the location of a significant event, historic occupation or activity, or a building or structure including aircraft or shipwrecks, whether standing, ruined, or vanished, and its debris field where the location itself retains historical or archeological value regardless of the value of any existing structure.

Artifact means any object or assemblage of objects found in an archeological context that yields or is likely to yield information of significance to the scientific study of culture or human history.

Cultural resource means the remains or records of districts, sites, structures, buildings, networks, objects, and events from the past. They may be historic, archeological, or architectural in nature. Cultural resources are an irreplaceable and nonrenewable aspect of our national heritage.

Gravesite means any natural or prepared physical location, whether originally below, on, or above the surface of the earth, where individual human remains are deposited.

Permit holder means any person authorized and given the exclusive right by the NHC to conduct any activity under these regulations.

Permitted activity means any activity that is authorized by the NHC under these regulations.

Research vessel means any vessel employed for scientific purposes under these regulations.

Shipwreck means the physical remains of a vessel, its cargo, and other contents.

Wrecksite means the location of a ship or aircraft that has been sunk, crashed, ditched, damaged, or stranded. The wreck may be intact or scattered, may be on land or in water, and may be a structure or a site. The site includes the physical remains of the wreck and all other associated artifacts.

Sec. 767.3 Policy.

(a) The NHC's policy has been to evaluate each Navy submerged cultural resource on an individual basis. In some cases, the removal of Navy submerged cultural resources may be necessary or appropriate to protect the resource and/or to fulfill other NHC goals, such as those encompassing research, education, public access, and appreciation. Recovery of Navy submerged cultural resources may be justified in specific cases where the existence of a resource may be threatened. Therefore, recovery of some or all of a resource may be permitted for identification and/or investigation to answer specific questions; or the recovery presents an opportunity for public research or education.

(b) Generally, submerged Navy cultural resources will be left in place unless artifact removal or site disturbance is justified and necessary to protect Navy cultural resources, to conduct research, or provide public education and information that is otherwise inaccessible. While the NHC prefers non-destructive, in situ research on submerged Navy shipwrecks and aircraft wrecks, it recognizes that site disturbance and/or artifact recovery is sometimes necessary. At such times, site disturbance and/or archeological recovery may be permitted, subject to conditions specified by NHC.

Subpart B--Permit Guidelines

Sec. 767.4 Application for permit.

(a) To request a permit application form, please write to:

Appendix 1

Department of the Navy
U.S. Naval Historical Center
Office of the Underwater Archeologist, Building 1
Washington Navy Yard
805 Kidderbreese Ave. SE
Washington DC 20374-5060
Telefax number: 202-433-2729

(b) Applicants must submit three copies of their completed application at least 90 days in advance of the requested effective date to allow sufficient time for evaluation and processing. Requests should be sent to the

Underwater Archeologist of the U.S. Navy
Naval Historical Center
Washington Navy Yard
805 Kidderbreese Ave. SE
Washington, DC 20374-5060

(c) If the applicant believes that compliance with one or more of the factors, criteria, or procedures in the guidelines contained in this part is not practicable, the applicant should set forth why and explain how the purposes of the NHC are better served without compliance with the specified requirements. Permits are valid for six months from the issue date.

Sec. 767.5 Evaluation of permit application.

(a) Permit applications for archeological research are reviewed for completeness, compliance with program policies, and adherence to these guidelines. Incomplete applications will be returned to the applicant for clarification. Complete applications are reviewed by NHC personnel and, when necessary, outside experts. In addition to the criteria set forth in Sec. 767.6. applications are also judged on the basis of: relevance or importance; archeological merits; appropriateness and environmental consequences of technical approach; whether the proposed effort would be more appropriately conducted outside of the NHC; and qualifications of the applicants.

(b) Under certain circumstances, it may be necessary to

consult with the State Historic Preservation Officer (SHPO) and the Advisory Council on Historic Preservation (ACHP) about the need to comply with section 106 of the NHPA. A section 106 review requires the NHC to consult with the appropriate SHPO and the ACHP. The ACHP review can take up to 60 days beyond the NHC's required 90-day review. Therefore, the entire review process may take up to 150 days.

(c) Applications for research at sites located in units of the National Park system, national wildlife refuge system, and national marine sanctuary system, shall be sent to the appropriate Federal land manager for review. Applications for research at sites located on state bottomlands should be sent to the appropriate state agency for review. The burden of obtaining any and all additional permits or authorizations, such as from a state or foreign government or agency, private individual or organization, or from another federal agency, is on the applicant.

(d) Based on the findings of the NHC evaluation, the NHC Underwater Archeologist will recommend an appropriate action to the NHC Director. If approved, the NHC will issue the permit; if denied, applicants are notified of the reason for denial and may appeal within 30 days of receipt of the denial. Appeals must be submitted in writing to:

Director of Naval History
Naval Historical Center
805 KidderBreese Ave. SE
Washington, DC 20374-5060.

Sec. 767.6 Credentials of principal investigator.

A resume or curriculum vitae detailing the professional qualifications and professional publications and papers of the principal investigator (PI) must be submitted with the permit application. The PI must have: a graduate degree in archeology, anthropology, maritime history, or a closely related field; at least one year of professional experience or equivalent specialized training in archeological research, administration or management; at least four months of supervised field and analytic experience in general North American historic archaeology and maritime history; the demonstrated ability to carry

Appendix 1

research to completion; and at least one year of full-time professional experience at a supervisory level in the study of historic marine archeological resources. This person shall be able to demonstrate ability in comprehensive analysis and interpretation through authorship of reports and monographs.

Sec. 767.7 Conditions on permits.

(a) Upon receipt of a permit, permit holders must countersign the permit and return copies to the NHC and the applicable SHPO prior to conducting permitted activities on the site. Copies of countersigned permits should also be provided to the applicable federal land manager when the sunken vessel or aircraft is located within a unit of the national park system, the national wildlife refuge system, or the national marine sanctuary system.

(b) Permits must be carried aboard research vessels and made available upon request for inspection to regional preservation personnel or law enforcement officials. Only persons named in the permit may participate in permitted activities. Permits are non-transferable. Permit holders must abide by all provisions set forth in the permit as well as applicable state or Federal regulations. Permit holders should abide by applicable regulations of a foreign government when the sunken vessel or aircraft is located in foreign waters. To the extent reasonably possible, the environment must be returned to the condition that existed before the activity occurred.

(c) Upon completion of permitted activities, the permit holder is required to submit to the NHC a working and diving log listing days spent in field research, activities pursued, and working area positions.

(d) The permit holder must prepare and submit a final report as detailed in Sec. 767.9, summarizing the results of the permitted activity.

(e) The permit holder must agree to protect all sensitive information regarding the location and character of the wreck site that could potentially expose it to non-professional recovery techniques, looters, or treasure hunters. Sensitive information includes specific location data such as latitude and longitude, and information about a wreck's cargo, the existence of armaments, or the knowledge of gravesites.

(f) All recovered DON cultural resources remain the property of the United States. These resources and copies of associated archaeological records and data will be preserved by a suitable university, museum, or other scientific or educational institution.

Sec. 767.8 Requests for amendments or extensions of active permits.

(a) Requests for amendments to active permits (e.g., a change in study design or other form of amendment) should conform to these guidelines. All necessary information to make an objective evaluation of the amendment should be included as well as reference to the original application.

(b) Permit holders desiring to continue research activities must reapply for an extension of their current permit before it expires. A pending extension or amendment request does not guarantee extension or amendment of the original permit. Therefore, you must submit an extension request to the NHC at least 30 days prior to the original permit's expiration date. Reference to the original application may be given in lieu of a new application, provided the scope of work does not change significantly. Applicants may apply for no more than two six-month extensions.

(c) Permit holders may appeal denied requests for amendments or extensions to the appeal authority listed in Sec. 767.5.

Sec. 767.9 Content of permit holder's final report.

The permit holder's final report shall include the following:

(a) A site history and a contextual history relating the site to the general history of the region;

(b) A master site map;

(c) Feature map(s) of the location of any recovered artifacts in relation to their position within the wrecksite;

(d) Photographs of significant site features and significant artifacts both in situ and after removal;

(e) A description of the conservation of artifact lists, labora-

Appendix 1

tory conservation records, and before and after photographs of significant artifacts at the conservation laboratory;

(f) A written report describing the historical background, environment, archeological field work, results, and analysis;

(g) A summary of the survey and/or excavation process;

(h) An evaluation of the completed permitted activity that includes an assessment of the permit holder's success of his/her specified goals.

Sec. 767.10 Monitoring of performance.

Permitted activities will be monitored to ensure compliance with the conditions of the permit. NHC on-site personnel, or other designated authorities, may periodically assess work in progress by visiting the study location and observing any activity allowed by the permit or by reviewing any required reports. The discovery of any potential irregularities in performance under the permit will be promptly reported and appropriate action will be taken. Permitted activities will be evaluated and the findings will be used to evaluate future applications.

Sec. 767.11 Violations of permit conditions.

The Director of the NHC, the Underwater Archeologist for DON, or his/her designee may amend, suspend, or revoke a permit in whole or in part, temporarily or indefinitely, if in his/her view the permit holder has acted in violation of the terms of the permit or of other applicable regulations, or for other good cause shown. Any such action will be communicated in writing to the permit holder and will set forth the reason for the action taken. The permit holder may appeal the action to the appeal authority listed in Sec. 767.5.

Sec. 767.12 References for submission of permit application to conduct archeological research.

(a) National Historic Preservation Act of 1966, as amended (NHPA), 16 U.S.C. 470 et seq. (1999), and Protection of Historic Properties, 36 CFR part 800 (1999). These regulations govern the Section 106 Review Process established by the NHPA.

(b) Secretary of the Interior's Standards and Guidelines for Archeology and Historic Preservation, 48 FR 44716 (1983). This publication establishes standards for the preservation planning process with guidelines on implementation.

(c) Archeological Resources Protection Act of 1979, as amended (ARPA), 16 U.S.C. 470aa et seq. (1999), and the Uniform Regulations, ARPA, 43 CFR part 7 (1998). These regulations establish basic government-wide standards for the issuance of permits for archeological research, including the authorized excavation and/or removal of archeological resources on public lands or Indian lands.

(d) Secretary of the Interior's Curation of Federally-Owned and Administered Archeological Collections, 36 CFR part 79 (1999). This publication establishes standards for the curation and display of federally-owned artifact collections.

(e) Antiquities Act of 1906, Pub. L. No. 59-209, 34 Stat. 225 (codified at 16 U.S.C. 431 et seq. (1999)).

(f) Executive Order No. 11593, 36 FR 8291, 3 CFR, 1971-1975 Comp., p. 559 (Protection and Enhancement of the Cultural Environment).

(g) Department of Defense Instruction 4140.21M (DoDI 4120.21M, August 1998). Subject: Defense Disposal Manual.

(h) Secretary of the Navy Instruction 4000.35 (SECNAVINST 4000.35, 17 August 1992). Subject: Department of the Navy Cultural Resources Program.

(i) Naval Historical Center Instruction 5510.4. (NAVHISTCENINST 5510.4, 14 December 1995). Subject: Disclosure of Information from the Naval Shipwreck Database. Christopher G. Carlson, Major, USMC, Alternate Federal Register Liaison Officer. [FR Doc. 99-30079 Filed 11-18-99; 8:45 am] BILLING CODE 3810-FF-P

Appendix 2

Archaeological Research Permit Application Guidelines
for
Ship and Aircraft Wrecks under the Jurisdiction of the
Department of the Navy

Policy

As stewards of the Navy's historic military craft, the Naval History & Heritage Command (NHHC) is responsible for managing these irreplaceable resources for the continued education and enjoyment of present and future generations. To ensure consistent and effective stewardship, the NHHC developed a comprehensive program that encompasses the following categories: preservation planning; wrecksite management; underwater archaeological research; conservation; curation; and public information, interpretation, and education. The NHHC strongly encourages cooperation with other agencies and individuals interested in preserving our maritime and aviation heritage.

Wrecked military craft will generally be left in place unless wrecksite disturbance or artifact removal is justified and necessary to protect the wrecksite, to conduct research, or provide public education and information that is otherwise inaccessible. While NHHC prefers non☐destructive, in situ research on wrecked military craft, it recognizes that disturbance and/or artifact recovery may become necessary. At such times, wrecksite disturbance and/or artifact recovery may be permitted, subject to conditions specified by NHHC as set forth in these regulations.

Permit Applications

Application forms are available on line at www.history.navy.mil or by writing to:

Department of the Navy
Naval History & Heritage Command
Underwater Archaeology Branch
805 Kidder Breese St., SE
Washington Navy Yard, DC 20374-5060.
Telefax number: 202-433-2729.

- Applicants must submit two (2) copies of their completed application at least 120 days in advance of the requested effective date to allow sufficient time for evaluation and processing.
-

Each permit application shall include:

A statement of research objectives, scientific methods, and significance of the proposed work to a particular geographical area. This should include discussion articulating clearly the archaeological, historical, or educational purposes of the proposed activity;

A summary of significant previous work in the area of interest;

A discussion of how the proposed activity could disturb, remove, or injure the wrecksite and the related physical environment;

A discussion of the methodology planned to accomplish the project's objectives. This should include a map showing the study location(s) and a description of the wrecksite(s) of particular interest;

An analysis of the extent and nature of potential environmental impacts on the resources from permitted activities, and any permits or authorizations required by foreign, federal, state, or local law;

A detailed plan for wrecksite restoration and remediation with recommendations on wrecksite preservation and protection of wrecksite location;

In addition, to identification of the Principal Investigator (PI), identification of all other members of the research team and their qualifications;

Sufficient data to substantiate, to the satisfaction of the NHHC, the applicant's financial capability to complete the proposed research and, if applicable, any conservation and curation costs;

Appendix 2

A proposed outlet for public dissemination of the results;

Where the application is for the excavation and/or removal of artifacts from a wrecksite, or the application is for the excavation and/or removal of the entire military craft:

A conservation plan and the name of the university, museum or laboratory, or other scientific or educational institution in which the material will be conserved, including written certification, signed by an authorized official of the institution, of willingness to assume conservation responsibilities must be included.

The name of the facility in which the recovered materials and copies of associated records derived from the work will be preserved. This will include written certification, signed by an authorized official of the institution, of willingness to assume curatorial responsibilities for the collection and to safeguard and preserve the materials as the property of the United States.

- The applicant is responsible for all conservation and curation costs, and for ensuring that the named repository meets the standards set forth in 36 CFR Part 79, Curation of Federally-Owned and Administered Archaeological Collections.

If the applicant believes that compliance with one or more of the factors, criteria, or procedures in the guidelines contained in the application are not practicable, the applicant should outline their objections, providing evidence to support their assertions, and explain how the purposes of NHHC are better served without compliance with the specified requirements. If the NHHC determines that the purposes of the Navy, its regulations, and its policies are better served without compliance, the NHHC will provide a written waiver to the applicant.

- Permits are valid for one year from the issue date.

Evaluation of Permit Applications
Permit applications are reviewed for completeness, compli-

ance with program policies, and adherence to the stated guidelines. Incomplete applications will be returned to the applicant for clarification. Complete applications are reviewed by NHHC personnel and, when necessary, outside experts. Applications are also judged on the basis of: relevance or importance of the proposed project; archaeological, historical or educational purposes; appropriateness; environmental consequences of technical approach; and qualifications of the applicants relative to the type and scope of the work proposed.

The NHHC shall send applications for research at sites located in units of the national park system, national wildlife refuge system, and national marine sanctuary system to the appropriate Federal resource manager for review. The applicable Federal land manager is responsible for ensuring that the proposed work is consistent with any management plan or established policy, objectives or requirements applicable to the federal management of the lands and waters concerned.

NHHC will send applications for research at wrecksites located on state bottomlands to the appropriate state agency for review.

The burden of obtaining any and all additional permits or authorizations, such as from a state or foreign government or agency, private individual or organization, or from another federal agency, is on the applicant.

Based on the findings of the NHHC evaluation, NHHC personnel will recommend an appropriate action to the NHHC Director. If approved, NHHC will issue the permit; if denied, applicants are notified of the reason for denial and denials may be appealed within 30 days of receipt of the denial. Appeals must be submitted in writing to:

Department of the Navy
Director of Naval History
Naval History & Heritage Command
805 Kidder Breese St., SE
Washington Navy Yard, DC 20374-5060

Appendix 2

Telefax number: 202-433-2729

Credentials of Principal Investigator

The principal investigator (PI) shall be suitably qualified as evidenced by training, education, and/or experience, and possess demonstrable competence in archaeological theory and method, and in collecting, handling, analyzing, evaluating, and reporting archaeological data, relative to the type and scope of the work proposed.

The PI must meet the following minimum requirements:
A graduate degree in archaeology, anthropology, maritime history, or a closely related field, or equivalent training and experience;

The demonstrated ability to plan, equip, staff, organize, and supervise the type and scope of activity proposed;

At least 16 months of full-time professional field experience at a supervisory level in the study of historic maritime archaeological resources or historic aviation archaeological resources, to include at least four months of supervisory field and analytic experience in the specific time period or subject matter of the work proposed;

The demonstrated ability to carry research to completion as evidenced by the timely submission of reports.

Conditions on Permits
Upon receipt of a permit, permit holders must counter-sign the permit and return one copy each to the NHHC and the applicable State Historic Preservation Office (SHPO), Federal or State land manager, or foreign government official prior to conducting permitted activities on the wrecksite. When the sunken military craft is located within a unit of the national park system, the national wildlife refuge system, or the national marine sanctuary system, copies of countersigned permits shall be provided to the applicable Federal resource manager.

-

Permits must be carried aboard research vessels and made available upon request for inspection to regional preservation personnel or law enforcement officials. Permits are non-transferable. Permit holders must abide by all provisions set forth in the permit as well as applicable state or Federal regulations. Permit holders should abide by applicable regulations of a foreign government when the sunken vessel or aircraft is located in the internal waters, territorial sea, or contiguous zone of a foreign nation, as defined by customary international law as reflected in the United Nations Convention on the Law of the Sea. To the extent reasonably possible, if the physical environment is impacted by the permitted activity, it must be returned to the condition that existed before the permitted activity occurred.

Upon completion of permitted activities, the permit holder shall submit to NHHC a work log/summary, listing days spent in field research, activities pursued, work area positions, and if applicable, a dive log summarizing dive personnel and specifics of each dive. Dive logs should use the "Command Smooth Diving Log" form found in the U.S. Navy Diving Manual (SS521-AG-PRO-010, 0910-LP-708-8000 REVISION 4, 20 January 1999, Change A dated 1 March 2001. A copy of this form is also available on line at www.history.navy.mil in the Underwater Archaeology Branch section.

The permit holder must prepare and submit a final report summarizing the results of the permitted activity to the NHHC, and the applicable SHPO, Federal or State resource manager, or foreign government official.

The permit holder's final report shall include the following:

A site history and a contextual history relating the site to the general history of the region

A master site map of the entire site and a project area map, indicating where the site is in relation to nearby landmarks

Site location datum should be in World Geographic System

Appendix 2

(WGS) 84 in the format of latitude/longitude. Any and all pertinent geographical information system data should be included

Feature map(s) of any recovered artifacts showing their positions within the wrecksite

Photographs of significant site features and significant artifacts both in situ and after removal

If applicable, a conservation report that includes an inventory of recovered artifacts, description of the conserved artifacts, laboratory conservation records, and photographs of the artifacts before and after conservation treatment

A written report describing the wrecksite's historical background, environment, archaeological field work, results, and analysis

A summary of the survey and/or excavation process

An evaluation of the completed permitted activity that includes an assessment of the permit holder's success of the project's specified goals.

Identification of any sensitive information that should be protected and withheld from public disclosure.

The permit holder shall agree to protect all sensitive information regarding the location and character of the wreck site that could potentially expose it to non☐professional recovery techniques, looters, or treasure hunters. Sensitive information includes specific location data such as latitude and longitude, and information about a wreck's cargo, the existence of armaments, or the knowledge of gravesites. Sensitive cargo information might include hazardous materials other than munitions.

All recovered DoN cultural resources remain the property of the United States. These resources and copies of associated archaeological records and data must be preserved by a suitable university, museum, or other scientific or educational institution that meets the standards set forth in 36 CFR 79, Curation of Federally Owned and Administered Archaeological Collections, at the expense of the applicant. Copies of associated archaeological records and data will be made available to the NHHC, and to the applicable SHPO, the Federal or State resource manager, or foreign government official upon request.

In the event that human remains are discovered, the permit holder shall cease all work and immediately notify the NHHC. Permitted work may not resume until permitted by the NHHC.

Requests for Amendments or Extensions of Active Permits
Requests for amendments to active permits (e.g., a change in study design or other form of amendment) should be directed to:

Department of the Navy
Director of Naval History
Naval History & Heritage Command
805 Kidder Breese St., SE
Washington Navy Yard, DC 20374-5060
Telefax number: 202-433-2729

All information deemed necessary by the NHHC to make an objective evaluation of the amendment must be included as well as reference to the original application.

Permit holders desiring to extend research activities must apply for an extension of their current permit before it expires. A pending extension or amendment request does not guarantee extension or amendment of the original permit. All requests for a permit extension must be submitted to the NHHC at least 30 days prior to the original permit's expiration date. Reference to the original application may be given in lieu of a new application, provided the scope of work does not change significantly. Applicants may apply for one-year extensions subject to annual review.

Appendix 2

Permit holders may appeal denied requests for amendments or extensions may appeal the decision. Appeals must be submitted in writing to:

Department of the Navy
Director of Naval History
Naval History & Heritage Command
805 Kidder Breese St., SE
Washington Navy Yard, DC 20374-5060
Telefax number: 202-433-2729

Monitoring of performance
Permitted activities will be monitored to ensure compliance with the conditions of the permit. NHHC on site personnel, or other designated authorities, may periodically assess work in progress by visiting the study location and observing any activity allowed by the permit or by reviewing any required reports. The discovery of any potential irregularities in performance under the permit will be promptly reported and appropriate action will be taken. Any such action will be communicated in writing to the permit holder and will set forth the reason for the action taken. Findings will be taken into consideration when evaluating future applications.

Violations of Permit Conditions
The Director of Naval History, or his/her designee may amend, suspend, or revoke a permit in whole or in part, temporarily or indefinitely, if in his/her view the permit holder has acted in violation of the terms of the permit or of other applicable regulations, or for other good cause shown. Any such action will be communicated in writing to the permit holder and will set forth the reason for the action taken. The permit holder may appeal the action. Appeals must be submitted in writing to:

Director of Naval History
Naval Historical Center
805 Kidder Breese St. SE
Washington, DC 20374-5060.
Telefax number: 202-433-2729

References for Submission of Permit Application

National Historic Preservation Act of 1966, as amended (NHPA),16 U.S.C. 470 et seq. (1999), and Protection of Historic Properties, 36 CFR part 800 (1999). These regulations govern the Section 106 Review Process established by the NHPA.

Secretary of the Interior's Standards and Guidelines for Archaeology and Historic Preservation, 48 FR 44716 (1983). This publication establishes standards for the preservation planning process with guidelines on implementation.

Archaeological Resources Protection Act of 1979, as amended (ARPA), 16 U.S.C. 470aa–mm, and the Uniform Regulations, ARPA, 43 CFR part 7 (1998). These regulations establish basic government–wide standards for the issuance of permits for archaeological research, including the authorized excavation and/or removal of archaeological resources on public or Indian lands.

Secretary of the Interior's Curation of Federally–Owned and Administered Archaeological Collections, 36 CFR part 79 (1999). This publication establishes standards for the curation and display of federally–owned collections of artifacts and associated documentation.

Antiquities Act of 1906, Pub. L. No. 59–209, 34 Stat. 225 (codified at 16 U.S.C. 431 et seq. (1999)).

Executive Order No. 11593, 36 FR 8291, 3 CFR, 1971–1975 Comp., p. 559 (Protection and Enhancement of the Cultural Environment).

Department of Defense Instruction 4140.21M (DoDI 4120.21M, August 1998). Subject: Defense Disposal Manual.

Secretary of the Navy Instruction 4000.35A (SECNAVINST 4000.35A, 9 April 2001). Subject: Department of the Navy Cultural Resources Program.

Appendix 2

Naval History & Heritage Command Instruction 5510.4. (NAVHISTCENINST 5510.4, 14 December 1995). Subject: Disclosure of Information from the Naval Shipwreck Database.

Definitions
Aircraft wreck means the physical remains of a vessel, intact or otherwise, its cargo, and other contents. Shipwrecks are classified as either historic structures or archaeological sites.

Archaeological site means a place, or group of physical sites, in which evidence of past human activity is preserved (either prehistoric, historic or contemporary), and which has been, or may be, investigated using archaeological techniques. A wreck site of a military craft, along with its debris field, has the potential to become an archaeological site when archaeological research methods are used for investigation and possible recovery of the wreck site.

Artifact means any portion of a military craft that is by itself or through its relationship to another object or assemblage of objects, regardless of age, whether in situ or not, that may carry archaeological or historical information that yields or is likely to yield information to the scientific study of culture or human history.

Cultural resource means any prehistoric or historic district, archaeological site, historic site, building, structure, or object, including artifacts, records, and material remains.

Gravesite means any natural or prepared physical location, whether originally below, on, or above the surface of the earth, where individual human remains are deposited.

Historic Structure means a structure made up of interdependent and interrelated parts in a definite pattern or organization. Constructed by humans, it is often an engineering project large in scale. An aircraft wreck or shipwreck is a historic structure when it is relatively intact and when it and its location retain historical, architectural, or associative value.

Permit holder means any person authorized and given the exclusive right by the NHHC to conduct any activity under these regulations.

Permitted activity means any activity that is authorized by the NHHC under these regulations.

Research vessel means any vessel employed for scientific purposes under these regulations.

Ship wreck means the physical remains of a vessel, intact or otherwise, its cargo, and other contents. Shipwrecks are classified as either historic structures or archaeological sites.

Wrecksite means the location of a military craft. The craft may be intact, scattered or completely deteriorated. The wreck site includes any physical remains of the military craft and all associated contents.

Appendix 3

H.R. 4200

Ronald W. Reagan National Defense Authorization Act for Fiscal Year 2005
(Enrolled as Agreed to or Passed by Both House and Senate)

TITLE XIV--SUNKEN MILITARY CRAFT

Sec. 1401. Preservation of title to sunken military craft and associated contents.
Sec. 1402. Prohibitions.
Sec. 1403. Permits.
Sec. 1404. Penalties.
Sec. 1405. Liability for damages.
Sec. 1406. Relationship to other laws.
Sec. 1407. Encouragement of agreements with foreign countries.
Sec. 1408. Definitions.

SEC. 1401. <<NOTE: 10 USC 113 note.>> PRESERVATION OF TITLE TO SUNKEN MILITARY CRAFT AND ASSOCIATED CONTENTS.

Right, title, and interest of the United States in and to any United States sunken military craft--
  (1) shall not be extinguished except by an express divestiture of title by the United States; and
  (2) shall not be extinguished by the passage of time, regardless of when the sunken military craft sank.

SEC. 1402. <<NOTE: 10 USC 113 note.>> PROHIBITIONS.

  (a) Unauthorized Activities Directed at Sunken Military Craft.--No person shall engage in or attempt to engage in any activity directed at a sunken military craft that disturbs, removes, or injures any sunken military craft, except--
    (1) as authorized by a permit under this title;
    (2) as authorized by regulations issued under this title;

this section.
- (b) Consistency With Other Laws.--The Secretary concerned shall require that any activity carried out under a permit issued by such Secretary under this section must be consistent with all requirements and restrictions that apply under any other provision of Federal law.
- (c) Consultation.--In carrying out this section (including the issuance after the date of the enactment of this Act of regulations implementing this section), the Secretary concerned shall consult with the head of each Federal agency having authority under Federal law with respect to activities directed at sunken military craft or the locations of such craft.
- (d) Application to Foreign Craft.--At the request of any foreign State, the Secretary of the Navy, in consultation with the Secretary of State, may carry out this section (including regulations promulgated pursuant to this section) with respect to any foreign sunken military craft of that foreign State located in United States waters.

SEC. 1404. <<NOTE: 10 USC 113 note.>> PENALTIES.

- (a) In General.--Any person who violates this title, or any regulation or permit issued under this title, shall be liable to the United States for a civil penalty under this section.
- (b) Assessment and Amount.--The Secretary concerned may assess a civil penalty under this section, after notice and an opportunity for a hearing, of not more than $100,000 for each violation.
- (c) Continuing Violations.--Each day of a continued violation of this title or a regulation or permit issued under this title shall constitute a separate violation for purposes of this section.
- (d) In Rem Liability.--A vessel used to violate this title shall be liable in rem for a penalty under this section for such violation.
- (e) Other Relief.--If the Secretary concerned determines that there is an imminent risk of disturbance of, re-

Appendix 3

or
(3) as otherwise authorized by law.

(b) Possession of Sunken Military Craft.--No person may possess, disturb, remove, or injure any sunken military craft in violation of--
(1) this section; or
(2) any prohibition, rule, regulation, ordinance, or permit that applies under any other applicable law.

(c) Limitations on Application.--
(1) Actions by united states.--This section shall not apply to actions taken by, or at the direction of, the United States.
(2) Foreign persons.--This section shall not apply to any action by a person who is not a citizen, national, or resident alien of the United States, except in accordance with--
(A) generally recognized principles of international law;
(B) an agreement between the United States and the foreign country of which the person is a citizen; or
(C) in the case of an individual who is a crew member or other individual on a foreign vessel or foreign aircraft, an agreement between the United States and the flag State of the foreign vessel or aircraft that applies to the individual.
(3) Loan of sunken military craft.--This section does not prohibit the loan of United States sunken military craft in accordance with regulations issued by the Secretary concerned.

SEC. 1403. <<NOTE: 10 USC 113 note.>> PERMITS.

(a) In General.--The Secretary concerned may issue a permit authorizing a person to engage in an activity otherwise prohibited by section 1402 with respect to a United States sunken military craft, for archaeological, historical, or educational purposes, in accordance with regulations issued by such Secretary that implement moval of, or injury to any sunken military craft, or that there has been actual disturbance of, removal of, or injury to a sunken military craft, the Attorney General, upon request of the Secretary concerned, may seek such relief as may be necessary to abate such risk or actual disturbance, removal, or injury and to return or restore the sunken military craft. The district courts of the United States shall have jurisdiction in such a case to order such relief as the public interest and the equities of the case may require.

(f) Limitations.--An action to enforce a violation of section 1402 or any regulation or permit issued under this title may not be brought more than 8 years after the date on which--

(1) all facts material to the right of action are known or should have been known by the Secretary concerned; and

(2) the defendant is subject to the jurisdiction of the appropriate district court of the United States or administrative forum.

SEC. 1405. <<NOTE: 10 USC 113 note.>> LIABILITY FOR DAMAGES.

(a) In General.--Any person who engages in an activity in violation of section 1402 or any regulation or permit issued under this title that disturbs, removes, or injures any United States sunken military craft shall pay the United States enforcement costs and damages resulting from such disturbance, removal, or injury.

(b) Included Damages.--Damages referred to in subsection (a) may include--

(1) the reasonable costs incurred in storage, restoration, care, maintenance, conservation, and curation of any sunken military craft that is disturbed, removed, or injured in violation of section 1402 or any regulation or permit issued under this title; and

(2) the cost of retrieving, from the site where the sunken military craft was disturbed, removed, or injured, any information of an archaeological, historical, or cultural

nature.

SEC. 1406. <<NOTE: 10 USC 113 note.>> RELATIONSHIP TO OTHER LAWS.

(a) In General.--Except to the extent that an activity is undertaken as a subterfuge for activities prohibited by this title, nothing in this title is intended to affect--
(1) any activity that is not directed at a sunken military craft; or
(2) the traditional high seas freedoms of navigation, including--
(A) the laying of submarine cables and pipelines;
(B) operation of vessels;
(C) fishing; or
(D) other internationally lawful uses of the sea related to such freedoms.
(b) International Law.--This title and any regulations implementing this title shall be applied in accordance with generally recognized principles of international law and in accordance with the treaties, conventions, and other agreements to which the United States is a party.
(c) Law of Finds.--The law of finds shall not apply to--
(1) any United States sunken military craft, wherever located; or
(2) any foreign sunken military craft located in United States waters.
(d) Law of Salvage.--No salvage rights or awards shall be granted with respect to--
(1) any United States sunken military craft without the express permission of the United States; or
(2) any foreign sunken military craft located in United States waters without the express permission of the relevant foreign state.
(e) Law of Capture or Prize.--Nothing in this title is intended to alter the international law of capture or prize with respect to sunken military craft.
(f) Limitation of Liability.--Nothing in sections 4281 through 4287 and 4289 of the Revised Statutes (46 U.S.C.

App. 181 et seq.) or section 3 of the Act of February 13, 1893 (chapter 105; 27 Stat. 445; 46 U.S.C. App. 192), shall limit the liability of any person under this section.

(g) Authorities of the Commandant of the Coast Guard.--Nothing in this title is intended to preclude or limit the application of any other law enforcement authorities of the Commandant of the Coast Guard.

(h) Prior Delegations, Authorizations, and Related Regulations.--Nothing in this title shall invalidate any prior delegation, authorization, or related regulation that is consistent with this title.

(i) Criminal Law.--Nothing in this title is intended to prevent the United States from pursuing criminal sanctions for plundering of wrecks, larceny of Government property, or violation of any applicable criminal law.

SEC. 1407. <<NOTE: 10 USC 113 note.>> ENCOURAGEMENT OF AGREEMENTS WITH FOREIGN COUNTRIES.

The Secretary of State, in consultation with the Secretary of Defense, is encouraged to negotiate and conclude bilateral and multilateral agreements with foreign countries with regard to sunken military craft consistent with this title.

SEC. 1408. <<NOTE: 10 USC 113 note.>> DEFINITIONS.

In this title:
  (1) Associated contents.--The term ``associated contents'' means--
    (A) the equipment, cargo, and contents of a sunken military craft that are within its debris field; and
    (B) the remains and personal effects of the crew and passengers of a sunken military craft that are within its debris field.
  (2) Secretary concerned.--The term ``Secretary concerned'' means--
    (A) subject to subparagraph (B), the Secretary of

Appendix 3

a military department; and

(B) in the case of a Coast Guard vessel, the Secretary of the Department in which the Coast Guard is operating.

(3) Sunken military craft.--The term ``sunken military craft'' means all or any portion of--

(A) any sunken warship, naval auxiliary, or other vessel that was owned or operated by a government on military noncommercial service when it sank;

(B) any sunken military aircraft or military spacecraft that was owned or operated by a government when it sank; and

(C) the associated contents of a craft referred to in subparagraph (A) or (B), if title thereto has not been abandoned or transferred by the government concerned.

(4) United states contiguous zone.--The term ``United States contiguous zone'' means the contiguous zone of the United States under Presidential Proclamation 7219, dated September 2, 1999.

(5) United states internal waters.--The term ``United States internal waters'' means all waters of the United States on the landward side of the baseline from which the breadth of the United States territorial sea is measured.

(6) United states territorial sea.--The term ``United States territorial sea'' means the waters of the United States territorial sea under Presidential Proclamation 5928, dated December 27, 1988.

(7) United states waters.--The term ``United States waters'' means United States internal waters, the United States territorial sea, and the United States contiguous zone.

Appendix 4

Code of Federal Regulations
Title 32 - National Defense
Volume: 5
Date: 2012-07-01
Original Date: 2012-07-01
Title: PART 767 - APPLICATION GUIDELINES FOR ARCHEOLOGICAL RESEARCH PERMITS ON SHIP AND AIRCRAFT WRECKS UNDER THE JURISDICATION OF THE DEPARTMENT OF THE NAVY
Context: Title 32 - National Defense.
Subtitle A - Department of Defense (Continued).
CHAPTER VI - DEPARTMENT OF THE NAVY.
SUBCHAPTER G - MISCELLANEOUS RULES.

Pt. 767
PART 767—APPLICATION GUIDELINES FOR ARCHEOLOGICAL RESEARCH PERMITS ON SHIP AND AIRCRAFT WRECKS UNDER THE JURISDICATION OF THE DEPARTMENT OF THE NAVY
Subpart A—Regulations and Obligations
Sec.767.1 Purpose.
767.2 Definitions.
767.3 Policy.
Subpart B—Permit Guidelines
767.4 Application for permit
.767.5 Evaluation of permit application.
767.6 Credentials of principal investigator.
767.7 Conditions of permits.
767.8 Requests for amendments or extensions of active permits.
767.9 Content of permit holder's final report.
767.10 Monitoring of performance.
767.11 Violations of permit conditions.
767.12 References for submission of permit application to conduct archeological research. Authority:5 U.S.C. 301; 16 U.S.C. 470. Source:65 FR 31080, May 16, 2000, unless otherwise noted.
Subpart A—Regulations and Obligations
§ 767.1 Purpose. (a) The purpose of this part is to establish the requirement and procedural guidelines for permits to con-

Appendix 4

duct research on and/or recover Department of the Navy (DON) ship and aircraft wrecks.(b) The U.S. Naval Historical Center's (NHC) Office of Underwater Archeology is the DON command responsible for managing DON ship and aircraft wrecks under the guidelines of the Federal Archeological Program. In order for the NHC's management policy to be consistent with the Federal Archeology Program, and the goals of the NHPA, DON has implemented a permitting process applicable to DON property consistent with and applying the Archeological Resources Protection Act of 1979 as amended (ARPA), 16 U.S.C. 470aa-mm, permitting criteria. Department of the Navy policies regarding its ship and aircraft wrecks are consistent with ARPA permitting requirements. Department of the Navy application of ARPA permitting criteria promotes consistency among federal agencies and meets DON's responsibilities under the NHPA while allowing qualified non-federal and private individuals and entities access to DON historic ship and aircraft wrecks.(c) To assist NHC in managing, protecting, and preserving DON ship and aircraft wrecks. § 767.2 Definitions. Aircraft wreck means the physical remains of an aircraft, intact or otherwise, its cargo, and other contents. Aircraft wrecks are classified as either historic structures or archeological sites.Archeological site means the location of an event, a prehistoric or historic occupation or activity, or a building or structure, whether standing, ruined, or vanished, where the location itself maintains historical or archeological value regardless of the value of any existing structure. A ship or aircraft wreck, along with its debris field, is an archaeological site when it lacks the structural integrity of an intact aircraft or vessel and when it and its location retain archeological or historical value regardless of the value of any existing remains.

Artifact means any object or assemblage of objects, regardless of age, whether in situ or not, that may carry archeological or historical information that yields or is likely to yield information to the scientific study of culture or human history.Cultural resource means any prehistoric or historic district, site, building, structure, or object, including artifacts, records, and material remains related to such a property or resource. Historic aircraft wrecks or shipwrecks are classified as either archeological sites or historic structures. Gravesite means any natural or prepared physical location, whether originally below, on, or above the surface of the earth, where individual human remains are deposited. Historic structure means a structure made up of interdependent and interrelated parts in a definite pattern or organization. Constructed by humans, it is often an engineering project large in scale. An aircraft wreck or shipwreck is a historic structure when it is relatively intact and when it and its location retain historical, architectural, or associative value. Permit holder means any person authorized and given the exclusive right by the NHC to conduct any activity under these regulations. Permitted activity means any activity that is authorized by the NHC under the regulations in this part. Research vessel means any vessel employed for scientific purposes under the regulations in this part. Ship wreck means the physical remains of a vessel, intact or otherwise, its cargo, and other contents. Shipwrecks are classified as either historic structures or archeological sites. Wrecksite means the location of a ship or aircraft that has been sunk, crashed, ditched, damaged, or stranded. The wreck may be intact or scattered, may be on land or in water, and may be a structure or a site. The site includes the physical remains of the wreck and all other associated artifacts. § 767.3 Policy. (a) The Naval Historical Center's policy has been to evaluate each DON ship and aircraft wreck on an individual basis. In some cases, the removal of DON ship and aircraft wrecks may be necessary or appropriate to protect the cultural resource and/or to fulfill other NHC goals, such as those encompassing research, education, public access, and appreciation. Recovery of DON ship and aircraft wrecks may be justified in specific cases where the existence of a cultural resource may be threatened. Therefore, recovery of some or all of a cultural resource may be permitted for identification and/or investigation to answer specific questions; or the recovery presents an opportunity for public research or education. (b) Generally, DON ship and aircraft wrecks will be left in place unless artifact removal or site disturbance is justified and necessary to protect DON ship and aircraft wrecks, to conduct research, or provide public education and information that is otherwise inaccessible. While NHC prefers non-destructive, in situ research on DON ship and air-

Appendix 4

craft wrecks, it recognizes that site disturbance and/or artifact recovery is sometimes necessary. At such times, site disturbance and/or archeological recovery may be permitted, subject to conditions specified by NHC. Subpart B—Permit Guidelines§ 767.4 Application for permit. (a) To request a permit application form, please write to: Department of the Navy, U.S. Naval Historical Center, Office of the Underwater Archeologist, 805 Kidder Breese St. SE, Washington Navy Yard, DC 20374-5060. Telefax number: 202-433-2729.(b) Applicants must submit three copies of their completed application at least 120 days in advance of the requested effective date to allow sufficient time for evaluation and processing. Requests should be sent to the Department of the Navy, U.S. Naval Historical Center, Office of the Underwater Archeologist, 805 Kidder Breese St. SE, Washington Navy Yard, DC 20374-5060.

(c) If the applicant believes that compliance with one or more of the factors, criteria, or procedures in the guidelines contained in this part is not practicable, the applicant should set forth why and explain how the purposes of NHC are better served without compliance with the specified requirements. Permits are valid for one year from the issue date.§ 767.5 Evaluation of permit application. (a) Permit applications for archeological research are reviewed for completeness, compliance with program policies, and adherence to the guidelines of this subpart. Incomplete applications will be returned to the applicant for clarification. Complete applications are reviewed by NHC personnel and, when necessary, outside experts. In addition to the criteria set forth in § 767.6, applications are also judged on the basis of: relevance or importance; archeological merits; appropriateness and environmental consequences of technical approach; and qualifications of the applicants.(b) Under certain circumstances, it may be necessary to consult with the State Historic Preservation Officer (SHPO) and the Advisory Council on Historic Preservation (ACHP) about the need to comply with section 106 of the NHPA. A section 106 review may require the NHC to consult with the appropriate SHPO and the ACHP. The ACHP review can take up to 60 days beyond the NHC's required 120-day review. Therefore, the entire review process may take up to 180 days.(c) The

NHC shall send applications for research at sites located in units of the national park system, national wildlife refuge system, and national marine sanctuary system to the appropriate Federal land manager for review. The Federal land manager is responsible for ensuring that the proposed work is consistent with any management plan or established policy, objectives or requirements applicable to the management of the public lands concerned. NHC shall send applications for research at sites located on state bottomlands to the appropriate state agency for review. The burden of obtaining any and all additional permits or authorizations, such as from a state or foreign government or agency, private individual or organization, or from another federal agency, is on the applicant.(d) Based on the findings of the NHC evaluation, the NHC Underwater Archeologist will recommend an appropriate action to the NHC Director. If approved, NHC will issue the permit; if denied, applicants are notified of the reason for denial and may appeal within 30 days of receipt of the denial. Appeals must be submitted in writing to: Director of Naval History, Naval Historical Center, 805 Kidder Breese St. SE, Washington Navy Yard, DC 20374-5060.§ 767.6 Credentials of principal investigator. A resume or curriculum vitae detailing the professional qualifications and professional publications and papers of the principal investigator (PI) must be submitted with the permit application. The PI must have: a graduate degree in archeology, anthropology, maritime history, or a closely related field; at least one year of professional experience or equivalent specialized training in archeological research, administration or management; at least four months of supervised field and analytic experience in general North American historic archaeology and maritime history; the demonstrated ability to carry research to completion; and at least one year of full-time professional experience at a supervisory level in the study of historic marine archeological resources. This person shall be able to demonstrate ability in comprehensive analysis and interpretation through authorship of reports and monographs.§ 767.7 Conditions of permits. (a) Upon receipt of a permit, permit holders must counter-sign the permit and return copies to the NHC and the applicable SHPO, Federal or State land manager, or foreign government official prior to conducting permitted activities on

Appendix 4

the site. Copies of countersigned permits should also be provided to the applicable federal land manager when the sunken vessel or aircraft is located within a unit of the national park system, the national wildlife refuge system, or the national marine sanctuary system.

(b) Permits must be carried aboard research vessels and made available upon request for inspection to regional preservation personnel or law enforcement officials. Permits are non-transferable. Permit holders must abide by all provisions set forth in the permit as well as applicable state or Federal regulations. Permit holders should abide by applicable regulations of a foreign government when the sunken vessel or aircraft is located in foreign waters. To the extent reasonably possible, the environment must be returned to the condition that existed before the activity occurred.(c) Upon completion of permitted activities, the permit holder is required to submit to NHC a working and diving log listing days spent in field research, activities pursued, and working area positions.(d) The permit holder must prepare and submit a final report as detailed in § 767.9, summarizing the results of the permitted activity.(e) The permit holder must agree to protect all sensitive information regarding the location and character of the wreck site that could potentially expose it to non-professional recovery techniques, looters, or treasure hunters. Sensitive information includes specific location data such as latitude and longitude, and information about a wreck's cargo, the existence of armaments, or the knowledge of gravesites.(f) All recovered DON cultural resources remain the property of the United States. These resources and copies of associated archaeological records and data will be preserved by a suitable university, museum, or other scientific or educational institution and must meet the standards set forth in 36 CFR part 79, Curation of Federally Owned and Administered Archeological Collections, at the expense of the applicant. The repository shall be specified in the permit application.§ 767.8 Requests for amendments or extensions of active permits. (a) Requests for amendments to active permits (e.g., a change in study design or other form of amendment) must conform to the regulations in this part. All necessary information to make an objective evaluation of the amendment should be included as well as reference to the original application.(b) Permit holders desiring to continue research activities must reapply for an extension of their current permit before it expires. A pending extension or amendment request does not guarantee extension or amendment of the original permit. Therefore, you must submit an extension request to NHC at least 30 days prior to the original permit's expiration date. Reference to the original application may be given in lieu of a new application, provided the scope of work does not change significantly. Applicants may apply for one-year extensions subject to annual review.(c) Permit holders may appeal denied requests for amendments or extensions to the appeal authority listed in § 767.5.§ 767.9 Content of permit holder's final report. The permit holder's final report shall include the following:(a) A site history and a contextual history relating the site to the general history of the region;(b) A master site map;(c) Feature map(s) of the location of any recovered artifacts in relation to their position within the wrecksite;(d) Photographs of significant site features and significant artifacts both in situ and after removal;(e) If applicable, a description of the conserved artifacts, laboratory conservation records, and before and after photographs of the artifacts at the conservation laboratory;(f) A written report describing the site's historical background, environment, archeological field work, results, and analysis;(g) A summary of the survey and/or excavation process; and(h) An evaluation of the completed permitted activity that includes an assessment of the permit holder's success of his/her specified goals.§ 767.10 Monitoring of performance. Permitted activities will be monitored to ensure compliance with the conditions of the permit. NHC on-site personnel, or other designated authorities, may periodically assess work in progress by visiting the study location and observing any activity allowed by the permit or by reviewing any required reports. The discovery of any potential irregularities in performance under the permit will be promptly reported and appropriate action will be taken. Permitted activities will be evaluated and the findings will be used to evaluate future applications.

§ 767.11 Violations of permit conditions. The Director of Naval

Appendix 4

History, the Underwater Archeologist for DON, or his/her designee may, amend, suspend, or revoke a permit in whole or in part, temporarily or indefinitely, if in his/her view the permit holder has acted in violation of the terms of the permit or of other applicable regulations, or for other good cause shown. Any such action will be communicated in writing to the permit holder and will set forth the reason for the action taken. The permit holder may appeal the action to the appeal authority listed in § 767.5.§ 767.12 References for submission of permit application to conduct archeological research. (a) National Historic Preservation Act of 1966, as amended (NHPA), 16 U.S.C. 470 et seq. (1999), and Protection of Historic Properties, 36 CFR part 800. These regulations govern the Section 106 Review Process established by the NHPA.(b) Secretary of the Interior's Standards and Guidelines for Archeology and Historic Preservation published on September 29, 1983 (48 FR 44716). These guidelines establish standards for the preservation planning process with guidelines on implementation.(c) Archeological Resources Protection Act of 1979, as amended (ARPA), 16 U.S.C. 470aa-mm, and the Uniform Regulations, 43 CFR part 7, subpart A. These regulations establish basic government-wide standards for the issuance of permits for archeological research, including the authorized excavation and/or removal of archeological resources on public lands or Indian lands.(d) Secretary of the Interior's regulations, Curation of Federally-Owned and Administered Archeological Collections, 36 CFR part 79. These regulations establish standards for the curation and display of federally-owned artifact collections.(e) Antiquities Act of 1906, Public Law 59-209, 34 Stat. 225 (codified at 16 U.S.C. 431 et seq. (1999)).(f) Executive Order 11593, 36 FR 8291, 3 CFR, 1971-1975 Comp., p. 559 (Protection and Enhancement of the Cultural Environment).(g) Department of Defense Instruction 4140.21M (DoDI 4120.21M, August 1998). Subject: Defense Disposal Manual.(h) Secretary of the Navy Instruction 4000.35 (SECNAVINST 4000.35, 17 August 1992). Subject: Department of the Navy Cultural Resources Program.(i) Naval Historical Center Instruction 5510.4. (NAVHISTCENINST 5510.4, 14 December 1995). Subject: Disclosure of Information from the Naval Shipwreck Database.

Appendix 5

Guidelines for Permitting Archaeological Investigations and Other Activities Directed at Sunken Military Craft and Terrestrial Military Craft Under the Jurisdiction of the Department of the Navy

A Proposed Rule by the Navy Department on 01/06/2014

Action
Proposed Rule.
Summary

The Department of the Navy (DoN) is revising its rules to assist the Secretary in managing sunken military craft under the jurisdiction of the DoN pursuant to the Sunken Military Craft Act (SMCA), and to issue revised application guidelines for research permits on terrestrial military craft under the jurisdiction of the DoN.

Unified Agenda

Permit Application Procedures for Archaeological Research and Enforcement Procedures of the Sunken Military Craft Act on Sunken Military Craft Under the Jurisdiction of the Department of the Navy

Table of Contents Back to Top

DATES:
ADDRESSES:
FOR FURTHER INFORMATION CONTACT:
SUPPLEMENTARY INFORMATION:
Executive Summary
Background
Matters of Regulatory Procedure
Unfunded Mandates Reform Act (Sec. 202, Pub. L. 104-4)
Public Law 96-354, "Regulatory Flexibility Act" (5 U.S.C. 601)
Public Law 96-511, "Paperwork Reduction Act" (44

Appendix 5

U.S.C. Chapter 35)
Federalism (Executive Order 13132)
List of Subjects in 32 CFR Part 767
PART 767—GUIDELINES FOR ARCHAEOLOGICAL INVESTIGATION PERMITS AND OTHER RESEARCH ON SUNKEN MILITARY CRAFT AND TERRESTRIAL MILITARY CRAFT UNDER THE JURISDICTION OF THE DEPARTMENT OF THE NAVY
Subpart A—Regulations and Obligations
Subpart B—Permit Requirements
Subpart C—Enforcement Provisions for Violations of the Sunken Military Craft Act and Associated Permit Conditions
Subpart A—Regulations and Obligations
Subpart B—Permit Requirements
Subpart C—Enforcement Provisions for Violations of the Sunken Military Craft Act and Associated Permit Conditions

DATES: Back to Top

Interested parties should submit written comments on or before March 7, 2014.

ADDRESSES: Back to Top

You may submit comments, identified by docket number and/or Regulatory Information Number (RIN) and title, by any of the following methods:

Federal eRulemaking Portal: http://www.regulations.gov.

Follow the instructions for submitting comments.

Mail: Federal Docket Management System Office, 4800 Mark Center Drive, East Tower, Suite 02G09, Alexandria, VA 22350-3100.

Instructions: All submissions received must include the

agency name and docket or RIN number for this Federal Register document. The general policy for comments and other submissions from members of the public is to make these submissions available for public viewing on the Internet at http://regulations.gov as they are received without change, including any personal identifiers or contact information.

FOR FURTHER INFORMATION CONTACT: Back to Top

Dr. Robert Neyland, Head, Underwater Archaeology Branch, Naval History & Heritage Command, Department of the Navy, 805 Kidder Breese Street SE., BL 57, Washington Navy Yard, DC 20374, email: NHHCUnderwaterArchaeology@navy.mil.

SUPPLEMENTARY INFORMATION: Back to Top

Executive Summary Back to Top

This proposed rule serves as a revision of the current 32 CFR part 767 and incorporates existing regulations together with the expanded authority provided to the Secretary of the Navy by the SMCA (Pub. L. 108-375, 10 U.S.C. 113 Note and 118 Stat. 2094-2098) in regards to permitting activities directed at sunken military craft that are otherwise prohibited by the SMCA (10 U.S.C. 1402(a)-1402(b)). The proposed rule replaces the current regulations and establishes a single permitting process for members of the public wishing to engage in activities that disturb, remove, or injure DoN sunken and terrestrial military craft for archaeological, historical, or educational purposes. As per the limitations on application expressed in (10 U.S.C. 1402(c)(1)), section 1402 shall not apply to actions taken by, or at the direction of, the United States.

The current rule is based on provisions of the National Historic Preservation Act (NHPA) (16 U.S.C. 470) which sets forth the responsibility for each agency to preserve

Appendix 5

and manage historic properties under their respective jurisdiction and control and 5 U.S.C. 301, which authorizes the DoN to promulgate regulations regarding the custody, use, and preservation of its records, papers and property. The rule institutes a permitting program that authorizes controlled access to disturb these historic properties, which remain property of the DoN, for prescribed purposes. It is the policy of the DoN to preserve these sites in situ unless site disturbance, removal, or injury is necessary for their protection or justified for research and educational purposes. Archaeological science and sound management principles support this strategy that affords the DoN the ability to efficiently oversee its more than 17,000 historic wrecks dispersed around the globe.

The existing regulations only apply to ships and aircraft that are classified as historic structures or archaeological sites, regardless of location, and do not carry the enforcement provisions necessary to serve as a deterrent to their unauthorized disturbance. The SMCA was enacted in 2004 and codified these existing principles of preservation of title and sovereign immunity in regards to sunken military craft. As defined in the SMCA, the term sunken military craft includes all sunken warships, all naval auxiliaries, and other vessels that were owned or operated by a government on military noncommercial service when they sank. The term also includes all sunken military aircraft or spacecraft owned or operated by a government when they sank. In addition, associated contents such as equipment, cargo, and the remains and personal effects of the crew and passengers are also protected if located within a craft's debris field. It is important to note that the SMCA is not limited to historic sunken military craft of the United States. All U.S. sunken military craft are covered, regardless of location or time of loss, while all foreign sunken military craft in U.S. waters, consisting of U.S. internal waters, the U.S. territorial sea, and the U.S. contiguous zone, are also afforded protection from disturbance by the

SMCA. A permitting process may be implemented by the Secretary of a military department or the department in which the Coast Guard is operating in order to permit activities directed at sunken military craft that are otherwise prohibited.

Sunken military craft are not only of historical importance to the Nation, having served in all of its most critical moments, but are also often war graves and memorials to the men and women who served aboard them. Many carry unexploded ordnance that can pose public safety hazards or oil and other materials that, if not properly handled, may cause substantial harm to the environment. Furthermore, many hold state secrets and technologies of significance to national security. Therefore, it is important for these sites to be respected and remain undisturbed and for the U.S. to promote the international law rules that sunken military craft are entitled to sovereign immunity and preservation of title. When otherwise prohibited activities are permitted, they must be conducted in a professional manner and with archaeological, historical or educational purposes in mind. Accordingly, the SMCA declares that the "law of finds" does not apply to any U.S. sunken military craft or any foreign sunken military craft in U.S. waters. No salvage rights or awards are to be granted with respect to U.S. sunken military craft without the express permission of the U.S., or with respect to foreign sunken military craft located in U.S. waters without the express permission of the relevant foreign state.

This proposed rule is promulgated based on the authority granted to the Secretary of the Navy by the SMCA to establish a permitting program allowing controlled public access to sunken military craft that is otherwise prohibited. As stewards of the DoN's historic ship and aircraft wrecks, the Naval History & Heritage Command (NHHC) continues its role as the authority responsible for administering this revised permitting program. As a result of the need to incorporate the existing regulations

Appendix 5

and provisions set forth in the SMCA, the proposed rule adopts the definition of sunken military craft present in the Act and develops a counterpart—terrestrial military craft—to refer to DoN wrecked craft located on land that are either historic structures or archaeological sites.

NHHC will serve as the permitting authority for the disturbance of non-historic DoN sunken and terrestrial military craft and consider such applications in the cases where there is a clear demonstrable benefit to the DoN under the special use permit provisions. Special use permits will only be issued in cases when internal DoN coordination does not result in any objection. Finally, the NHHC will also serve as the permitting authority for those foreign sunken military craft located in U.S. waters that through and under the terms of an agreement with the respective foreign state are included within NHHC's management purview. Non-intrusive activities including diving adjacent to or remotely documenting sites do not require a permit or authorization from the NHHC though this does not preclude the obligation to obtain permits or other authorizations otherwise required by law. The regulations stipulate an application process for disturbance of historic sunken military craft and terrestrial military craft. Applicants must meet certain requirements and qualifications which are set forth in the proposed rules in order to demonstrate careful planning, professional credentials, and a long-term view of the effects of the proposed activities on the craft and any recovered material.

The proposed rule also incorporates provisions for a special use permit to be issued in the case of certain activities directed at sunken military craft that would result in the wrecksite's disturbance, removal, or injury but otherwise be minimally intrusive. The standards that must be met for special use permits are more easily attainable as are the reporting requirements, though data collected must be shared with NHHC.

As more than half of the DoN's sunken military craft rest beyond U.S. waters, the U.S. government has an interest in reaching agreements with foreign nations, and in particular the major maritime powers, seeking assurances that our sunken military craft will be respected and protected and offering foreign nations reciprocal treatment. In order to encourage universal respect and such mutually-beneficial treatment of sunken military craft, the Secretary of the Navy, in consultation with the Secretary of State, may consider requests by foreign states to incorporate their military craft located in U.S. waters within the DoN permitting program. The foreign state must assert its sovereign immunity over its craft, request assistance by the U.S. government, and acknowledge the provisions that will apply to their sunken military craft if incorporated into the DoN permitting program. Following such a request and appropriate consultation, an understanding to this effect may be reached with that foreign state.

The final major provision of the proposed rule affects violations of the SMCA or of the permitting program and outlines penalties and enforcement procedures. Violators may be punished by a fine not to exceed $100,000 per violation, with each day of a violation counting as a separate incident, may be liable for damages, and may suffer loss of their vessel and other equipment associated with the violation.

The proposed revision to the rule codifies existing legislation and stated public policy and does not carry a significant burden of cost to the public. With stricter enforcement provisions acting as a deterrent and a management policy based on the principle of in situ preservation, the proposed rule makes the protection of war-related and other maritime graves, the preservation of historical resources, the proper handling of safety and environmental hazards, and the safeguarding national security interests more effective, efficient, and affordable. At the same time, the proposed rule enables the

Appendix 5

public to have controlled intrusive access to sites otherwise prohibited from disturbance, bringing to light new knowledge about the Nation's maritime heritage, and honoring the service of those Sailors lost at sea.

The revisions to this rule are part of DoD's retrospective plan under EO 13563 completed in August 2011. DoD's full plan can be accessed at http://exchange.regulations.gov/exchange/topic/eo-13563.

Background Back to Top

The DoN is revising 32 CFR part 767 pursuant to the SMCA in order to implement a permitting system regulating research activities directed at DoN sunken military craft that otherwise are prohibited by the SMCA. The proposed rule also revises existing regulations by incorporating those permitting provisions stemming from 5 U.S.C. Chapter 301, 16 U.S.C. Chapter 470, and the SMCA into a single comprehensive set of rules for research activities directed at sunken military craft and terrestrial military craft under the jurisdiction of the DoN, regardless of location or passage of time. Sunken military craft and terrestrial military craft are non-renewable cultural resources that often serve as war-related and other maritime graves, safeguard state secrets, carry environmental and safety hazards such as oil and ordnance, and hold significant historical and archaeological value. Access to these sites requires DoN oversight to ensure site preservation, the sanctity of war and other maritime graves, public safety, and sound environmental stewardship. In addition, DoN oversight ensures that research carrying the potential to disturb such sites is conducted to professional standards under existing laws and guidelines such as those of the Federal Archaeology Program and the NHPA. The proposed rule allows for theincorporation of foreign sunken military craft in this permitting system upon request and agreement with the foreign state. Furthermore, it identifies penalties and enforcement procedures to be followed in the event of violations to the proposed rule affecting sunken military craft. The proposed rule will replace the existing section to reflect current agency regulations. Interested persons are invited to comment in writing on this amendment. All written comments received will be considered in making the proposed amendments to this part. It has been determined that this proposed rule amendment is not a major rule within the criteria specified in Executive Order 12866, as amended by Executive Order 13258, and does not have substantial impact on the public.

Matters of Regulatory Procedure Back to Top

Executive Order 12866, "Regulatory Planning and Review" and Executive Order 13563, "Improving Regulation and Regulatory Review"

It has been determined that 32 CFR Part 767 is not a significant regulatory action. The rule does not:

(1) have an annual effect on the economy of $100 million or more or adversely affect in a material way the economy, a sector of the economy, productivity, competition, jobs, the environment, public health or safety, or state, local, or tribal governments or communities;

(2) create a serious inconsistency or otherwise interfere with an action taken or planned by another agency;

(3) materially alter the budgetary impact of entitlements, grants, user fees, or loan programs, or the rights and obligations of the recipients thereof; or

(4) raise novel legal or policy issues arising out of legal mandates, the President's priorities, or the principles set forth in these Executive Orders.

Unfunded Mandates Reform Act (Sec. 202, Pub. L. 104-4) Back to Top

Appendix 5

It has been certified that 32 CFR Part 767 does not contain a Federal Mandate that may result in the expenditure by State, local, and tribal governments, in aggregate, or by the private sector, of $100 million or more in any one year.

96, "Regulatory Flexibility Act" (5 U.S.C. 601) Back to Top

It has been certified that 32 CFR Part 767 is not subject to the Regulatory Flexibility Act (5 U.S.C. 601) because it would not, if promulgated, have a significant economic impact on a substantial number of small entities.

96, "Paperwork Reduction Act" (44 U.S.C. Chapter 35) Back to Top

It has been certified that 32 CFR Part 767 does not impose any reporting or recordkeeping requirements under the Paperwork Reduction Act of 1995 (44 U.S.C. Chapter 35).

Federalism (Executive Order 13132) Back to Top

It has been certified that 32 CFR Part 767 does not have federalism implications, as set forth in Executive Order 13132. This rule does not have substantial direct effects on:

(1) The States;

(2) The relationship between the National Government and the States; or

(3) The distribution of power and responsibilities among the various levels of government.

List of Subjects in 32 CFR Part 767 Back to Top

- Evaluation of permit applications

- Historic sunken military craft and terrestrial military craft site permits
- Special use permits
- Foreign sunken military craft
- Civil penalties
- Liability for damages
- Enforcement actions
- Prohibited acts
- Permit requirements

For the reasons set forth in the preamble, the Department of the Navy proposes to revise 32 CFR part 767 to read as follows:

begin regulatory text

PART 767—GUIDELINES FOR ARCHAEOLOGICAL INVESTIGATION PERMITS AND OTHER RESEARCH ON SUNKEN MILITARY CRAFT AND TERRESTRIAL MILITARY CRAFT UNDER THE JURISDICTION OF THE DEPARTMENT OF THE NAVY Back to Top

Sec.
767.1 Purpose.
767.2 [Reserved].
767.3 Definitions.
767.4 Prohibited acts.
767.5 Policy.
767.6 Historic sunken military craft and terrestrial military craft permit application.
767.7 Evaluation of permit application.
767.8 Credentials of principal investigator.
767.9 Conditions of permits.
767.10 Requests for amendments or extensions of active permits.
767.11 Content of permit holder's final report.
767.12 Special use permit application.
767.13 Monitoring of performance.
767.14 Amendment, suspension, or revocation of permits.

Appendix 5

767.15 Application to foreign sunken military craft and U.S. sunken military craft not under the jurisdiction of the DoN.

767.16 Civil penalties for violations of Act or permit conditions.

767.17 Liability for damages.

767.18 Notice of Violation and Assessment (NOVA).

767.19 Procedures regarding service.

767.20 Requirements of respondent or permit holder upon service of a NOVA.

767.21 Hearings.

767.22 Final administrative decision.

767.23 Payment of final assessment.

767.24 Compromise of civil penalty, enforcement costs and/or liability for damages.

767.25 Factors considered in assessing penalties.

767.26 Criminal law.

767.27 References.

Authority:

10 U.S.C. 113 note; Pub. L. 108-375, Title XIV, sections 1401 to 1408, Oct. 28, 2004, 118 Stat. 2094; 5 U.S.C. 301; 16 U.S.C. 470.

Subpart A—Regulations and Obligations Back to Top

§ 767.1 Purpose.

The purpose of this part is:

(a) To assist the Secretary in managing sunken military craft under the jurisdiction of the Department of the Navy (DoN) pursuant to the Sunken Military Craft Act (SMCA), 10 U.S.C. 113 note; Public Law 108-375, Title XIV, sections 1401 to 1408, Oct. 28, 2004, 118 Stat. 2094, and to provide application rules for research permits on applicable military craft under the jurisdiction of the DoN.

(b) To establish the procedural rules for the issuance of permits authorizing persons to engage in activities directed at sunken military craft and terrestrial military craft under the jurisdiction of the DoN for archaeological, historical, or educational purposes, when the proposed activities may disturb, remove, or injure the sunken military craft or terrestrial military craft.

(c) To ensure DoN consistency with other applicable Federal laws. The Secretary is responsible for managing DoN historic military craft, including those that also qualify as sunken military craft, under the guidelines of the Federal Archeology Program. In order for the Secretary's management policy to be consistent to the extent practicable with the Federal Archeology Program, the NHPA (16 U.S.C. 470), Protection of Archaeological Resources: Uniform Regulations (32 CFR part 229), and Curation of Federally-Owned and Administered Archaeological Collections (36 CFR part 79), the DoN has implemented a permitting process applicable to DoN historic military craft consistent with and applying theArchaeological Resources Protection Act (ARPA) of 1979 as amended, 16 U.S.C. 470aa-mm, permitting criteria. The DoN's application of ARPA's permitting criteria promotes consistency among federal agencies. The regulations provide qualified individuals and entities with access to DoN historic military craft for purposes consistent with ARPA and the SMCA.

(c) To set forth the procedures governing administrative proceedings for assessment of civil penalties or liability damages in the case of a sunken military craft permit violation or violation of section 1402 of the SMCA.

§ 767.2 [Reserved]

§ 767.3 Definitions.

Agency means the Department of the Navy.

Appendix 5

Archaeological site means the place or places where the remnants of a past culture survive in a physical context that allows for the interpretation of these remains. A historic sunken military craft or a terrestrial military craft is considered an archaeological site when it lacks the structural integrity of an intact craft and when its wrecksite retains archaeological or historical value.

Artifact means any portion of a sunken military craft or terrestrial military craft that by itself or through its relationship to another object or assemblage of objects, regardless of age, whether in situ or not, may carry archaeological or historical data that yields or is likely to yield information that contributes to the understanding of culture or human history.

Associated Contents means:

(1) The equipment, cargo, and contents of a sunken military craft or terrestrial military craft that are within its debris field; and

(2) The remains and personal effects of the crew and passengers of a sunken military craft or terrestrial military craft that are within its debris field.

Disturb or Disturbance means directly or indirectly affecting the physical condition of any portion of a sunken military craft or terrestrial military craft, altering the position or arrangement of any portion of a sunken military craft or terrestrial military craft, or influencing the wrecksite or its immediate environment in such a way that any portion of a craft's physical condition is affected or its position or arrangement is altered.

Debris field means an area, whether contiguous or noncontiguous, that consists of portions of one or more sunken military craft or terrestrial military craft distributed due to, or as a consequence of, a wrecking event and post-depositional site formation processes. An artifact field forms part of a debris field.

Historic in the case of a sunken military craft or a terrestrial military craft means fifty (50) years have elapsed since the date of its loss and/or the craft is listed on, eligible for, or potentially eligible for listing on the National Register of Historic Places.

Historic structure means a structure made up of interdependent and interrelated parts in a definite pattern or organization that has been deemed historic. Constructed by man, it is often an engineering project large in scale. If a historic structure has lost its historic configuration or pattern of organization through deterioration or demolition, it is considered an archaeological site. A historic sunken military craft or terrestrial military craft is a historic structure when it is relatively intact and when it and its location retain historical, architectural, or associative value.

Injure or injury means to inflict material damage on or impair the soundness of any portion of a sunken military craft or terrestrial military craft.

Permit holder means any person authorized and given the right by the Naval History and Heritage Command (NHHC) to conduct activities authorized under these regulations.

Permitted activity means any activity that is authorized by the NHHC under the regulations in this part.

Person means an individual, corporation, partnership, trust, institution, association; or any other private entity, or any officer, employee, agent, instrumentality, or political subdivision of the United States.

Possession or in possession of means having physical custody or control over any portion of a sunken military craft or terrestrial military craft.

Appendix 5

Remove or removal means to move or relocate any portion of a sunken military craft or terrestrial military craft by lifting, pulling, pushing, detaching, extracting, or taking away or off.

Respondent means a vessel or person subject to a civil penalty, enforcement costs and/or liability for damages based on an alleged violation of this part or a permit issued under this part.

Secretary means the Secretary of the Navy or his or her designee. The Director of the NHHC is the Secretary's designee for DoN ship and aircraft wreck historical and archaeological policy; the permitting of activities that disturb foreign sunken military craft in U.S. waters and DoN sunken military craft; the initiation of enforcement actions; and, assessment of civil penalties or liability for damages. The Secretary's designee for appeals of Notices of Violations is the Defense Office of Hearings and Appeals (DOHA).

Secretary concerned means:

(1) The Secretary of a military department;

(2) In the case of a sunken Coast Guard military craft, the Secretary of the Department in which the Coast Guard is operating.

Sunken Military Craft means all or any portion of—

(1) Any sunken warship, naval auxiliary, or other vessel that was owned or operated by a government on military noncommercial service when it sank;

(2) Any sunken military aircraft or military spacecraft that was owned or operated by a government when it sank;

(3) The associated contents of a craft referred to in para-

graph (1) or (2) of this definition;

(4) Any craft referred to in paragraph (1) or (2) of this definition which may now be on land or in water, if title thereto has not been abandoned or transferred by the government concerned.

Sunken Military Craft Act refers to the provisions of 10 U.S.C. 113 note; Pub.L. 108-375, Title XIV, sections 1401 to 1408, Oct. 28, 2004, 118 Stat. 2094.

Terrestrial military craft means the physical remains of all or any portion of a historic ship, aircraft, spacecraft, or other craft, intact or otherwise, manned or unmanned, along with all associated contents, located on land and under the jurisdiction of the DoN. Terrestrial military craft sites are classified as either historic structures or archaeological sites and are distinguished from sunken military craft by never having sunk in a body of water.

United States Contiguous Zone means the contiguous zone of the United States declared by Presidential Proclamation 7219, dated September 2, 1999. Accordingly, the contiguous zone of the United States extends to 24 nautical miles from the baselines of the United States determined in accordance with international law, but in no case within the territorial sea of another nation.

United States Internal Waters means all waters of the United States on the landward side of the baseline from which the breadth of the United States territorial sea is measured.

United States sunken military craft means all or any portion of a sunken military craft owned or operated by the United States.

United States Territorial Sea means the waters of the

Appendix 5

United States territorial sea claimed by and described in Presidential Proclamation 5928, dated December 27, 1988. Accordingly, the territorial sea of the United States extends to 12 nautical miles from the baselines of the United States determined in accordance with international law.

United States Waters means United States internal waters, the United States territorial sea, and the United States contiguous zone.

Wrecksite means the location of a sunken military craft or terrestrial military craft. The craft may be intact, scattered or completely deteriorated, may presently be on land or in water, and may be a historic structure or an archaeological site. The wrecksite includes any physical remains of the craft and all associated contents.

§ 767.4 Prohibited acts.

(a) Unauthorized activities directed at sunken military craft or terrestrial military craft. No person shall engage in or attempt to engage in any activity directed at a sunken military craft or terrestrial military craft that disturbs, removes, or injures any sunken military craft or terrestrial military craft, except—

(1) As authorized by a permit issued pursuant to these regulations;

(2) As otherwise authorized by these regulations; or

(3) As otherwise authorized by law.

(b) Possession of sunken military craft or terrestrial military craft. No person may possess, disturb, remove, or injure any sunken military craft or terrestrial military craft in violation, where applicable, of—

(1) Section 1402 of the SMCA; or

(2) Any regulation set forth in this part or anypermit issued under it; or

(3) Any prohibition, rule, regulation, ordinance, or permit that applies under any other applicable law.

(c) Limitations on Application. Prohibitions in section 1402 of the SMCA shall not apply to—

(1) Actions taken by, or at the direction of, the UnitedStates.

(2) Any action by a person who is not a citizen, national,or resident alien of the United States, except in accordancewith—

(i) Generally recognized principles of international law;

(ii) An agreement between the United States and the foreign country of which the person is a citizen;

(iii) In the case of an individual who is a crew member or other individual on a foreign vessel or foreign aircraft, an agreement between the United States and the flag State of the foreign vessel or aircraft that applies to the individual.

§ 767.5 Policy.

(a) As stewards of the DoN's historic sunken military craft and wrecksites, the NHHC is responsible for managing these irreplaceable resources for the continued education and appreciation of present and future generations. To ensure consistent and effective stewardship, the NHHC has developed a comprehensive program that encompasses the following categories: preservation planning; wrecksite management; curation; and public information, interpretation, and education. The NHHC strongly encourages cooperation with other Department of Defense commands, Federal and State

Appendix 5

agencies, educational institutions, and individuals interested in preserving DoN's maritime and aviation heritage.

(b) Historic sunken military craft and terrestrial military craft will generally be managed in place unless wrecksite disturbance, recovery, or injury is justified and necessary to protect the craft or the environment, to conduct research, or provide for public education. While the NHHC prefers non-destructive, in situ research on sunken military craft and terrestrial military craft, it recognizes that wrecksite disturbance, removal, or injury may become necessary or appropriate. At such times, wrecksite disturbance, removal, or injury may be permitted by the NHHC with respect to DoN sunken military craft for archaeological, historical, or educational purposes, subject to conditions set forth in accordance with these regulations. Historic shipwrecks under the jurisdiction of the DoN that do not qualify as sunken military craft are to be provided the same consideration and treatment as terrestrial military craft.

(c) In addition to managing historic sunken military craft and terrestrial military craft, the NHHC will serve as the permitting authority for the disturbance of non-historic DoN sunken military craft. Permit applications will only be issued in instances where there is a clear demonstrable benefit to the DoN, and only special use permits can be issued in the case of non-historic sunken military craft. In such instances, prior to issuing a special use permit, the NHHC will consult with appropriate DoN offices within affected commands or offices, including, but not limited to, the Naval Sea Systems Command, Naval Air Systems Command, Space and Naval Warfare Systems Command, Naval Supply Systems Command, Naval Facilities Engineering Command, Navy Personnel Command, Supervisor of Salvage and Diving, Office of the Judge Advocate General of the Navy, the Office of the Chief of Naval Operations, or any other interested office.

(d) The NHHC will serve as the permitting authority for disturbance of those foreign state sunken military craft located in U.S. waters addressed in § 767.15 of this part. The NHHC, in consultation with the Department of State as appropriate, will make a reasonable effort to inform the applicable agency of a foreign state of the discovery or significant changes to the condition of its sunken military craft upon becoming aware of such information.

(e) The DoN recognizes that, in accordance with section 1402(a)(3) of the Act, certain federal agencies have statutory authority to permit specific activities directed at DoN sunken military craft. The NHHC will coordinate, consult, and enter into interagency agreements with those federal agencies to ensure effective management of DoN sunken military craft and compliance with applicable law.

(f) Notwithstanding any other section of this part, no act by the owner of a vessel, or authorized agent of the owner of a vessel, under a time charter, voyage charter, or demise charter to the DoN and operated on military service at the time of its sinking, provided that the sunken military craft is not considered historic as determined by the NHHC, shall be prohibited by, nor require a permit under, the SMCA or these regulations. This paragraph (f) shall not be construed to otherwise affect any right or remedy of the United States existing at law, in equity, or otherwise, in regard to any such sunken military craft, in regard to cargo owned by the United States on board or associated with any such craft, or in regard to other property or contents owned by the United States on board or associated with any such sunken military craft.

(g) The NHHC reserves the right to deny an applicant a permit if the proposed activity does not meet the permit application requirements; is inconsistent with DoN policy or interests; does not serve the best interests of the sunken military craft or terrestrial military craft in question; in the case of foreign sunken military craft, is inconsistent with the desires of a foreign sovereign; is inconsistent with an existing resource management plan; is directed towards a sunken military craft or terrestrial military craft upon which other activities are being considered or have been authorized; will be undertaken in such a manner as will not permit the applicant to meet final report requirements; raises ethicalconduct concerns or concerns over commercial exploitation; raises concerns over national security, foreign policy, environmental or ordnance issues; or out of respect for any human remains that may be associated with a wrecksite. The NHHC also reserves the right to deny an applicant a permit if the applicant has not fulfilled requirements associated with preceding permits issued by NHHC to the applicant.

Subpart B—Permit Requirements Back to Top

§ 767.6 Historic sunken military craft and terrestrial military craft permit application.

(a) Any person seeking to engage in an activity otherwise prohibited by section 1402 of the SMCA with respect to a historic sunken military craft or any activity that might affect a terrestrial military craft under the jurisdiction of the DoN shall apply for a permit for the proposed activity and shall not begin the proposed activity until a permit has been issued. The Secretary or his designee may issue a permit to any qualified person, in accordance with these regulations, subject to appropriate terms and conditions.

(b) To request a permit application form, please write to: Department of the Navy, U.S. Naval History and Heritage Command, Underwater Archaeology Branch, 805 Kidder Breese St. SE., Washington Navy Yard, Washington, DC 20374-5060. Application forms and guidelines can also be found on the NHHC's Web site at: www.history.navy.mil.

(c) Applicants must submit two printed copies of their completed application, as well as a digital version, at least 120 days in advance of the requested effective date to allow sufficient time for evaluation and processing. Completed applications should be sent to the Department of the Navy, U.S. Naval History and Heritage Command, Underwater Archaeology Branch, 805 Kidder Breese St. SE., Washington Navy Yard, Washington, DC 20374-5060.

(d) Each permit application shall include:

(1) A statement of research objectives, scientific methods, and significance of the proposed work to the U.S. Navy or the nation's maritime cultural heritage. This should include discussion articulating clearly the archaeological, historical, or educational purposes of the proposed activity;

(2) A summary of significant previous work in the area of interest;

(3) A discussion of how the proposed activity could disturb, remove, or injure the sunken military craft or the terrestrial military craft and the related physical environment;

(4) A discussion of the methodology planned to accomplish the project's objectives. This should include a map showing the study location(s) and a description of the wrecksite(s) of particular interest;

(5) An analysis of the extent and nature of potential environmental impacts from permitted activities and any associated permits or authorizations required by foreign, federal, state, or local law;

(6) A detailed plan for wrecksite restoration and remediation with recommendations on wrecksite preservation and protection of the wrecksite location;

Appendix 5

(7) In addition to identification and qualifications of the Principal Investigator (PI), required by Sec. 767.8 of this part, identification of all other members of the research team and their qualifications. Changes to the primary research team subsequent to the issuance of a permit must be authorized via a permit amendment request as per § 767.10(a) of this part;

(8) A proposed budget, identification of funding source, and sufficient data to substantiate, to the satisfaction of the NHHC, the applicant's financial capability to complete the proposed research and, if applicable, any conservation and curation costs associated with or resulting from that activity;

(9) A proposed plan for the public interpretation and professional dissemination of the proposed activity's results;

(10) Where the application is for the excavation and/or removal of artifacts from a sunken military craft or terrestrial military craft, or for the excavation and/or removal of a sunken military craft or terrestrial military craft in its entirety:

(i) A conservation plan, estimated cost, and the name of the university, museum, laboratory, or other scientific or educational institution in which the material will be conserved, including written certification, signed by an authorized official of the institution, of willingness to assume conservation responsibilities must be included.

(ii) A plan for applicable post-fieldwork artifact analysis, including an associated timetable.

(iii) The name of the facility in which the recovered materials and copies of associated records derived from the work will be preserved. This will include written certification, signed by an authorized official of the institution, of willingness to assume curatorial responsibilities for the collection. The named repository must, at a minimum, meet the standards set forth in 36 CFR part 79, Curation of Federally-Owned and Administered Archaeological Collections as per § 767.9(h) of this part.

(iv) Acknowledgement that the applicant is responsible for all conservation-related and long-term curation costs.

(11) A proposed project timetable to incorporate all phases of the project through to the final report and/or any other project-related activities.

(e) If the applicant believes that compliance with one or more of the factors, criteria, or procedures in the regulations contained in this part are not practicable, the applicant should set forth why and explain how the purposes of the SMCA (if applicable), these regulations, and the policies of the DoN are better served without compliance with the specified requirements. If the NHHC determines there is merit in the request and that full compliance is not required to meet these priorities, the NHHC will provide a written waiver to the applicant stipulating which factors, criteria, or procedures may be foregone or amended. However, NHHC will not waive statutory procedures or requirements.

(f) Persons carrying out official NHHC duties under the direction of the NHHC Director, or his/her designee, or conducting activities at the direction of or in coordination with the NHHC as recognized through express written permission by the NHHC Director, or his/her designee, need not follow the permit application procedures set forth in this section and §§ 767.7 and 767.9 to 767.12 of this part if those duties or activities are associated with the management of archaeological resources. Where appropriate, such persons will coordinate with Federal Land Managers, the Bureau of Ocean Energy Management, and/or State Historic Preservation Offices prior to engaging in the aforementioned activities. The NHHC Director, or his/her designee, shall ensure that the provisions of §§ 767.6(d), 767.8, and 767.11 of this part have been met by other documented means consistent with the Federal Archeology Program and, that such documents and all resulting data will be archived within the NHHC.

§ 767.7 Evaluation of permit application.

(a) Permit applications are reviewed for completeness, compliance with program policies, and adherence to the regulations of this subpart. Incomplete applications will be returned to the applicant for clarification. Complete applications are reviewed by NHHCpersonnel who, when appropriate, may seek outside guidance or peer reviews. In addition to the criteria set forth in §§ 767.6(d) and 767.8 of this part, applications are also judged on the basis of: project objectives being consistent with DoN policy and the near- and long-term interests of the DoN; relevance or importance of the proposed project; archaeological, historical, or educational purposes achieved; appropriateness and environmental consequences of technical approach; conservation and long-term management plan; qualifications of the applicants relative to the type and scope of the work proposed; and funding to carry out proposed activities. The NHHC will also take into consideration the historic, cultural, or other concerns of a foreign state when considering an application to disturb a foreign sunken military craft of that state located within U.S. waters, subsequent to an agreement with the foreign state as per § 767.15 of this part. The same consideration may be applied to U.S. sunken military craft that are not under the jurisdiction of the DoN, following an agreement with the Secretary of any military department, or in the case of the Coast Guard, the Secretary of the Department in which the Coast Guard is operating, as set forth in § 767.15(e) of this part.

(b) The NHHC will consult with the appropriate federal

resource manager when it receives applications for research at wrecksites located in areas that include units of the National Park System, National Wildlife Refuge System, National Marine Sanctuary System, Marine National Monuments, within lease blocks managed by the Bureau of Ocean Energy Management, or within areas of responsibility of other Federal Land Managers.

(c) The NHHC will consult with the appropriate State Historic Preservation Office (SHPO) or Tribal Historic Preservation Office (THPO) when it receives applications for research at wrecksites located on state lands, including lands beneath navigable waters as defined in the Submerged Lands Act, 43 U.S.C. 1301-1315, or tribal lands.

(d) The applicant is responsible for obtaining any and all additional permits or authorizations, such as but not limited to those issued by another federal or state agency, or foreign government. In the case of U.S. sunken military craft or terrestrial military craft located within foreign jurisdictions, the NHHC may review and issue a conditional permit authorizing activities upon receipt of the appropriate permits and authorizations of the applicable foreign government by the applicant. The applicant must file a copy of the foreign government authorization with the NHHC when submitting the preliminary report stipulated in § 767.9(d) of this part and final report stipulated in § 767.9(f) of this part. Failure to do so will be considered a permit violation.

(e) Based on the findings of the NHHC evaluation, NHHC personnel will recommend an appropriate action to the NHHC Deputy Director. If approved, the NHHC Deputy Director, or his or her designee, will issue the permit; if denied, applicants are notified of the reason for denial and may request reconsideration within 30 days of receipt of the denial. Requests for reconsideration must be submitted in writing to: Director of Naval History, Naval History and Heritage Command, 805 Kidder Breese St.

Appendix 5

SE., Washington Navy Yard, Washington DC 20374-5060.

§ 767.8 Credentials of principal investigator.

The principal investigator shall be suitably qualified as evidenced by training, education, and/or experience, and possess demonstrable competence in archaeological theory and method, and in collecting, handling, analyzing, evaluating, and reporting archaeological data, relative to the type and scope of the work proposed. A resume or curriculum vitae detailing the professional qualifications of the principal investigator must be submitted with the permit application. Additionally, the principal investigator will be required to attest that all persons on the project team shall be qualified and have demonstrated competence appropriate to their roles in the proposed activity. The principal investigator must, at a minimum, meet the following requirements:

(a) The minimum professional qualification standards for Archeology as determined by the Secretary of the Interior's Standards and Guidelines for Archeology and Historic Preservation (http://www.cr.nps.gov/local-law/arch_stnds_0.htm).

(b) At least one year of full-time professional supervisory experience in the archaeological study of historic maritime resources or historic aviation resources. This experience requirement may concurrently account for certain stipulations of § 767.8(a);

(c) The demonstrated ability to plan, equip, fund, staff, organize, and supervise the type and scope of activity proposed;

(d) If applicable, the demonstrated ability to submit post-operational archaeological or other technical reports in a timely manner.

§ 767.9 Conditions of permits.

(a) Permits are valid for one year from the date of issue.

(b) Upon receipt of a permit, permit holders shall counter-sign the permit and return copies to the NHHC and the applicable SHPO, THPO, or foreign government official prior to conducting permitted activities on the wrecksite. When the sunken military craft or terrestrial military craft is located within federal areas such as a unit of the National Park System, the National Wildlife Refuge System, the National Marine Sanctuary System, or Marine National Monuments, the permit holder shall provide copies of countersigned permits to the applicable federal resource manager. Upon NHHC confirming receipt of the counter-signed permit, the permitted activities may commence, provided that any other regulatory and permitting requirements that may be applicable are met.

(c) Permits shall be carried on-site and made available upon request for inspection to regional preservation personnel or federal or state law enforcement officials. Permits are non-transferable. Permit holders are expected to remain on-site for the duration of operations prescribed in the permit. In the event a permit holder is unable to directly oversee operations, the permit holder must nominate a suitable qualified representative who may only serve in that function upon written approval by NHHC.

(d) Permit holders must abide by all provisions set forth in the permit as well as applicable state or federal regulations. Permit holders must abide by applicable regulations of a foreign government for activities directed at a sunken military craft when the sunken military craft is located in the internal waters, territorial sea, or contiguous zone of a foreign State, as defined by customary international law as reflected in the United Nations Convention on the Law of the Sea. If the sunken military

Appendix 5

craft is located on the continental shelf of a foreign nation, there may also be laws or regulations pertaining to the foreign nation's sovereign rights and jurisdiction relating to its continental shelf or EEZ that may apply to the proposed activities. To the extent possible, if the physical environment is impacted by the permitted activity, it must be returned to the condition that existed before the activity occurred.

(e) Upon completion of permitted activities and at least 30 days prior to the original permit expiring, the permitholder shall submit to the NHHC a preliminary report that includes a working and diving log, the latter where appropriate, listing days spent conducting field research, activities pursued, working area locations including precise coordinates, an inventory of artifacts observed or recovered, and preliminary results and conclusions.

(f) In the case of one or more permit extensions received through the process identified in § 767.10(b) of this part, a preliminary report that includes all the information stated in paragraph (d) of this section is to be submitted by the permit holder annually at least 30 days prior to the renewed permit's expiration date.

(g) The permit holder shall prepare and submit a final report as detailed in Sec. 767.11 of this part, summarizing the results of the permitted activity to the NHHC, and the applicable SHPO, THPO, federal or state resource manager, or foreign government official within an appropriate time frame as specified in the permit. Failure to submit a final report within the specified timeframe will be considered a permit violation. If the final report is not due to be submitted within two years of commencement of a permitted activity, interim reports must be filed biannually, with the first interim report submitted within two years of commencement of the activity. The interim report must include information required by § 767.11 of this part to the maximum extent possible, a report on the progress that has been achieved to date, as well as the remaining objectives to be accomplished until submission of the final report.

(h) The permit holder shall agree to protect all sensitive information regarding the location and character of the wrecksite that could potentially expose it to non-professional recovery techniques, looters, or unauthorized salvage. Sensitive information includes specific location data and information about the cargo of a sunken military craft or terrestrial military craft, the existence of armaments and munitions, or the presence of or potential presence of human remains. Sensitive cargo might also include hazardous materials other than munitions.

(i) All recovered DoN sunken military craft, terrestrial military craft, and their associated contents, remain the property of the United States. These resources and copies of associated archaeological records and data must be preserved by a suitable university, museum, or other scientific or educational institution that, at a minimum, meets the standards set forth in 36 CFR part 79, Curation of Federally-Owned and Administered Archaeological Collections, at the expense of the applicant or facility, unless otherwise agreed upon in writing by the NHHC. The curatorial facility must establish a loan of resources agreement with the NHHC and maintain it in good standing. If a loan of resources agreement is not established, or at the discretion of the NHHC, resources are to be managed, conserved and curated directly by the NHHC at the expense of the applicant and at no cost to the government, unless otherwise agreed upon in writing by the NHHC. Copies of associated archaeological and conservation records and data will be made available to the NHHC, and to the applicable SHPO, THPO, the federal or state resource manager, or foreign government official upon request.

(j) The disposition of foreign sunken military craft or associated contents shall be determined on a case-by-case basis in coordination with the foreign state prior to the issuance of a NHHC permit.

(k) In the event that credible evidence for or actual human remains, unexploded ordnance, or environmental pollutants such as oil are discovered during the course of research, the permit holder shall cease all work and immediately notify the NHHC. Permitted work may not resume until authorized by the NHHC.

(l) The permittee shall purchase and maintain comprehensive general liability insurance, or post an equivalent bond, against claims arising out of activities conducted under the permit and agrees to hold the United States harmless against such claims.

§ 767.10 Requests for amendments or extensions of active permits.

(a) Requests for amendments to active permits (e.g., a change in study design or research personnel) must conform to the regulations in this part. All information deemed necessary by the NHHC to make an objective evaluation of the amendment must be included as well as reference to the original application. Requests for amendments must be sent to the Deputy Director, Naval History and Heritage Command, 805 Kidder Breese St. SE., Washington Navy Yard, Washington DC 20374-5060. A pending amendment request does not guarantee approval. Proposed activities cannot commence until approval is granted. All requests for permit amendments must be submitted during the period within which an existing permit is active and at least 30 days prior to the desired effect date of the amendment. Time-sensitive amendments must be submitted in writing to the contact information included in the permit and will be considered and expedited on a case-by-case basis.

(b) Permit holders desiring to continue research activities beyond the original permit expiration date must apply for an extension of a valid permit prior to its expiration. A pending extension request does not guarantee an extension of the original permit. All requests for a permit extension must be sent to the Deputy Director, Naval History and Heritage Command, 805 Kidder Breese St. SE., Washington Navy Yard, Washington DC 20374-5060, at least 30 days prior to the original permit's expiration date. Reference to the original application may be given in lieu of a new application, provided the scope of work does not change significantly. Applicants may apply for one-year extensions subject to annual review.

(c) Permit holders may appeal denied requests for amendments or extensions to the appeal authority listed in § 767.7(e) of this part.

§ 767.11 Content of permit holder's final report.

The permit holder's final report shall at minimum include the following:

(a) A wrecksite history and a contextual history relating the wrecksite to the general history of the region;

(b) A master wrecksite map;

(c) Feature map(s) of any recovered artifacts showing their position within the wrecksite;

(d) Where environmental conditions allow, photographs of significant wrecksite features and significant artifacts both in situ and after removal;

(e) If applicable, a section that includes an inventory of recovered artifacts, description of the conserved artifacts, laboratory conservation records, documentation of analyses undertaken, photographs of the artifacts before and after conservation treatment, and recommended curation conditions;

Appendix 5

(f) A written report describing the wrecksite's discovery, environment, past and current archaeological fieldwork, results, and analysis;

(g) A summary of the survey and/or excavation process including methods and techniques employed, an account of operational phases, copies of applicable logs, as well as thorough analysis of the recovered data.

(h) An evaluation of the completed permitted activity that includes an assessment of the success of the goals specified in the permit application;

(i) Recommendations for future activities, if applicable.

(j) An account of how the public interpretation or dissemination plandescribed in the permit application has been or is being carried out. Additionally, identification of any sensitive information that should be protected and withheld from public disclosure as detailed in § 767.9(g) of this part; and

(k) If a wrecksite is deemed by the NHHC to be eligible or potentially eligible for the National Register of Historic Places then a completed draft National Register of Historic Places nomination form must be attached as an appendix to the final report. The eligibility determination will be made by the NHHC upon review of the preliminary report that is to be submitted by the permit holder.

§ 767.12 Special use permit application.

(a) Any person proposing to engage in an activity to document a sunken military craft utilizing remotely-operated or autonomously-operated equipment or collect data or samples from a wrecksite that would result in the wrecksite's disturbance but otherwise be minimally intrusive may apply for a special use permit. Any person proposing to engage in an activity that would disturb, remove, or injure a non-historic sunken military craft may apply for a special use permit.

(b) To request a special use permit application form, please refer to § 767.6(b) and (c) of this part. Special use permit applications must be sent to the Deputy Director, Naval History and Heritage Command, 805 Kidder Breese St. SE., Washington Navy Yard, Washington DC 20374-5060.

(c) Each special use permit application shall include:

(1) A statement of the project's objectives and an explanation on how they would serve the NHHC's objectives stated in § 767.5 of this part;

(2) A discussion of the methodology planned to accomplish the project's objectives. This should include a map showing the study location(s) and a description of the wrecksite(s) of particular interest;

(3) An analysis of the extent and nature of potential direct or indirect environmental impacts on the resources from permitted activities;

(4) Where appropriate, a plan for wrecksite restoration and remediation with recommendations on wrecksite preservation and protection of the wrecksite location;

(5) Any permits or authorizations required by foreign, federal, state, tribal, or local law.

(d) The NHHC Deputy Director, or his or her designee, may authorize a special use permit under the following conditions:

(1) The proposed activity is compatible with NHHC policies and in the case of non-historic sunken military craft is not opposed by consulted DoN parties;

(2) The activities carried out under the permit are con-

Appendix 5

ducted in a manner that is minimally intrusive and does not purposefully or significantly disturb, destroy or injure the sunken military craft or wrecksite;

(3) When applicable, the pilot(s) of remotely-operated equipment holds a commercial certificate of operation from a nationally-recognized organization;

(4) The principal investigator must hold a graduate degree in archaeology, anthropology, maritime history, oceanography, marine biology, marine geology, other marine science, closely related field, or possess equivalent training and experience. This requirement may be waived by the NHHC on a case by case basis depending on the activity stipulated in the application.

(e) The permittee shall submit the following information subsequent to the conclusion of the permitted activity within an appropriate time frame as specified in the permit:

(1) A summary of the activities undertaken that includes an assessment of the goals specified in the permit application;

(2) Identification of any sensitive information that should be protected and withheld from public disclosure as detailed in § 767.9(g) of this part;

(3) Complete and unedited copies of any and all documentation and data collected (photographs, video, remote sensing data, etc.) during the permitted activity and results of any subsequent analyses.

(f) The following additional sections of subpart B shall apply to special use permits: §§ 767.7(e); 767.9(a), (b), (c), (e), (f), (g), (I,) (j), and (k); 767.10(a), (b), and (c); 767.13; and 767.14 of this part.

(g) All sections of subpart A shall apply to special use

permits and all sections of subpart C shall apply to special use permits pertaining to sunken military craft.

(h) Unless stipulated in the special use permit, the recovery of artifacts associated with any wrecksite is strictly prohibited.

§ 767.13 Monitoring of performance.

Permitted activities will be monitored to ensure compliance with the conditions of the permit. In addition to remotely monitoring operations, NHHC personnel, or other designated authorities, may periodically assess work in progress through on-site monitoring at the location of the permitted activity. The discovery of any potential irregularities in performance under the permit by NHHC on-site personnel, other designated authorities, or the permit holder, must be promptly reported to the NHHC for appropriate action. Adverse action may ensue as per § 767.14 of this part. Findings of unauthorized activities will be taken into consideration when evaluating future permit applications.

§ 767.14 Amendment, suspension, or revocation of permits.

The NHHC Deputy Director, or his/her designee may amend, suspend, or revoke a permit in whole or in part, temporarily or indefinitely, if in his/her view the permit holder has acted in violation of the terms of the permit or of other applicable regulations, or for other good cause shown. Any such action will be communicated in writing to the permit holder or the permit holder's representative and will set forth the reason for the action taken. The permit holder may request the Director of NHHC reconsider the action as per § 767.7(e) of this part.

§ 767.15 Application to foreign sunken military craft and U.S. sunken military craft not under the jurisdiction of the DoN.

Appendix 5

(a) Sunken military craft are generally entitled to sovereign immunity regardless of where they are located or when they sank. Foreign governments may request, via the Department of State, that the Secretary of the Navy administer a permitting program for a specific or a group of its sunken military craft in U.S. waters. The request must include the following:

(1) The foreign government must assert its sovereign immunity over a specified sunken military craft or group of sunken military craft;

(2) The foreign government must request assistance from the United States government;

(3) The foreign government must acknowledge that Subparts B and C of this Part will apply to the specified sunken military craft or group of sunken military craft for which the request is submitted.

(b) Upon receipt and favorable review of a request from a foreign government, the Secretary of the Navy, or his or her designee, in consultation with the Department of State, will proceed to accept the specified sunken military craft or group of sunken military craft into the present permitting program. The Secretary of the Navy, or his or her designee, in consultation with the Department of State, reserves the right to decline a request by the foreign government. Should there be a need toformalize an understanding with the foreign government in response to a submitted request stipulating conditions such as responsibilities, requirements, procedures, and length of effect, the Secretary of State, or his or her designee, in consultation with the Secretary of Defense, or his or her designee, will proceed to formalize an understanding with the foreign government. Any views on such a foreign government request or understanding expressed by applicable federal, tribal, and state agencies will be taken into account.

(c) Persons seeking a permit to disturb foreign sunken military craft located in U.S. waters that have been accepted into the present permitting program or are covered under a formalized undertanding as per Sec. 767.15(b) of this section, may submit a permit application for consideration by the NHHC as per subparts B and C of this part.

(d) In the case where there is reasonable dispute over the sovereign immunity status of a foreign sunken military craft, the Secretary of the Navy maintains the right to postpone action on §§ 767.6 and 767.12 of this part, as well as requests under § 767.15(a) of this part, until the dispute over the sovereign immunity status is resolved.

(e) The Secretary of any military department or in the case of the Coast Guard, the Secretary of the Department in which the Coast Guard is operating, may request that the Secretary of the Navy administer a permitting program for sunken military craft under his or her cognizance. Upon the agreement of the Secretary of the Navy, subparts B and C of this part shall apply to those agreed upon craft.

Subpart C—Enforcement Provisions for Violations of the Sunken Military Craft Act and Associated Permit Conditions Back to Top

§ 767.16 Civil penalties for violation of Act or permit conditions.

(a) In general. Any person who violates the SMCA, or any regulation or permit issued thereunder, shall be liable to the United States for a civil penalty.

(b) Assessment and amount. The Secretary may assess a civil penalty under this section of not more than $100,000 for each violation.

(c) Continuing violations. Each day of a continuing violation of the SMCA or these regulations or any permit issued hereunder constitutes a separate violation.

(d) In rem liability. A vessel used to violate the SMCA shall be liable in rem for a penalty for such violation.

§ 767.17 Liability for damages.

(a) Any person who engages in an activity in violation of section 1402 or any regulation or permit issued under the Act that disturbs, removes, or injures any U.S. sunken military craft shall pay the United States enforcement costs and damages resulting from such disturbance, removal, or injury.

(b) Damages referred to in paragraph (a) of this section may include:

(1) The reasonable costs incurred in storage, restoration, care, maintenance, conservation, and curation of any sunken military craft that is disturbed, removed, or injured in violation of section 1402 or any regulation or permit issued under the Act; and

(2) The cost of retrieving, from the site where the sunken military craft was disturbed, removed, or injured, any information of an archaeological, historical, or cultural nature.

§ 767.18 Notice of Violation and Assessment (NOVA).

(a) A NOVA will be issued by the Director of NHHC and served in person or by registered, certified, return receipt requested, or express mail, or by commercial express package service, upon the respondent, or in the case of a vessel respondent, the owner of the vessel. A copy of the NOVA will be similarly served upon the permit holder, if the holder is not the respondent. The NOVA will contain:

(1) A concise statement of the facts believed to show a violation;

(2) A specific reference to the provision(s) of the SMCA, regulation, or permit violated;

(3) The findings and conclusions upon which the Director of NHHC bases the assessment;

(4) The amount of civil penalty, enforcement costs and/or liability for damages assessed; and

(5) An advisement of the respondent's rights upon receipt of the NOVA, including a citation to the regulations governing the proceedings.

(b) The NOVA may also contain a proposal for compromise or settlement of the case.

(c) Prior to assessing a civil penalty or liability for damages, the Director of NHHC will take into account information available to the Agency concerning any factor to be considered under the SMCA and any other information required by law or in the interests of justice. The respondent will have the opportunity to review information considered and present information, in writing, to the Director of NHHC. At the discretion of the Director of NHHC, a respondent will be allowed to present information in person.

§ 767.19 Procedures regarding service.

(a) Whenever this Part requires service of a document, such service may effectively be made on the respondent, the respondent's agent for service of process or on a representative designated by that agent for receipt of service. Refusal by the respondent, the respondent's agent, or other designated representative to be served, or refusal by his or her designated representative of service of a document will be considered effective service of the

Appendix 5

document as of the date of such refusal. Service will be considered effective on the date the document is mailed to an addressee's last known address.

(b) Any document served upon a respondent must be signed by:

(1) The person or persons serving the same; or

(2) Other person having authority to sign.

(c) A document will be considered served and/or filed as of the date of the postmark; or (if not mailed) as of the date actually delivered in person; or as shown by electronic mail transmission.

(d) Time periods begin to run on the day following service of the document or date of the event. Saturdays, Sundays, and Federal holidays will be included in computing such time, except that when such time expires on a Saturday, Sunday, or Federal holiday, such period will be extended to include the next business day. This method of computing time periods also applies to any act, such as paying a civil penalty or liability for damages, required by this part to take place within a specified period of time.

§ 767.20 Requirements of respondent or permit holder upon service of a NOVA.

(a) The respondent or permit holder has 45 days from service receipt of the NOVA in which to reply. During this time the respondent or permit holder may:

(1) Accept the penalty or compromise penalty, if any, by taking the actions specified in the NOVA;

(2) Seek to have the NOVA amended, modified, or rescinded under paragraph (b) of this section;

(3) Request a hearing before a DOHA Administrative Judge under paragraph (f) of this section;

(4) Request an extension of time to respond under paragraph (c) of this section; or

(5) Take no action, in which case the NOVA becomes final in accordance with § 767.22(a) of this part.

(b) The respondent or permit holder may seek amendment, modification, orrescindment of the NOVA to conform to the facts or law as that person sees them by notifying the Director of NHHC in writing at the address specified in the NOVA. If amendment or modification is sought, the Director of NHHC will either amend the NOVA or decline to amend it, and so notify the respondent, permit holder, or vessel owner, as appropriate.

(c) The respondent or permit holder may, within the 45-day period specified in paragraph (a) of this section, request in writing an extension of time to respond. The Director of NHHC may grant an extension in writing of up to 30 days unless he or she determines that the requester could, exercising reasonable diligence, respond within the 45-day period.

(d) The Director of NHHC may, for good cause, grant an additional extension beyond the 30-day period specified in paragraph (c) of this section.

(e) Any denial, in whole or in part, of any request under this section that is based upon untimeliness will be in writing.

(f) If the respondent or permit holder desires a hearing, the request must be in writing, dated and signed, and must be sent by mail to the Director, Defense Office of Hearings and Appeals, 875 North Randolph St., Suite 8000, Arlington VA, 22203. The Director, Defense Office of Hearings and Appeals may, at his or her discretion,

Appendix 5

treat any communication from a respondent or a permit holder as a proper request for a hearing. The requester must attach a copy of the NOVA. A single hearing will be held for all parties named in a NOVA and who timely request a hearing.

§ 767.21 Hearings.

(a) Hearings before a DOHA Administrative Judge are de novo reviews of the circumstances alleged in the NOVA and penalties assessed. Hearings are governed by procedures established by the Defense Office of Hearings and Appeals. Hearing procedures will be provided in writing to the parties and may be accessed on-line at http://www.dod.mil/dodgc/doha/. Hearings shall be held at the Defense Office of Hearings and Appeals, Arlington VA, either in person or by Video Teleconference. Each party shall bear their own costs.

(b) In any DOHA hearing held in response to a request under § 767.20(f) of this part, the Administrative Judge will render a final written Decision which is binding on all parties.

§ 767.22 Final administrative decision.

If no request for a hearing is timely filed as provided in § 767.20(f) of this part, the NOVA becomes effective as the final administrative decision and order of the Agency on the 45th day after service of the NOVA or on the last day of any delay period granted.

§ 767.23 Payment of final assessment.

(a) Respondent must make full payment of the civil penalty, enforcement costs and/or liability for damages assessed within 30 days of the date upon which the assessment becomes effective as the final administrative decision and order of the Agency. Payment must be made by mailing or delivering to the Agency at the address specified in the NOVA a check or money order made payable in U.S. currency in the amount of the assessment to the "Treasurer of the United States," or as otherwise directed.

(b) Upon any failure to pay the civil penalty, enforcement costs and/or liability for damages assessed, the Agency may request the Department of Justice to recover the amount assessed in any appropriate district court of the United States, or may act under any law or statute that permits recovery, arrest, attachment, or garnishment of property and/or funds to satisfy a debt owed to the United States.

§ 767.24 Compromise of civil penalty, enforcement costs and/or liability for damages.

(a) The Director of NHHC, in his/her sole discretion, may compromise, modify, remit, or mitigate, with or without conditions, any civil penalty or liability for damages imposed, or which is subject to imposition, except as provided in this Subpart.

(b) The compromise authority of the Director of NHHC under this section is in addition to any similar authority provided in any applicable statute or regulation, and may be exercised either upon the initiative of the Director of NHHC or in response to a request by the respondent or other interested person. Any such request should be sent to the Director of NHHC at the address specified in the NOVA.

(c) Neither the existence of the compromise authority of the Director of NHHC under this section nor the Director's exercise thereof at any time changes the date upon which an assessment is final or payable.

§ 767.25 Factors considered in assessing penalties.

(a) Factors to be taken into account in assessing a

Appendix 5

penalty may include the nature, circumstances, extent, and gravity of the alleged violation; the respondent's degree of culpability; any history of prior offenses; ability to pay; and such other matters as justice may require.

(b) The Director of NHHC may, in consideration of a respondent's ability to pay, increase or decrease a penalty from an amount that would otherwise be warranted by other relevant factors. A penalty may be increased if a respondent's ability to pay is such that a higher penalty is necessary to deter future violations, or for commercial violators, to make a penalty more than the profits received from acting in violation of the SMCA, or any regulation or permit issued thereunder. A penalty may be decreased if the respondent establishes that he or she is unable to pay an otherwise appropriate penalty amount.

(c) Except as provided in paragraph (d) of this section, if a respondent asserts that a penalty should be reduced because of an inability to pay, the respondent has the burden of proving such inability by providing verifiable, complete, and accurate financial information to the Director of NHHC. The Director of NHHC will not consider a respondent's inability to pay unless the respondent, upon request, submits such financial information as the Director of NHHC determines is adequate to evaluate the respondent's financial condition. Depending on the circumstances of the case, the Director of NHHC may require the respondent to complete a financial information request form, answer written interrogatories, or submit independent verification of his or her financial information. If the respondent does not submit the requested financial information, he or she will be presumed to have the ability to pay the penalty.

(1) Financial information relevant to a respondent's ability to pay includes, but is not limited to, the value of respondent's cash and liquid assets and non-liquid assets, ability to borrow, net worth, liabilities, income, prior and

anticipated profits, expected cash flow, and the respondent's ability to pay in installments over time. A respondent will be considered able to pay a penalty even if he or she must take such actions as pay in installments over time, borrow money, liquidate assets, or reorganize his or her business. The Director of NHHC's consideration of a respondent's ability to pay does not preclude an assessment of a penalty in an amount that would cause or contribute to the bankruptcy or other discontinuation of the respondent's business.

(2) Financial information regarding respondent's ability to pay should besubmitted to the Director of NHHC as soon after receipt of the NOVA as possible. In deciding whether to submit such information, the respondent should keep in mind that the Director of NHHC may assess de novo a civil penalty, enforcement costs and/or liability for damages either greater or smaller than that assessed in the NOVA.

§ 767.26 Criminal law.

Nothing in these regulations is intended to prevent the United States from pursuing criminal sanctions for plundering of wrecks, larceny of Government property, or violation of applicable criminal law, whether the infringement pertains to a sunken military craft, a terrestrial military craft or other craft under the jurisdiction of the DoN.

§ 767.27 References.

References for submission of permit application, including but not limited to, and as may be further amended:

(a) NHPA of 1966, as amended, 16 U.S.C. 470 et seq. (1999), and Protection of Historic Properties, 36 CFR part 800. These regulations govern the section 106 review process established by the NHPA.

Appendix 5

(b) National Environmental Policy Act of 1969, as amended, 42 U.S.C. 4321 et seq., and Protection of the Environment, 40 CFR 1500-1508. These regulations require agencies to consider the effects of their actions on the human environment.

(c) Secretary of the Interior's Standards and Guidelines for Archeology and Historic Preservation, available at http://www.cr.nps.gov/local-law/arch_stnds_0.htm. These guidelines establish standards for the preservation planning process with guidelines on implementation.

(d) ARPA of 1979, as amended, 16 U.S.C. 470aa-mm, and the Uniform Regulations, 43 CFR part 7, subpart A. These regulations establish basic government-wide standards for the issuance of permits for archaeological research, including the authorized excavation and/or removal of archaeological resources on public lands or Indian lands.

(e) Secretary of the Interior's regulations, Curation of Federally-Owned and Administered Archaeological Collections, 36 CFR part 79. These regulations establish standards for the curation and display of federally-owned artifact collections.

(f) Antiquities Act of 1906, 59, 34 Stat. 225 (codified at 16 U.S.C. 431 et seq. (1999)).

(g) Executive Order 11593, 36 FR 8291, 3 CFR, 1971-1975 Comp., p. 559 (Protection and Enhancement of the Cultural Environment).

(h) Department of Defense Instruction 4140.21M (DoDI 4140.21M, August 1998). Subject: Defense Disposal Manual.

(i) Secretary of the Navy Instruction 4000.35A (SECNAVINST 4000.35A, 9 April 2001). Subject: Department of the Navy Cultural Resources Program.

(j) Naval History and Heritage Command Instruction 5510.4. (NAVHISTCENINST 5510.4, 14 December 1995). Subject: Disclosure of Information from the Naval Shipwreck Database.

N.A. Hagerty-Ford,

Commander, Office of the Judge Advocate General, U.S. Navy,Federal Register Liaison Officer.

Index

Accelerate: 8
Admiralty law: 112, 194
Advisory Council on Underwater Archaeology: 159
Airacobra: 212
Air Force, U.S.: 168, 175, 195, 210
Akers, Gina: 37
Alabama: 99, 114-124, 222
Alexandria, Virginia: 84, 85
Almirante: 66
Anacostia River: 35
"Application Guidelines for Underwater Archeological Research Permits on Submerged Cultural Resources Under the Jurisdiction of the Department of the Navy": 17, 181-189, 190
Arizona: 158, 223
Arlington National Cemetery: 220, 223
Army Corps of Engineers: 8, 97, 156
Army, U.S.: 168, 195, 210
Asserton, P.C.: 93
Atlantis II: 130
Automated Wreck and Obstruction Information System: 143
B-17: 167
Bahia, Brazil: 99-100
Ballistic Experimental Target 'A': 69
Bartone, Dan: 144-146
Bass: 75
Battle of Hampton Roads: 92-93
Battle of Roanoke Island: 71
Bederman, David: 120-121
Bilinski, Marcie: 10, 12-13, 15, 16, 23
Boston, Massachusetts: 101
Boston Harbor: 8, 13, 15, 27
Boston Iron & Metal Company: 68-69, 72

Brazil: 99-101, 106, 112, 222
Breese, Denny: 37-39
Brown, Captain Clements: 94-95
Bulkoil: 141-147
Bushnell: 78
C: 69
Captain Wrong Way Peachfuzz: 220
Casey, Senator Robers: 44
Cavalcante, Bernard: 36, 38-39
Cervoni, Robert: 194
Channel Islands National Marine Sanctuary: 204
Charleston, South Carolina: 149, 161
Charleston Harbor: 152, 154, 155, 157
Chauncey, Commodore Isaac: 125
Cherbourg, France: 122-123
Cherry Point, North Carolina: 178
Chesapeake Bay: 105
Chicago World's Fair: 68-69
Chrestensen, Francis: 69
Christman, Eugene: 104-109
Churchill, Winston: 137
City of Rockland: 12
Coast Guard, U.S.: 176, 178
Cohan, Representative Mark
Cold Harbor Civil War Museum: 103, 105, 108
College of William and Mary: 97
College Park, Maryland: 49
Columbus, Georgia: 106
Confederate Naval Historical Society: 106
Confederate Naval Museum: 106
Confederate States of America: 118-119
Congress: 180, 182
Congressional and Public Affairs Office: 21
Constitution of the United States: 112, 181, 190
Corsair: 165, 178-180
Cralley, Lex: 179-180
Crooks, James and William: 126-127
Cumberland: 92-98, 101, 103, 106, 108, 109, 111, 113, 221-222
Curacao: 141
Curtis Helldiver: 169

Index

Cussler, Clive: 38, 96-98, 101-102, 106, 156-157, 160
Daily Press: 109-111
Dauntless: 171, 173-175, 187
David and Goliath: 151
Debevoise, District Judge Dickenson: 119-121
Deerhound: 114
Department of Justice: 171
Department of the Interior: 112, 113
Dictionary of American Naval Fighting Ships: 23, 64-81, 114, 116, 125
Dixon, Lieutenant George: 150
Dragonet: 67
Dudley, Bill: 40, 53-54, 56-57
Dutton, Harry: 12-13
Eagle 56: 76-77
Eastern Sea Frontier: 46, 143
Ehrhardt, Captain Dieter: 138
England: 167
Enoree: 141
Epps, Pat: 167
Espiritu Santo: 166
Etiwan: 149
Ex-German Submarine Expeditionary Force: 78
Explosive Ordnance Disposal Mobile Unit 12: 22
Falcon: 67, 77
Federal Bureau of Investigation: 60, 103, 106-107, 110-113, 171
Federal Register: 191
Felix Taussig: 76
Fields, W.C.: 155
Finney, Ed: 81-83
Florida: 96, 97, 99-114, 222
Flying Fortress: 167
Fort Warren: 101
fossils: 214
Foster, Kevin: 106, 113
France: 115, 123
Frankfurt: 78-80
Frankwitz, Ensign Vincent: 176-177
Freedom of Information Act: 27, 28, 30, 31, 33, 61-62, 90

French navy: 122
Fuentes, Larry: 173, 175
Fuhrer's U-boats in American Waters, The: 76
Fulham, Master's Mate: 118
G-1: 73, 182, 221
G-2: 73
G-102: 78
General Services Administration: 103, 112, 118, 122, 156, 158, 159
Gentian: 37-39
German Submarine Activities on the Atlantic Coast of the United States and Canada: 48
Gestapo: 171
Gettysburg Address: 158
Government Printing Office: 48
Granite State: 72
Greenland: 166-167
Grumman Wildcat: 169
"Guidelines for Permitting Archaeological Investigations and Other Activities Directed at Sunken Military Craft and Terrestrial Military Craft Under the Jurisdiction of the Department of the Navy" (proposed 2014): 18, 199-226
Haberlein, Chuck: 81-83
Halifax, Nova Scotia: 24
Hall, Wes: 157
Hamilton: 125-128, 222
Hamilton, City of: 127-128
Hampton Roads, Virginia: 95, 100, 103, 109, 113
Hampton Roads Naval Museum: 107
Hastings, Joseph: 104-109
Havana Harbor, Cuba: 216
Hebrew, John A.: 93
Hellcat: 176-178, 187
Herndon: 8, 27, 65
Hesperides: 211
Hess, Peter: 120-121, 171-178
Hisko: 66
Hitler, Adolf: 49, 164
H.L. Hunley: 148-164
Hoist: 129

Index

Hooey, Kevin: 171, 175
Hooper, Vice Admiral Edwin: 48-50
Housatonic: 151-154, 164
Hummel, Jeffrey: 169
Hunley, Horace Lawson: 148, 150
Hunley Commission: 159
Icarus: 129
Iceland: 167
Independence: 144
Indian Chief: 150
Ironclad Legacy: Battles of the USS Monitor: 93
Isle of Guernsey: 116-117, 124
Jacob Bell: 111
Jacob Jones: 25
James River: 111, 113
J.C.: 94, 95
Johnson, Kenneth: 46-47
Jones, Representative Walter B.: 180
Judge Advocate General: 27, 84-91, 98
Jupiter, Florida: 171
Kaiser's U-boats in American Waters, The: 50, 77, 78
Katahdin: 69
Katsuda, G.: 79
Karen Lynn: 105
Kearsarge: 114-117, 121
Kell, Lieutenant John: 117
Kohler, Richie: 143-147
Kuhn, J.K.: 21-23, 26, 31-32, 61-62
L-8: 74-75
Lady Jennifer: 105
Larkins, Gary: 175
Lake Washington: 169
Lamont-Doherty Geological Observatory: 38
Langley Field, Virginia: 79
Law of Finds: 194
Law of Salvage: 194
Law of the Sea Convention: 181, 185
Lawrence, Captain James: 7
Lawson, William: 117
Lee, Karston: 138
Lightfoot, Virginia: 103

Lightning: 167-168
Lincoln, President Abraham: 158
Lize, Patrick: 50-51
Lloyd, Kathy: 37, 40, 41-42, 45-47, 50, 55
Lockwood: Vice Admiral Charles A.: 78
Lord Nelson: 126
Lost Squadron: 167
Lovegreen, Magistrate Donald: 177
Lozano, District Judge Rudy: 174-175
Lusitania Controversies, The: 80
Luters Nautical Antiques Emporium: 159
Macon, Buddy: 173
Maffit, Captain John: 102
Maillefert, Benjamin: 153
Maine: 216
Mallard: 67
Marchitelli, T.T.: 21
Mariners' Museum, The: 97, 101, 110, 158
Marmer Rooke Gallery: 117
Marshal's Service, U.S.: 171
Martha's Vineyard, Massachusetts: 176
Massachusetts Board of Underwater Archaeological Resources: 14, 15
Mastone, Vic: 14
Maxter Metals: 54, 57
McCauley, Matthew: 169
McClintock, James R.: 148
Merrimack: 93, 96
Merritt-Chapman & Scott: 8
Ministry of Love: 46
Ministry of Truth: 124
Mitchell, Billy: 77-80
Mobile, Alabama: 148, 159
Monitor: 158, 204
Monitor National Marine Sanctuary: 204
Monroe, President James: 127
Morehead City, North Carolina: 130
Mulholland Machinery Corp.: 72
Murphy: 85, 141-147, 174
National Archives: 20-21, 43, 49, 50, 55, 85, 144
National Archives, Navy Records Branch: 48

Index

National Historic Preservation Act: 185, 188
National Museum of Naval Aviation (alias National Naval Aviation Museum): 169, 173, 175, 177, 178, 187, 220
National Oceanic and Atmospheric Association: 158, 160, 204, 206
National Park Service: 158, 159, 204, 206
National Register of Historic Places: 186-187
National Underwater and Marine Agency: 96-98, 156
Nautilus: 148
Naval Academy, U.S.: 117
Naval Criminal Investigative Service: 16, 106, 145-147, 173-175
Naval Expeditionary Combat Command: 29-30, 31, 32, 91
Naval Historical Center: 7, 16, 17, 19-22, 33, 35-62, 91, 123, 144-146, 157, 175, 208
Naval History and Heritage Command: 6, 14, 21-22, 30, 31-34, 53, 80-81, 83, 84, 98, 114, 118-119, 122, 124, 142-143, 148-150, 161, 164, 165, 169, 176, 183, 185, 189, 190-195, 200, 205, 207, 208, 210, 212-213, 219-221, 223, 224-226
Naval Mine Warfare Proving Ground: 69
Naval Photographic Center: 33, 35-36, 74-75, 81-84
Naval Sea Systems Command: 21, 29, 32, 33
Navy Department Library: 35-36, 47-48
Navy Register (and Navy list): 8, 21, 65, 69, 73
Navy Wreck List: 143
Nelson: 141
Nelson, Daniel: 126
New Hampshire: 72
New Hebrides: 166
Newport Naval Station: 183, 221
Newport News, Virginia: 97, 101
Newport, Rhode Island: 183, 221
Neyland, Bob: 56
Nina: 65-66
Norfolk Naval Museum: 97-98
Norfolk Navy Yard: 97
North South Trader: 106
O.E. Maltby & Company: 94

Official Records of the Union and Confederate Navies in the War of the Rebellion: 71
Ohio: 66
Oneida: 126
Operational Archives: 35-62
Operation Drumbeat: 38
Orangeburg Times & Democrat: 155
Oreto: 99
Orzech, Otto: 55-56, 58
Ostfriesland: 78-80
P-38: 167-168
P-39: 212
Park and Lyons: 148
Passaic-class: 154
Patapsco: 154
Pennington, Lieutenant Robin: 178
Perth Amboy: 72
Petrel: 77
Popular Dive Guide Series: 9, 55
Portsmouth Navy Yard: 78
Potsdam Agreement: 137-138
Publication No. 1: 48, 49
Public Law 108-375, Section 1083: 180
Purifoy, George: 129
Queen Wilhelmina: 95
Quonset Air Museum: 176-178
Rappahannock Spit, Virginia: 69
Rhode Island: 176
Riley, Wilbur: 96
Rilley, Harry E.: 44, 47-48, 62-63
Robert A. Owens: 77
Ronald W. Reagan National Defense Authorization Act for Fiscal Year 2005: 191
Royal Ontario Museum: 127-128
Rudd, Theron: 126
S-5: 66-68
S-16: 21
S-49: 68-69
S-132: 78
Sackville: 24
Salvador, Brazil: 99

Index

San Diego: 51-59, 223
Sands, John: 97-98
SC-60: 76
SC-209: 76
Schwartz, Representative Allyson: 44
Scourge: 125-128, 222-223
SeaDuctress: 10
Semmes, Captain Raphael: 114-118
Ships Histories Branch: 23, 35-36, 62-64, 74, 80, 81, 183
Shipwreck Heresies: 143
Shipwrecks of Delaware and Maryland: 66-67
Shipwrecks of Massachusetts: North: 8, 13-14, 15, 18, 72
Shipwrecks of Massachusetts: South: 72-73
Shipwrecks of New Jersey: North: 76
Shipwrecks of New Jersey: South: 66, 76
Shipwrecks of New York: 76
Shipwrecks of North Carolina: 37
Shipwrecks of North Carolina: from Hatteras Inlet South: 72
Shipwrecks of North Carolina: from the Diamond Shoals North: 71
Shipwrecks of Rhode Island and Connecticut: 73-75
Shipwrecks of South Carolina and Georgia: 161
Shipwrecks of Virginia: 70, 80
Shipwrecks of the Chesapeake Bay in Maryland Waters: 67, 69
Shipwrecks of the Chesapeake Bay in Virginia Waters: 69-70, 99
Sikorsky helicopter: 179
Smith, Angus: 153
Smithsonian Institution: 159
Sonoma: 78
South Carolina Institute of Archaeology and Anthropology: 156, 157, 159-160
South Carolina, State of: 159
Specter, Senator Arlen: 44
Spence, Lee: 153-156, 159, 160
Spikefish: 76
Stevens, Larry: 104-108

Steinmetz, Richard: 116-124
Stephenson, Robert: 155
Stolen Heritage: 128
Suitland, Maryland: 85
Sullivan's Island, South Carolina: 153
"Sunken Military Craft" rider: 20, 22, 191-193, 196
Supreme Court: 111
Tangier Sound: 69
Tarpon: 21, 72, 218
Taylor, Richard: 167
Texas (Second Class Battleship): 69-70, 182-183
Texas (Battleship No. 35): 141
Theophanis, Peter: 169-176
Theophanic, Peyton: 171
Third Reich: 49
Tobin, Admiral Paul: 40-45
Toomey, Senator Pat: 18-21, 27, 30, 61
Townley, John: 106-113
Track of the Gray Wolf: 37, 41, 43, 46, 76
Triana: 72
U-85: 139-140, 223
U-111: 77, 78, 79-80
U-117: 78, 79
U-140: 78
U-352: 26, 129-138, 221, 223
U-534: 138
U-853: 77
U-701: 70
U-2513: 77
UB-88: 78
UB-148: 78
"U-boat Operations in the Western Atlantic During World War I": 40-41, 48-50
UC-97: 78
Underwater Archaeological Joint Ventures: 98
United Fruit Company: 66
U.S.S. San Diego: the Last Armored Cruiser: 55, 57, 209
V-43: 78
Vanuatu: 166
Verne, Jules: 148
Virginia: 92-93, 96, 97

Index

Virginia Capes: 70
Vision State (of the NHC and NHHC): 60
von Doenhoff, Richard A.: 44, 47-48
Wachusett: 99-101, 114
Walker, Governor Gilbert C.: 93
Walker, Mike 36, 38-39
Walker, Mr.: 116
warbirds: 165-168, 198
War Shipping Administration: 196
Washington: 70
Washington National Records Center: 85-89
Washington Navy Yard: 35, 47, 61
Watson, Baxter: 148
Weehawken: 154
Weicker, Senator Lowell: 129, 138
Washington Navy Yard Museum: 67-68
Welles, Gideon: 98, 100
West, Mr.: 94
Wheeler, Captain Peter: 44
Wilbanks, Ralph: 157
Wildlife and Marine Resources Department: 160
Wilson, Thomas: 99
Wilkes-Barre: 21
William Lawrence: 160
Willis, Mr. E.: 153
Williams, Gary: 105-108
Williamsburg, Virginia: 97, 103
Winfield Scott: 204
Wreck Information List: 143
YF-415: 72
YMS-14: 7, 8-34, 65, 221, 223
Young, Christina: 143-146
YP-387: 76
YP-389: 70-71
YSD-56: 72-73
Zinkowski, Nicholas: 75

Books by the Author

The Popular Dive Guide Series
Shipwrecks of Massachusetts: North
Shipwrecks of Massachusetts: South
Shipwrecks of Rhode Island and Connecticut
Shipwrecks of New York
Shipwrecks of New Jersey (1988)
Shipwrecks of New Jersey: North
Shipwrecks of New Jersey: Central
Shipwrecks of New Jersey: South
Shipwrecks of Delaware and Maryland (1990 Edition)
Shipwrecks of Delaware and Maryland (2002 Edition)
Shipwrecks of the Chesapeake Bay in Maryland Waters
Shipwrecks of the Chesapeake Bay in Virginia Waters
Shipwrecks of Virginia
Shipwrecks of North Carolina: from the Diamond Shoals North
Shipwrecks of North Carolina: from Hatteras Inlet South
Shipwrecks of South Carolina and Georgia

Shipwreck and Nautical History
Andrea Doria: Dive to an Era
Deep, Dark, and Dangerous: Adventures and Reflections on the Andrea Doria
Great Lakes Shipwrecks: a Photographic Odyssey
The Great Navy Wreck Scam
The Fuhrer's U-boats in American Waters
Ironclad Legacy: Battles of the USS Monitor
The Kaiser's U-boats in American Waters
The Lusitania Controversies: Atrocity of War and a Wreck-Diving History (Book One)
The Lusitania Controversies: Dangerous Descents into Shipwrecks and Law (Book Two)
The Nautical Cyclopedia
NOAA's Ark: the Rise of the Fourth Reich
Shadow Divers Exposed: the Real Saga of the U-869
Shipwreck Heresies
The Shipwreck Research Handbook
Shipwreck Sagas
Stolen Heritage: the Grand Theft of the Hamilton and Scourge
Track of the Gray Wolf
Underwater Reflections
USS San Diego: the Last Armored Cruiser
Wreck Diving Adventures

Dive Training
Primary Wreck Diving Guide

Books by the Author

Advanced Wreck Diving Guide
The Advanced Wreck Diving Handbook
Ultimate Wreck Diving Guide
The Technical Diving Handbook

Nonfiction
The Absurdity Principle
Lehigh Gorge Trail Guide
Wilderness Canoeing

Science Fiction
A Different Universe
A Different Dimension
A Different Continuum
Entropy (a novel of conceptual breakthrough)
A Journey to the Center of the Earth
The Mold
Return to Mars
Second Coming
Silent Autumn
Subaqueous
Tesla and the Lemurian Gate
The Time Dragons Trilogy
    A Time for Dragons
    Dragons Past
    No Future for Dragons

Sci-Fi Action/Adventure Novels
Memory Lane
Mind Set
The Peking Papers

Supernatural Horror Novel
The Lurking: Curse of the Jersey Devil

Vietnam Novel
Lonely Conflict

Videotape or DVD
The Battle for the USS Monitor

Visit the GGP website for availability of titles:
http://www.ggentile.com

www.ingramcontent.com/pod-product-compliance
Lightning Source LLC
Chambersburg PA
CBHW051037160426
43193CB00010B/968